AF324301

State Capitalism's Uncertain Future

State Capitalism's Uncertain Future

Scott B. MacDonald
and
Jonathan Lemco

An Imprint of ABC-CLIO, LLC
Santa Barbara, California • Denver, Colorado

Library of Congress Cataloging-in-Publication Data
MacDonald, Scott B., author.
   State capitalism's uncertain future / Scott B. MacDonald and Jonathan Lemco.
      pages cm
   Includes bibliographical references and index.
   ISBN 978-1-4408-3107-2 (print : alk. paper) — ISBN 978-1-4408-3108-9 (e-book)
1. Capitalism—Government policy. 2. Globalization—Economic aspects.
3. Economic policy—History—21st century. I. Lemco, Jonathan, author. II. Title.
HB501.M21875 2015
330.12'2—dc23   2015007507

ISBN: 978-1-4408-3107-2
EISBN: 978-1-4408-3108-9

19 18 17 16 15   1 2 3 4 5

This book is also available on the World Wide Web as an eBook.
Visit www.abc-clio.com for details.

Praeger
An Imprint of ABC-CLIO, LLC

ABC-CLIO, LLC
130 Cremona Drive, P.O. Box 1911
Santa Barbara, California 93116-1911

This book is printed on acid-free paper (∞)
Manufactured in the United States of America

Contents

Preface

Since the end of the Cold War the global political economy has been in a state of disequilibrium. That state of affairs is related to the redefinition of relationships between countries, peoples, and markets. The era has witnessed the rise of China as a global power, the relative decline of the United States as the dominant power, Europe's slippage into a crisis of identity, a critical reassessment of their roles in the world by Japan and Russia, and the emergence of a number of other countries into the upper rungs of global power. Among the latter group are Brazil, India, Indonesia, Saudi Arabia, Turkey, and Mexico. While one interpretation of this is that the global South, the swath of countries that constitute the southern hemisphere, is finally on the rise and reaching a convergence with the more industrialized and developed West, another view is that the end of the Cold War released more traditional forces. Globalization created a "new world order" based on a community of countries that had a stake in the system, but also left them reaching for the commanding heights of the new and poorly defined world community.

The question raised in the following pages points to the issue of what has emerged from the end of the Cold War and the extended period of globalization that commenced in the 1980s. Along these lines, the global community is one that is less held together by the benefits of globalization, in which shareholding has a little less meaning and nationalism has returned as a force. Indeed, as reflected by the 2014 Scottish independence referendum and the movement for Catalonia's independence in Spain, proto-nationalism is alive and well. The issue of nationalism also points back to what kind of political economy is the best. In advanced economies, the dominant model is democratic capitalism—a capitalist economic system, led by the private sector. Although there are variations between the Anglo-American economies and continental Europe and Japan, the key tenets are electoral politics, rule of law, respect for contracts, and a well-defined and extensive space for the private sector.

The competing model is autocratic capitalism. The political system is authoritarian, and the economy is capitalist, but large state-owned companies play a major role in the creation of national wealth. In such a system, the government may be willing to hold elections, occasionally allowing an opposition, and promotes a private sector—but the core group of political and economic actors are drawn from the ranks of the ruling party or the ruling elite. Decisions are usually made promptly, talent is appreciated, and state companies are often competitive with their foreign private sector counterparts. This system has brought considerable advances to China, Russia, and Singapore (by far the most successful), but also carries with it a hardnosed approach to opposing ideas. Moreover, there is a downside to autocratic capitalism if it slips beyond professionalism and pragmatism into crony capitalism.

The catalyst for this book came from the events of 2008's global financial panic and Great Recession, which shook the foundations of the democratic capitalist system in the West and Japan. The excessive dependence on financial capitalism in the United States, the United Kingdom, and Ireland eroded claims of the superiority of those economic models and, with the upsurge in the economic clout of China and the other BRICS (Brazil, Russia, India, and South Africa), lent credence to the idea that state capitalism might be the future. This claim was reinforced by China's willingness to implement a massive stimulus program in 2008–2009 that did much to prevent the world from slipping into a new Great Depression similar to the 1930s. Most significantly, the rise of China advanced the argument that state capitalism, especially with an autocratic bent, was set to knock private sector companies out of business and threaten the world with a new brand of authoritarian government. Indeed, state capitalism appeared to be the core of a "new normal" of geo-economics that was like a juggernaut on the world stage.

Our view is that although state capitalism's surge in the aftermath of the 2008 financial panic and Great Recession was impressive, this is not the threat to the world community purported by some. Instead state capitalism has an uncertain future, considering the massive economic, demographic, and political challenges confronting governments in China,

Russia, and Saudi Arabia. This creates a landscape in which volatility and risk are magnified. Many state capitalist systems are going to be severely challenged by the temptations of cronyism, reflected in the cozy relations between many of China's economic elites and its state-owned companies, or the same matrix in Russia. This problem is evident even in democracies such as Brazil, which became painfully obvious in the Petrobras scandal of 2015. Democratic capitalism, faults and all, is hardly finished. This is important to recognize as younger generations of students, businesspeople, and policymakers are going to be forced to deal with the challenges represented by autocratic state capitalism.

The authors wish to thank their families for their patience with the finishing of the book. Special appreciation is extended to M.-M. Kateri Scott-MacDonald for her reading and editing each chapter. Vitmar Harizaj's help in editing is also appreciated. We have also appreciated the patience of Hilary Claggett, our editor. Her faith in us to finish the book has been vindicated. All responsibility for this book is ours and ours alone. We should also add that the views expressed in the following pages do not necessarily represent those of MC Asset Management Holdings LLC or Vanguard.

ONE

Introduction

In the aftermath of the Great Recession (2007–2008), the term "new normal" came into vogue. Often attributed to PIMCO's (Pacific Investment Management Company) Bill Gross and Mohamed El-Erian, the term reflected a new era of long-term high unemployment, questions over the future viability of citizens' per capita income, and the carnage in international markets that threatened the collapse of the global financial system. From that ominous premise, the "new normal" definition broadened to include the idea of protracted slow growth in advanced economies, faster growth in emerging markets, and ongoing volatility in international securities and commodity markets. Attached to these developments was the presumption that the economy or market forces no longer drove markets, but that governments would intervene with various policy instruments— be it through support for "national champions," strategically timed public statements, quantitative easing from central banks, or financial lifelines from sovereign wealth funds for troubled companies. The big difference between these national champions and old-line socialist companies is that most of the former are listed on stock markets and subject to global competition.

In 2012, *The Economist* called state-owned enterprises (SOEs) the "new masters of the universe." Although the new normal gave way to the "new neutral" in 2014, the idea of the enhanced role of state capitalism as a powerful force has not gone away.[1] The implication is that it is time to throw away Adam Smith, David Ricardo, and Joseph Schumpeter, and pick up a copy of a government handbook on managing the commanding heights of the global economy through SEOs. In many of the most important nations in the world, the public sector is driving economic development strategies. These models of "state capitalism" include Brazil, China, and Russia, among others, and are characterized by varying degrees of government involvement in economic policymaking. State capitalism has existed throughout history in various forms, but it has never been employed on such a grand scale as it is in the early twenty-first century. It is well financed, run by highly professional teams, and, in many cases, innovative. The alternative view of private sector–driven capitalism is most evident in the advanced economies—the United States, the United Kingdom, Canada, Japan, Australia, and the Eurozone—a group of countries often regarded as "the West." Through much of the twentieth century and into the first decade of the next, the private sector–driven model was held up as the most successful path to climbing the economic heights, something that was reinforced by multilateral lending institutions like the International Monetary Fund, World Bank, and Inter-American Development Bank. But emerging-market countries employing state capitalist models are a very meaningful challenger to that view. Furthermore, the financial crisis of 2007 to 2008 in the United States and United Kingdom, and the Eurozone crisis of 2010 to 2013, are challenging the credibility of conventional market/private sector–driven capitalist models.

For anyone looking across the global economic landscape, the obvious appeal and the success of many developing countries employing state capitalist models is impressive. In the past twenty years, hundreds of millions of people in China, for example, have been elevated from the depths of poverty to the lower middle class. Singapore has become a wealthy city-state, with a standard of living better than many countries considered "advanced." In emerging markets, the "middle class" has risen in countries like Brazil, India, and even in parts of Africa.[2] However, state capitalism is no panacea either. We believe that its very success holds the seeds of its decline. If its objective is to create more affluent, better-educated and globally-aware populations, then we suspect that these will become increasingly difficult in those countries with authoritarian or quasi-authoritarian political systems (which make up a hefty number) as ruling elites strive to maintain the political status quo. Over time and as middle classes emerge, official corruption becomes less tolerated. Middle-class expectations for equality of opportunity emerge, and conventional capitalist models become more attractive. This does not mean that emerging markets will become carbon copies of the U.S., Canadian, or Swedish economies, but that they select elements of those systems that work best for them within the context of greater transparency, disclosure, and accountability by the socioeconomic elites.

It is the purpose of this book to examine the rise of state capitalism and its uncertain future. Particular attention will be devoted to the challenges that state capitalism poses to private sector capitalist models in the global economy and to multinational corporations in many sectors, such as oil and gas, mining, aerospace, and, increasingly, finance. The emergence of sovereign wealth funds (SWFs) are an obvious example of the last factor. SWFs have given many emerging market economies the ability to use their riches to expand into the global economy either to secure natural resource supplies, enhance the competitiveness of their national companies (either state-owned or private), and extend influence into friends' and rivals' economic lives—just as the advanced economies accomplished before them. To observe the mixing of economic and political influence is nothing new, as the emergence of state capitalism is a necessary condition associated with the economic and political development in many emerging market countries (and some developed countries, such as South Korea, Israel, and Scandinavia). At the same time, the state capitalism model has serious limitations, which are often downplayed. These limitations include the channeling of resources to favored companies, skewed distribution of income to the elite, official corruption that erodes legitimacy, and controlled political systems that provide few outlets for the public dissatisfaction caused by some of these factors. The control factor can also stifle healthy debate over inefficiencies and possible alternative strategies, as well as maintaining unhealthy favoritism toward entrenched elites. Last but hardly least in challenges facing state capitalism is the difficulty, at times, of discerning where corporate and government goals overlap. Is Company X looking for corporate objectives, or is it an extension of government foreign policy aimed at gaining strategic resources, garnering desirable technology, or staking a geographical claim to some disputed territory? Considering these factors, the threatening state-led and allied business juggernaut may still look imposing, but its defects also indicate that the demise of private sector–led market capitalism is being overstated.

One other factor to consider is that the tensions between state capitalism, in particular the autocratic type, and private sector–oriented economies in democratic systems are creating a new normal in global geopolitics. Along these lines, the new geopolitical normal is one in which the international system is multi-polar, with states more readily willing to use military means as part of achieving national interest goals (e.g., Russia in Eastern Europe). Directly related to this, the competition between private sector and state-owned enterprises is more intense and increasingly entangled in foreign policy deliberations. Simply stated, the relative decline of U.S. power, and the rise (or return) of other powers to center stage, has injected more political risk into the daily conduct of international business and investment. This is true for both state-owned companies and their private sector counterparts. It clearly underscores that the new geopolitical normal is more high-risk, as volatility is now not just an issue for bond and stock markets, but also political stability in a more rough-and-tumble world that will severely challenge the political and economic systems of state capitalism.

THE HISTORICAL CONTEXT

The twentieth century was locked in competition between three forces: communism, national socialism/fascism, and democratic capitalism. World War II saw the end of national socialism/fascism; the Cold War ended in 1989–1991 with the defeat of communism, leaving democratic capitalism the victor. However, history did not end, and capitalism proved to be a house with many rooms, something that was pushed along by globalization. Globalization required countries, governments, and companies to respond to a dramatic transformation in how economies work, encompassing everything from manufacturing, logistical supply lines, and marketing. While capitalism was and remains the dominant economic force, it is varied between free market–oriented capitalism, with its emphasis on the privately owned enterprise, practiced by the majority of advanced economies and a number of emerging market countries, and state capitalism with varying degrees of government involvement, including large state-owned multinational corporations. There is also an overlay of democratic versus autocratic political systems, which becomes very evident when comparing the experiences of the United States, Canada, and Germany vis-à-vis China, Russia, and Saudi Arabia. Indeed the democratic-versus-autocratic dimension has injected a higher degree of tension in international relations in the first half of the twenty-first century.

While there are differences between free market–oriented capitalism and state capitalism, there are also variations within the state capitalistic camp. State capitalism ranges from what is practiced by what are called the "resource nationalist" countries of Argentina, Bolivia, Saudi Arabia, and Venezuela, to countries like China and Singapore that are more driven by manufacturing and services. Financial power is increasingly important in the latter cases as the SWFs of both countries are important sources of capital for many publicly traded companies in Asia and the West. This book, therefore, argues that state capitalism has become a major rival of private sector–driven free market capitalism, with a strong political overlay of authoritarianism versus democracy. This rivalry will only intensify as the century advances. Both in industry and in finance, state capitalist economies have clout and threaten to overrun free market capitalism based on the dominance of the private sector. Linked to this is the over-hyped question of whether state capitalism means the end of free market capitalism in the twenty-first century.

Although state capitalism represents a powerful force in the global economic system, it is ultimately a flawed economic model, in large part due to its reliance on an autocratic political elite that is constantly under pressure to balance reaping the benefits of the system and spreading enough of the wealth to remain in power. State capitalism can work for a long time, but in parts of the world where it was long-entrenched, like Tunisia, Libya, and Egypt, the inequities of the system lead to its downfall. This can extend even to China and Russia, the two most ardent models of this approach to capitalism. Ultimately the competition between state capitalism and free market capitalism is one of ideas, pitting a belief of a corporate autocratic society built up around economic growth and increasing nationalism against a limited state–private sector society that is also pushed along by the need for corporate growth. Although the free market model was bruised and battered by the Great Recession, and the following recovery was fragile, it is capable of tremendous revitalization, something which will happen over time. Most importantly, as Ian Bremmer, author of *The End of the Free Market*, correctly observed: "the private sector is the only reliable long-term engine of robust and sustainable growth."[3]

What makes state capitalism as practiced by China and Russia so competitive is that its practitioners do not want the old Cold War-era communist companies that were inefficient, bloated with extra personnel, and unprofitable. Rather, they want, create, and promote well-managed, efficient, and profitable companies. A university degree in Marxist ideology does not cut it; an MBA from Wharton or Harvard Business School does. Out of China and Russia have come some of the twenty-first century's largest, most powerful globe-trotting companies, such as the petro-giants CNOOC (China National Offshore Oil Company), Sinopec, Lukoil, and Gazprom, to name a few. There is also the financial arm of the state: banks and sovereign wealth funds. There remains ongoing demand for talent to help fuel greater economic growth. These intermixes between the political class and economic stewards in countries like China, Russia, and, to some degree, the United Arab Emirates, Qatar, and Saudi Arabia, are what we call the state capitalists. They are playing a far more significant role than in the past in the global economy and, according to some, represent "the end of the free market." A key point is that democracy is not a prerequisite for attracting foreign direct investment, achieving high levels of growth, or creating multinational corporations.[4] At the very least, the state capitalist approach, in its broadest sense, represents a strong competitor to the liberal market views long held as sacrosanct in the Anglo-American economies.

Considering that capitalism is inherently competitive, the state capitalists and free market capitalists are locked in a battle over who will control the commanding heights of the global economy in the aftermath of the Great Recession. It certainly raises a valid question about how private sector companies are able to compete with state-owned enterprises that are backed by political support (declared or undeclared), vast stockpiles of foreign exchange reserves, and easy access to state-owned banks and SWFs. According to data from CNN Money, in 2006 there were six state-owned companies in the top 100 companies by revenues.[5] These companies came from China (2), Venezuela, Mexico, and Brazil, and were largely linked to energy. By 2013, the number of state-owned companies grew to 20, with China leading the way at 11, followed by Russia (3), and then spread out among Brazil, Mexico, India, Malaysia, Thailand, and Venezuela. While oil companies maintained a dominant representation, banks and telecommunications companies also had risen through the ranks. In the top ten companies by revenues, state-owned companies rose from zero in 2006 to three in 2013, with those being the Sinopec group, China National Petroleum, and the State Grid Corporation of China.

State capitalism gained considerable influence and attraction by the self-inflicted wounds of the more free-wheeling free market capitalism embraced by the United States and the United Kingdom, as well as Ireland. From the 1980s to the first decade of the twenty-first century, the global economy was transformed by a wide-ranging acceptance of Anglo-American market-oriented economics, an extensive globalization of transport, communications, and culture, and the penetration of finance into almost every facet of economic life, including food, energy, and housing. With this also came the rising power of the BRICs (Brazil, Russia, India, and China), which became important pillars of a new world capitalist system, especially as they are key producers of either goods, services, or commodities. What was stunning about the frothy days of market-driven global economics was how three major countries, Russia, India, and China, willingly left behind inward-looking development models and embraced capitalism, albeit of varying state-dominated strategies.

The dominance of private sector–driven market economics came to an abrupt end in 2008 when the free market economic express collided with the disaster caused by a greedy, overreaching, and overleveraged financial sector. The crisis in free market capitalism was marked by the near-collapse of the U.S. financial system and a descent into the worst economic crisis since the 1930s, which quickly spread around the globe. A new Great Depression was averted, but the Great Recession of 2007–08 left its own upheaval in the form of collapsing banks, large ranks of the unemployed, and a discrediting in many circles of the free market system. That discrediting included growing distrust with how the legislative process in the United States became hostage to the lobbyists, big business' oversized role in campaign finance, and extreme income inequality related to an explosive escalation of boardroom pay while average earnings have stagnated.[6] It also led to the intervention of the state in the UK, the United States, and Ireland into the economy, in the form of propping up the banking systems. In the UK and Ireland, the government ended owning majority shares in the countries' largest banks, while in the United States, it was buying partial ownership in the banks but a takeover (via a negotiated bankruptcy) of two out of three of the major automobile corporations.

The Great Recession also hit Continental Europe, the other major bastion of capitalism. Europe initially fared better with the Great Recession, as it was less dependent on finance playing a dominant role in the economy. Continental capitalism, if we want to call it that, was more comfortable with a somewhat larger state role in the economy and society, though still wed to private sector–driven capitalism. Germany, for example, was a firm believer in making products, not in financial innovation, and remained one of the world's major exporters. The weakness in the Continental capitalist model was heavy social spending (showing up in recurring fiscal deficits and large public sector debts), coziness between the banks and government, and a culture of entitlement among an aging population that was resistant to most changes. Continental capitalism was to find the second decade of the twenty-first century a brutal period and a time of reckoning in its dependency on borrowing.

The post-2008 global economy is different from the preceding 30 years—at least for now. The Anglo-American and European Continental models of capitalism are discredited or at least being rethought. As one of the authors noted in 2008, "Now that the U.S. model has had its comeuppance, what kind of capitalism should emerge? There is a smorgasbord—quasi-authoritarian capitalism (Russia), authoritarian capitalism (China) and within democratic-capitalism, you have Anglo-American, Continental and Japanese-Asian versions."[7] While there was not a rush to adopt the old shibboleths of communism and fascism in the global arena (except for a few diehards and fellow travelers), the appeal of the free market and the related dimensions of its political economy in the advanced economies (i.e., an acceptance of democratic institutions and practices) lost ground. There was some shock value to the greed and arrogance tied to elements of Western financial capitalism. Equally important, there was a willingness on the part of some countries, such as China, Russia, and Brazil, not only to promote state capitalism in their local "spheres of influence," but to globally proclaim that the days of U.S. and Western dominance are over and that there is now the "rise of the rest," a term used by geopolitical commentator Fareed Zakaria in his bestselling *The Post-American World and the Rise of the Rest.*

The theme was picked up by former Brazilian president Luiz Inacio Lula da Silva, who stated in 2011: "For too long, rich countries saw us as peripheral, problematic, even dangerous. Today we are an essential, unde-niable part of the solution to the biggest crisis of the last decade—a crisis that emerged from the great centers of world capitalism."[8] Even Europe took its share of criticism. Historian Timothy Garton Ash wrote in 2012: "As European leaders stagger into yet another round of crisis summitry, this potential superpower is widely viewed as the sick man of the devel-oped world."[9] And economic recovery since 2012 has been fragile.

The free market approach to economic development runs the risk of being eclipsed. It is crucial to clarify that state capitalism is a very dif-ferent beast from the state-run planned economy under communism. It is also very different from the ideas of socialism, as the state capitalism approach is meant to attract the best and brightest, reward their efforts, and maximize profits, usually at the expense of another country's companies. Parag Khanna, a Senior Research Fellow at the New America Founda-tion, provides some color in regard to China: "The Party is more powerful, sophisticated and complex than any Chinese dynasty in history. Rather than child emperors for whom the nation itself was a personal asset, today there are MBA emperors who think in terms of business plans—and are co-opting the business elites into consulting roles."[10]

The nature of the challenge is further emphasized by Martin Jacques, in *When China Rules the World: The End of the Western World and the Birth of a New Global Order.* As he notes of China: "It is the bearer and driver of the new world, with which it enjoys an increasingly hegemonic relationship, its tentacles having stretched across East Asia, Central Asia, South Asia, Latin America and Africa in a little more than a decade."[11] It is not just China that is busy reshaping the world. Saudi Arabia plays a critical role, much akin to the old Hapsburg Empire of the Austro-Hungarian Empire, in keeping a conservative, non-democratic state capitalist system in place in parts of the Middle East. Qatar punches well above its geographic and demographic size, playing an active role in Libya's overthrow of the Gadaffi regime, support of the short-lived Muslim Brotherhood government in Egypt in 2013, and backing of rebel forces in Syria. Russia is active in supporting authoritarian regimes, such as in Belarus, Syria, and Venezuela, and used military force in carving away parts of Georgia in 2008, and taking Crimea from neighboring Ukraine and sponsoring separatists in the eastern part of the same country in 2014 and 2015.

There is also an attractiveness to the state capitalist model in China's achievements, in terms of lifting millions out of poverty and converting an agricultural economy into the workshop of the world. As one Brazilian diplomat noted of the decline of Europe and the rise of China: "It used to be that all of Latin America looked to Europe as its ideal model, and that one day Brazil, Argentina and Colombia would become a Portugal, Italy, Greece or Spain, if it was lucky. But now, given the eurozone crisis, that is no longer the case. And, increasingly, China is becoming a more attractive or plausible model."[12]

It should be added that a number of countries in Latin America fit into the state capitalism world. In that region, resource nationalism plays an important role, especially as observed in the historical context where many local leaders feel that their development was stunted in some capacity by first Europe and then the United States, both of which imposed economic and social mores. Countries such as Argentina, Brazil, Bolivia, Ecuador, and Venezuela in the past decade moved to assert greater government control over extractive natural resource companies. While this takes on more socialist rhetoric in Bolivia, Ecuador, and Venezuela, it boils down to the same situation of government officials asserting greater control or total control over key parts of the national economy but still competing in the global economy within a capitalist construct. Although not out-and-out socialism (to which Cuba still seeks to adhere and Venezuela has disastrously sought to implement), the large role of the state is clearly a factor throughout much of Latin America, but it varies considerably between how Brazil treats Petrobras, majority state-owned oil and gas company, and Argentina's heavy-handed nationalization of Spain's Repsol, or how the Venezuelan state treats PDVSA, its state oil company, as the purse of social benefits policies.

While it is easy to proclaim that the free market is dead, the private sector has an incredibly resilient nature. Despite a lengthy period of communist rule in China, there now exists a vibrant private sector. There is also a strong entrepreneurial dimension to Chinese capitalism that cannot be entirely explained by the size and scope of state-owned corporate behemoths. The rebirth of Chinese capitalism, commencing in 1978, released huge, pent-up energy that was stimulated by competition, incentives of self-betterment through hard work, and the opportunity to accumulate wealth. The survival and ultimately the resurgence of free market capitalism is not limited to China's private sector. More significantly there is a critical ability of free market–oriented capitalism to reinvent itself. This is occurring in the United States, where the financial sector is downsizing and manufacturing has returned as a growth sector. Out of crisis is coming reinvention. With reinvention comes restructuring. With restructuring comes revitalization and a new phase of private sector–led growth.

The greatest chances for the revitalization of free market–oriented capitalism ultimately come from the attractiveness of what it has to offer. Despite the major stumble in 2007–2008, many of the attributes for private sector–led growth are evident in state capitalism: incentives, promotions, transparency, and disclosure that are meant to provide a level playing field, and lengthy periods of economic growth that can pull entire societies along. This also includes a willingness to allow competition—including over ideas. And this is where state capitalism has its limitations. There is an encouragement of some free exchange and competition of ideas, but the discourse is often limited in economic matters. This explains the extensive controls exercised in China vis-à-vis the internet, and the stubborn opposition to the controlled political system in Russia. In China, the most successful of state capitalist models, the ruling Communist Party lives with a deep-seated worry over the political situation slipping out of control, which earlier threatened in the form of the Tiananmen Square demonstrations in 1989. Ultimately, control of the economy itself is a form of control. Political scientists Steven Levitsky and Lucan A. Way have observed: "Discretionary economic power furnishes incumbents with powerful tools to compel compliance and punish opposition. Where the livelihoods, careers, and business prospects of much of the population can be affected easily and decisively by government decisions, opposition activity becomes a high-risk venture."[13] The risk for such a system of control is that at some point the state capitalist model's strong points turn against it, and there can be a shift from considerable resilience to a dangerous brittleness directly linked to the regime's ability to maintain growth and share the economic spoils.

OPERATIONALIZING THE BOOK'S TERMS

Before proceeding, it is necessary to further operationalize our term, "state capitalism." It is also important to define capitalism. In this, economic historian Joyce Appleby provides an insightful view: "Capitalism—a system based on individual investments in the production of marketable goods—slowly replaced the traditional ways of meeting the material needs of a society. From early industrialization to the present global economy, a sequence of revolutions relentlessly changed the habits and habitats of human beings."[14] Two key elements come from this definition: the importance of the individual endeavor (as opposed to that of the state) and the revolutionary nature of capitalism as a catalyst of change. To this, we would add the Protestant ideals of hard work, thrift, and pride in one's productive efforts. To round out this picture, it is necessary also to assert the importance of the rule of law and respect for property rights.

Free market capitalism refers to the belief in letting market forces run free of government or political interference. It encompasses a belief that the markets are always right in seeking out efficiencies and inefficiencies. Central to this is the belief that the private sector is best equipped to take advantage of market conditions, not the government. Depending on the country, there may be acceptance of the need for regulation to maintain a level playing field for private sector participants. In this, the state has a role as a referee to agreed-upon rules of the game and is not a player. The rules of the game, of course, include respect of property rights, the right to a safe workplace, and rule of law.

The hallmarks of state capitalism are a fundamental acceptance of capitalism but also a large, guiding state role in the economy, state shareholder ownership in major companies, and a co-mingling of political and economic interests. Significantly, there is emphasis on the political dimension, as the political class's ability to rule hinges on its ability to maintain economic growth and spread the wealth to the rest of the population. Adrian Wooldridge, in a Special Report in *The Economist*, observed of state capitalism: "It depends on the government to pick winners and promote economic growth. It also uses capitalist tools such as listing state-owned companies on the stock market and embracing globalism. Elements of state capitalism have been seen in the past, for example, in the rise of

Japan in the 1950s and even Germany in the 1970s, but never before has it operated on such a scale and with such sophisticated tools."[15]

Woolridge's last point, concerning the scale of state capitalism and sophisticated tools, points to a stunning array of state-owned enterprises in a wide variety of businesses. The energy sector is decidedly top-heavy with state-owned companies, ranging from Saudi Arabia's Saudi Aramco to China's PetroChina and Russia's Rosneft and Lukoil. It also includes mining companies, large banks, and, of course, sovereign wealth funds. The last two add a powerful tool to the arsenal of emerging market countries that have gained from the upheaval of the global economy and the discrediting of the free market model. It is estimated that SWFs (including those in advanced economies) have roughly $5 trillion in assets (according to the SWF Institute as of June 2012). That translates into a considerable amount of cash. Yet sovereign wealth funds need some type of free market in which to invest—a certain irony and directly related to the weakness of state capitalism, in that many of its regimes have proven willing to change the rules concerning foreign investment.

The financial clout of billion-dollar sovereign wealth funds allows countries like China, Russia, and Saudi Arabia to purchase stakes of companies in sectors their countries regard as strategic. It also raises significant questions as to where business interests end and foreign policy begins. As the *Financial Times'* Hal Weitzman observed of SWFs and the lack of transparency of many of their number: "What's more, given that they were essentially piggy banks of governments, their motivations weren't necessarily the usual profit and loss goals of private sector companies, so one reason they inspired fear in the developed world was that it wasn't clear what their goals actually were."[16] This trip-wire was hit in the United States when China's government-owned CNOOC sought to purchase Unocal Corp. for $18.4 billion in 2005. It has been an issue in Canada as well when foreign companies, some of them state-owned, have sought to purchase local firms, most recently in 2011 with Sinopec and CNOOC obtaining small and medium-sized oil and gas companies in the North American country. It is also becoming an issue in global agriculture, which has emerged with Arab countries in recent years, via their SWFs or government-related companies, buying in Africa.

One last point is that a state presence in the economy does not automatically make a country part of the state capitalist camp. Norway has a large state-owned oil company, Statoil, and a number of other enterprises, including Norsk Hydro and Telenor, all of which give the state control of over 30 percent of the economy. Norway's SWF, the Government Pension

Fund Global, is also regarded as a major player in global markets, with around $890 billion in assets, equal to an estimated 1 percent of all the world's stocks and bonds. At the same time, Norway's political elite are not using these companies to keep themselves in power or to keep their political parties in office. They are regarded as non-corrupt as well. Moreover, the wealth generated benefits the rest of Norwegian society in the form of generous social benefits, while the country has a functioning private sector. Along these lines, there are substantial differences between Norway and China, the least of which is that the former is democratic and has a well-defined and active civil society.

STRUCTURE OF THE BOOK

The book has eight chapters, including an introduction and a conclusion. Chapter one asks the question, what does the rise of state capitalism portend for the global economy? Related to that is the question, what kind of futures do market capitalism and private companies have? The two stripes of capitalism are likely to increasingly compete aggressively against each other, especially as the state capitalist approach blurs the lines between the corporate and political worlds. Chapter two provides a brief historical note pertaining to state capitalism. Chapter three is focused on the state capitalist experiment in China, which has developed state champion-type companies and SWFs. Chapter four discusses Russia, and chapter five the Middle East, focusing on Saudi Arabia, the United Arab Emirates, and Qatar. The Middle Eastern variation is generally monarchial, is reinforced by a unifying religion (Islam), relies on resource nationalism, and makes extensive use of SWFs.

Chapter six explores state capitalism in Latin America, which has a wider range of regime styles. While Brazil has many aspects of state capitalism, it is democratic on the political side of the equation and has a history of strong private sector companies that have thrived alongside state-owned firms. It is important to emphasize the return of democracy in 1985, as its consolidation brought greater transparency and disclosure of state-owned companies and supportive economic policies. The corruption factor, however, still lingers, as reflected by the Petrobras scandal in 2014. There are also the "resource nationalists," such as Argentina, Bolivia, Ecuador, and Venezuela. These are political halfway houses, dominated by populist leaders and focused on state control over national resources. They also border on "crony capitalism," especially in the cases of Argentina and Venezuela.

Chapter seven discusses the limits of state capitalism. This is an important consideration, as there is no guarantee that state capitalism will triumph over free market economics. State capitalism faces many challenges, such as a weakness of the institutions central to the functioning of a market economy. These institutions encompass a modern legal system and a constitutional order that can protect property rights and enforce contracts, as well as a political system that enforces accountability and limits state opportunism. Another challenge facing the state capitalist model is that there is too much mutual self-interest of government and business, which constantly raises the issues of corporate governance and of cronyism. This plays into the massive problems of corruption that plague China, Russia, and Venezuela. According to Transparency International, in 2013 China ranks 80 out of 177 countries in terms of corruption, with Russia lagging behind at 127 and Venezuela at 160, compared to Norway at 5, the United States at 19, and the United Kingdom at 14. Without a level playing field for businesses, there will eventually be problems of political decisions trumping practical business decisions. If state capitalist companies seek to compete and play by mutually accepted international rules, their political connections are used against them. This has already factored into business rulings over foreign takeovers in Australia, Canada, and the United States. The state capitalist model can also stifle innovation and incentive.

Chapter eight is the conclusion and discusses the future of capitalism in the twenty-first century, with a view that competition between the two rival forms of capitalism will become more intense. Despite the stumble of free market economics from 2008 to 2013, it is wrong to count this type of capitalism out. Moreover, democratic capitalism (in all its variations) is likely to remain an attractive force, especially as it reinvents itself, probably in a world driven less by finance and leverage and more by manufacturing and technology services. The financial system's excesses will be further curbed. State capitalism will likely maintain its adherents, but two of the key countries in this category, Russia and China, confront major political challenges in the years ahead that could detract from their economic trajectories. Russia's 2011 Duma elections or the following 2012 presidential elections were not the easy rubberstamp that the Putin elite believed they would be, while China lives in the shadow of 1989's Tiananmen Square. Why is it that the so-called "Big Data" companies have been founded in the United States and South Korea, rather than China or Russia? Moreover, for all of the state capitalist countries' ownership of large multinational corporations heavily engaged in natural resources, the threatening juggernaut of state-owned companies is less evident in such sectors as agriculture, technology, retail, biotechnology, and infrastructure. When athletes go to put on their soccer or basketball shoes, they reach for Nike or Adidas, not Vlad Putin Supersneakers.

In the short term, state capitalism is likely to be a dominant factor in global economic development. Even in the bastions of free market capitalism, the state role has grown, and calls in the United States for industrial policy have become more vocal, especially considering the nature of the challenge posed by state-owned capitalist enterprises and sovereign wealth funds. In the early twenty-first century, capitalism is in a crisis defined by the battle between private sector companies and their statist counterparts. It is a battle over natural resources, human talent, and profits, with the endgame increasingly looking to beggar-thy-neighbor policies. Free market capitalism is not dead, but it badly needs to reinvent itself and restructure its regulatory systems with an eye to maintaining a more level playing field. Equally important, free marketeers need to give serious attention to the egregiously widening income levels between those at the top and the rest of the planet. This issue has become a political hot button in U.S., UK, and European politics, and it will not easily go away. At the same time, looking at state capitalism as an unbeatable juggernaut is wrong and politically short-sighted. State capitalism has numerous flaws, many of which have been glossed over in the discrediting of free market capitalism. Those flaws are not inconsequential and leave the door open to the potential for major stumbles. Indeed, in 2013-2015 the dynamic expansion of the BRICs gave way to slower economic growth and questions over long-term sustainability.

The rise of state capitalism and how to accommodate it is an issue that is going to be around for some time to come. While globalization has its share of critics, it has left us with a far more interconnected world. That world is increasingly going to be shaped by the emerging market countries, which makes it critical to have a better understanding of the political and economic dynamics affecting the several billion people living there and how the Brazilians, Chinese, and others are going to interact with the rest of the planet. This book will provide readers with a guide to those dynamics shaping the global economy and possible outcomes.

NOTES

1. In 2014, PIMCO moved away from the new normal to the "new neutral," in which economic growth globally will be converging toward

lower yet more stable top speeds, and central banks' interest rates will remain stuck below their pre-crisis equilibrium.

2. For an example of the discussion over emerging markets' middle class, see Ernst & Young, *Hitting the Sweet Spot: The Growth of the Middle Class in Emerging Markets*, 2013.

3. Ian Bremmer, *The End of the Free Market: Who Wins The War Between States and Corporations?* (New York: Penguin, 2010), p. 186.

4. This point is made by Yu Zheng, *Governance and Foreign Investment in China, India, and Taiwan: Credibility, Flexibility, and International Business* (Michigan: University of Michigan Press, 2014).

5. Data from Global 500CNN Money, http://money.cnn.com/magazines/fortune/global500/2013/full_list/?iid.

6. See John Plender, "Nostalgia for the Land of Opportunity," *Financial Times*, April 16, 2002.

7. Scott B. MacDonald, "Global Crisis: How Far to Go? Part III," Yale Global Online, October 14, 2008. http://yaleglobal.yale.edu/content/global-crisis-how-far-go-part-iii.

8. Quoted from Rukmini Callimaatti, "'Capitalism is dead,' Lula Tells Forum," Associated Press, February 7, 2011. www.the.star.com/news/world/2011/02/07/capitalism_is_sdead_lula_tells_forum.html.

9. Timothy Garton Ash, "Can Europe Survive the Rise of the Rest?" *The York Times Sunday Review*, September 1, 2012. http://www.nytimes.com/2012/09/02/opinion/sunday/can-europre-surive-the-rise-of-the-rest.

10. Parag Khanna, *The Second World: Empires and Influence in the New Global Order* (New York: Random House, 2008), pp. 318–19.

11. Martin Jacques, *When China Rules the World: The End of the Western World and the Birth of a New Global Order* (New York: The Penguin Press, 2009), p. 11.

12. Quoted from Joe Leahy, "Brazil—After the Carnival," *Financial Times*, July 10, 2012, p. 7.

13. Steven Levitsky and Lucan A, Way, *Competitive Authoritarianism: Hybrid Regimes After the Cold War* (New York: Cambridge University Press, 2010), p. 66.

14. Joyce Appleby, *The Relentless Revolution: A History of Capitalism* (New York: W. W. Norton & Company, 2010), pp. 3–4.

15. Adrian Wooldridge, "The Visible Hand: State Capitalism," Special Report, *The Economist*, p. 3.

16. Hal Weitzman, *Latin Lessons: How South America Stopped Listening to the United States and Started Prospering* (Hoboken, NJ: John Wiley & Sons, Inc, 2011), p. 97.

TWO

A Short History of State Capitalism

The purpose of this chapter is to provide a brief historical context to the drama that is being played out in the early twenty-first century, of competition between state capitalism and private sector–led capitalism. State capitalism has a long and colorful history. It has gone through a number of transformations as political and economic elites have sought to find better ways to reap the riches of trade, commerce, and industry. In this usually elaborate game, princes and merchants have been both allies and enemies through much of the modern era, with state-backed trading companies setting sail into the far-flung waters of the White Sea and the Atlantic, Indian, and Pacific oceans. The same could be said of industrialists and bankers, who have been friends and allies with merchants and princes as well as bumping heads with labor over changing profit-making paradigms. While the state role, in a broadly defined sense, was often dominant in parts of Europe, the rise of private entrepreneurs, beginning with the Italian merchants and bankers in the fifteenth and sixteenth centuries, increasingly weighed on the direction and rewards of global trade and commerce. Many times this opened fierce debates as to whether business should follow the flag or the opposite. The political influence of corporate leaders, be they of state-owned or private enterprises, became another factor in the march of economic development. Along these lines, a critical link between the developments of the modern market economy, from its early days in the late fifteenth century to the twenty-first century, remains the friction between state-owned businesses and the private sector in those economies that have defined themselves as capitalist. Indeed, the competition between state capitalist companies and private sector companies must be seen through a long historical lens.

IN THE BEGINNING

When the great transformation of Europe into a market economy commenced in the fifteenth century, tremendous opportunities arose for trade and commerce. Significantly, there was a shift from the Middle Ages' arrangement of an economy generally founded upon a social system of rights and obligations to one based on an acquisitive profit-oriented economy of buying and selling.[1] There was also a shift from family-based enterprises and banks to more sophisticated organizations that included non-family shareholders. An additional factor in the economic transformation was the geographical discoveries that brought a massive flow of gold and silver from the Americas to the Iberian kingdoms of Europe. This had the impact of pumping a huge amount of wealth into Spain and Portugal. While the Iberian countries placed an emphasis on their military and religious establishments, they failed to develop strong business organizations or an entrepreneurial business culture, something that took root in the Low Lands, in particular, among the Dutch in the seventeenth century, and across the English Channel in Great Britain. To generalize, a new business culture emerged, based on the idea of putting savings back into businesses, carefully calculating prices and costs, and willingness to assume risks to make gains.

One example of this change was the creation of the Amsterdam Exchange Bank (Wisselbank) in 1609. The bank was supported by the City of Amsterdam, which provided a committee of city government officials to run it. This was a pragmatic market solution to the problem of merchants having to deal with multiple currencies brought in by the trade activities in the city. The bank created a place for merchants to deposit different currencies, which could be drawn from the bank in the form of cheques and debits, or transferred in what rapidly became a standardized currency (called bank money). The result of having a prudently run bank, providing a key service, was that the idea of using the Bank of Amsterdam as a payment agent gained ground, and the volume of trading increased, helping put the Dutch at the forefront of the new capitalism that was taking root.

The development of the market economy in Europe also brought changes in political structures. Kings and princes embarked upon the process of nation-building, creating new alliances. In particular, merchants benefited from larger unified markets, something that came more quickly with political unity—which, in turn, came from a group of strong monarchs asserting their power vis-à-vis the nobility and the Roman Catholic Church. Furthering a mingling of monarch–merchant interests, the latter increasingly served as a source of capital for the former, either through loans or through taxes. As the monarch, merchants, and elements of the gentry worked to establish strong, unified states, backed by military naval strength and capable of opening up new avenues to wealth generation, ideas pertaining to the role of the state in the economy emerged.

MERCANTILISM

One of the first schools of economic thought was mercantilism, which pulled together ideas pertaining to nationalism, self-sufficiency, and national power, around the idea of an actively engaged state. State involvement in the economy came in multiple forms. Economist Daniel R. Fusfeld provides an excellent summary of what become known as mercantilism: "Manufacturing was encouraged by subsidies, special privileges, patents, and monopolies. Foreign trade was stimulated by acquisition of colonies and efforts to keep wages down and regulated by tariffs, navigation laws and trade restrictions. Agriculture was fostered by a variety of policies: In England imports of food were taxed in order to keep out foreign competition, while in France exports of agricultural products were taxed in order to keep domestic production at home."[2]

There were national variations on the mercantilist theme. In France the name most closely associated to mercantilism was the powerful Jean Baptiste Colbert (1619–1683). Born of a merchant family and a close associate of the dominant political figure Cardinal Mazarin, the hardworking Colbert was the minister of finance for more than twenty years under Louis XIV, the Sun King. Colbert's rise occurred at a time when the power of the French throne was dominant and France was aggressively seeking to expand its power throughout Europe and into the Atlantic. This expansion came with a number of wars, which were costly and kept French government finances under pressure. This put Colbert in the position of seeking to increase the national wealth, reduce the country's debt burden, and bolster royal authority.

Colbert gave considerable attention to overhauling the state's finances (by raising taxes on a wide range of items), improving French industry, creating a favorable balance of trade (partially through protectionist measures), and expanding the country's colonial empire.[3] Among his market-oriented reforms was the establishment of the Manufacture Royale de Glaces de Miroirs in 1665. France was spending considerable money on importing highly regarded Venetian glass, which was a drain on the country's finances. Colbert believed that France could produce its own glass; hence his turn to a royal factory. The venture was successful. The Manufacture Royale supplied the glass for Louis XIV's Hall of Mirrors at Versailles, and Venetian imports fell, saving France money. The company was the cornerstone for present-day Saint-Gobain, which traces its roots to 1665 and states its ambition "to become a world leader on the habitat and construction markets, providing innovative solutions to the key challenges of our age: growth, energy and the environment."[4] There is no doubt that Colbert would be proud.

Colbert also sought to attract Flemish clothmakers to France, founded a royal tapestry works, provided regulation of the country's numerous guilds, and pursued protective trade policies to help nurture domestic industry. Public works projects sought to improve infrastructure and reinforce manufacturing and trade policies. Furthermore, the French crown under Colbert created a merchant marine and two trading companies, the French East India Company and the French West India Company, both in 1664. Colbert was stimulated to this action by his observation that British and Dutch trading companies had been successful in stealing a march on the French. The French West India Company's mandate was comprehensive, as it received French possessions on the Atlantic coasts of Africa and the Americas, had a monopoly on trade in the Americas for forty years, and was mandated to settle Canada.

Not all of Colbert's economic policies were successful. The French West India Company failed within a decade, though the French East India Company would last in one form or another until 1790. Colbert, however, left a strong imprint on the idea that the state had a constructive role to play in the country's economic development. In France this tendency came to be referred to as *dirigisme*, broadly defined as a capitalist economic system in which the state exerts a strong directive influence over investment. Indeed, France followed a *dirigisme* approach to its economic development in the post-World War II era, as there was a pressing need to jumpstart a national infrastructure decimated by aerial bombardments, battles, and sabotage, and a business sector struggling with a shortage of capital and facing superior U.S. competition. Consequently French *dirigisme* policies encompassed state-directed investment, economic planning to supplement the market economy, and the creation of state enterprises in strategic sectors, ideas that are still very much alive in the global economy.

THE RISE OF THE CLASSICALISTS

Not everyone believed in mercantilism along Colbert's lines. Some of the earliest anti-mercantilists were the Physiocrats, fellow Frenchmen who believed that wealth came from the land, not commerce. They failed to make much of an impression in French decision-making circles.[5] But it was in England that a more well-articulated response was to take form and give an answer to mercantilism. Indeed, in that seafaring trading nation, mercantilism was initially popular and devoted largely to the expansion of trade and promotion of manufacturing, which led to the withering away of guilds (in contrast to France, where the guilds remained an impediment to industrialization). More significantly, more market-driven ideas were to surface, such as those advanced by Dudley North (1641–1691), a wealthy merchant, who wrote *Discourses upon Trade.* North strongly favored free trade, which promoted specialization, division of labor, and the increase of wealth. As for the role of the state, regulation impeded trade, which ultimately limited the accumulation of wealth. North's views were reinforced by others such as David Hume (1711–1776) and Bernard de Mandeville (1670–1733). The latter's *The Fable of the Bees* was regarded as scandalous, in that de Mandeville argued that economic progress came from the selfish interests of the individual. Indeed, prosperity and economic growth would be expanded by free play to the selfish motives of the individual, limited only by the maintenance of justice (the role of the state limited to that of a referee/keeper of law and order).[6] The classical school also added thoughts about the role of labor and property, including the importance of property rights. By the early eighteenth century, mercantilism was increasingly viewed as a force that restricted individual initiative, limiting the upside to wealth creation.

No discussion about free markets would be complete without a mention of Adam Smith (1723–1790). Central to his legacy was a "system of natural liberty." By this, the Scottish economist meant that individuals would be left free to pursue and advance their own economic interests, a system which would produce the greatest wealth for the individual as well as society. This placed Smith in sharp contrast to those favoring mercantilism and heavy government regulation. Smith noted: "It is not from the benevolence of the butcher, the brewer, or the baker, that we expect our dinner, but from their regard to their own interest. We address ourselves, not to their humanity, but to their self-love, and never talk to them of our own necessities but of their advantages."

Smith acknowledged that government had a role, albeit a limited one. He believed the state existed for the establishment and maintenance of justice, national defense, and the creation and maintenance of certain public works and public institutions. The last point translated into state support for roads and communications, but the cost should be largely shouldered by tolls on users and not the taxpayer. Smith was adamant that anything beyond justice, defense, and certain public works was more of a hindrance to economic growth and wealth creation than a benefit. While the state was to play a limited role, self-interest worked via a system of self-adjusting markets, which took into consideration competitive supply and demand factors to reach a "natural price."

There is one other concept worth noting from Smith's *Wealth of Nations*, the "invisible hand." This directly relates to the role of the individual and the lack of an active state. The concept itself is defined as occurring when individuals seek to maximize their own good and become wealthier; through their trade and entrepreneurship, society as a whole benefits. In a sense, as the wealthier get wealthier, they will create more jobs and allow other people access to the opportunity to seek their own fortune. Along these lines, government intervention in the economy is not necessary; the invisible hand is the best guide for the economy. Smith wrote: "By pursuing his own interest he frequently promotes that of the society more effectively than when he really intends to promote it. I have never known much good done by those who affected to trade for the public good."

Adam Smith's works were followed by others, who came to be called the "classical school" of economics. Some of the best-known include Thomas Malthus (1776–1834), David Ricardo (1772–1823), Jeremy Bentham (1748–1832), and Jean-Baptiste Say (1767–1832). They reinforced the fundamental thrust of free markets, limited government, and individual self-interest. Each economist added certain twists, probably the most significant being Malthus' work on the dangers of overpopulation (which could be held in check by a good dose of "misery and vice") and David Ricardo's comparative advantage (something gained if someone can produce a product or service at a lower cost than anyone else). Against the backdrop of the industrial revolution, first in Great Britain and then in France, Germany, and the United States, the classical school was a dominant approach to economic affairs. For the British, classical economics also fit well into their expansion across the globe, based on trade, industry, and investment. Considerable wealth was accumulated, and through the nineteenth and into the early twentieth century, London was the world's financial, economic, and political capital.

KARL MARX AND ALL THAT

Not everyone was enamored of the free market, industrialization, and the "Invisible Hand." The very different economic world created by capitalism created massive new wealth, freed people from the land, and brought into play a massive surge in globalization that connected far-flung markets and people. At the same time, the march into industrialization came with bad, even brutish, working conditions for labor, environmental pollution, slums, and disparities between rich and poor. Historian Joyce Appleby observed of the industrial revolution: "High-pressure work become the norm, not just because of the operation of the machinery but also because machine owners wanted their capital investment to pay off every second. As mines sank deeper so did the danger from explosives, and all mechanized work filled lungs with contaminants."[7] It should be added that the advance of trade sometimes was forced on unwilling local populations and could have a pernicious side, as in the slave trade and later in opium.

Reactions to the brave new world of machines, regimented labor, and industrial pollution were many. In England, Charles Dickens wrote *Hard Times* in 1854, reflecting the impact of industrialization on his country. Dickens provides insight on the grittiness of industrialization in his depiction of Coketown: "It was a town of machinery and tall chimneys, out of which interminable serpents of smoke trailed themselves forever and ever, and never get uncoiled. It had a black canal in it, and a river that run purple with ill-smelling dye, and vast piles of buildings full of windows where there was a rattling and a trembling all day long, and where the piston of the steam-engine worked monotonously up and down, like the head of an elephant in a state of melancholy madness."

On the political front, however, German-born Karl Marx (1818–1883) and Friedrich Engels (1820–1895) penned *The Communist Manifesto*, a violent denunciation of capitalism and why it would eventually fail. To Marx and Engels, the capitalist system had two key components, capitalists and workers or proletariat, with the former exploiting the latter. The workers produced labor, which was used by the capitalists, who converted into capital. This process, however, left workers exploited and alienated. What ultimately emerges from this system, according to Marx and Engels, is a two-faced economic system, with one side defined by capital accumulation and growth, and the other characterized by exploitation and alienation.

Marx and others came to offer an alternative vision of economic life, based on the view that capitalism would witness increasingly periodic crises, with the biggest capitalists devouring the smaller ones and the middle class or bourgeois, until only a handful of capitalists remain, facing a vast working class. This, of course, sets the stage for world revolution, which would be a total refutation of the free market and the self-serving private sector. The Marxist agenda called for the abolition of private ownership of property (it would be taken over by the state), abolition of all right of inheritance, and the centralization of credit in the hands of a single state-owned bank (which would effectively have a monopoly). All means of communication and transport would also be centralized, and both agriculture and industry would fall under the control of the state. Led by a vanguard of the proletariat (a term later added by Russian Bolshevik leader Vladimir Lenin), human society would move in the direction of a classless utopian society.

Marxism made an impression in the late nineteenth century, a period marked by considerable societal ferment, as many countries moved into a new phase of large-scale industrialization. The socioeconomic upheaval included the 1870 Paris Commune, the wars surrounding the unification of Italy and Germany, respectively, and the rise of an active bomb-throwing anarchist movement that targeted world leaders. Marxism focused on the role of labor, seeking to carve out a more dignified position for workers in the harshness of the industrial revolution. It also gave a boost to the unionization of labor in Europe. Marxism would play an important role in the years ahead, forming thoughts about economic and social development that were to run sharply counter to capitalism, including state capitalism. It was also the intellectual wellspring for an upcoming generation of leaders, such as Lenin, Leon Trotsky, Rosa Luxembourg, and Mao Zedong, who embraced the idea of violent revolution.

THE TWENTIETH-CENTURY LABORATORY

Although communists and fellow travelers (like anarchists and socialists) added an element of societal turmoil, the global economy entered the twentieth century with a decidedly capitalist global political economy, characterized by liberal democracies presiding over large empires. To be sure, autocratic empires still existed—Austro-Hungary, the Ottomans, and Tsarist Russia. One of the world's largest empires, China, was ruled by the feeble Xing dynasty, soon (in 1911) to limp into the mists of history. India was under British rule. The rest of the world was tied together through trade and investment, with London functioning as the financial hub. British, American, German, French, and Dutch capital fueled the creation of rubber plantations, diamond mining, and grain shipments, while technologies improved communications within and between countries. Large privately owned companies strode the globe in search of tea and sugar, critical items to Britain's working-class daily existence. The same companies imported bananas from the Caribbean and Central Americas to the United States and brought Argentine beef to the British. Even rivals like Germany and Britain had high levels of trade and investment with each other.

The world that emerged by the early twentieth century was captured by British journalist and politician Normal Angell (1872–1967), who wrote *The Great Illusion: A Study of the Relation of Military Power in Nations to their Economic and Social Advantage.* What was significant about Angell's writing was that he ruled out the possibility of war between the world's powers, due to what he perceived as a high level of interdependence via economic and financial systems. He observed: "The complexity of modern finance makes New York dependent on London, London upon Paris, Paris upon Berlin, to a greater degree than has ever yet been the case in history. This interdependence is the result of the daily use of contrivances of civilization which date from yesterday—the rapid post, the instantaneous dissemination of financial and commercial information by means of telegraphy, and generally the incredible progress of rapidity in communications which has put the half-dozen chief capitals of Christendom in closer contact financially, and has rendered them more dependent the one upon the other than were the chief cities of Great Britain than a hundred years ago."[8]

Indeed, according to Angell, economic integration between Europe's powers made militarism obsolete. In a sense, he believed, markets and capitalism were so advanced that no one would opt for the insanity of nationalism and war to disrupt it. Sadly Angell's vision was to prove tragically wrong. By 1914 the world plunged into a global conflict that came close to ending free market capitalism, did end a number of empires (the Hapsburgs, Romanovs, and Ottomans), killed more than 8 million people, and left another 21 million wounded.

It also opened the door to a twentieth century initially defined by three competing ideological views concerning economic development: fascism, communism, and democratic capitalism (the latter practiced in the United States, the UK, and France). Fascism was a system dominated by a powerful state, backed by a controlled and limited private sector. This varied between the racial-nationalist welfare system pushed to extremes by Nazi

Germany to the more corporatist experiments in Italy, Spain, Portugal, and Brazil, that sought to organize society along the lines of major interest groups (or corporate groups). These groups included agriculture, business, and labor, with a view of how to achieve common interests.[9]

The recovery from World War I was protracted and greatly complicated by the Great Depression. Democratic-capitalism was under siege from many quarters, and even in the United States, the role of the state was great expanded by President Franklin Delano Roosevelt's New Deal. With the slippage of Germany, Italy, Spain, and Portugal under the fascist flag in the 1930s, and the Soviet Union under the hammer and sickle, the ideas of Adam Smith and other free market economists became questionable in a highly uncertain world order. There was a political element, in that hard times seemed to call for strong leaders, something that appeared lacking in many of the economically struggling democracies, like Weimar Germany, Fourth Republic France, and the British Empire. Leaders like Adolph Hitler and Benito Mussolini simplified complex problems, provided clear-cut solutions, and stirred nationalistic pride.

The Soviet Union's approach to economic development derived from Marx, adding the views of Vladimir I. Lenin, who saw the Communist Party as the vanguard of the proletariat, leading the workers to Utopia. Translated into economic policy, this meant the elimination of the private sector, state planning, and the creation of new party elite who led the way. As these policies did little to help the economy, Lenin and Stalin, who followed him at the helm of the fledgling Soviet state, were more than ready to use force to eliminate opposing voices. Stalin's purges in the 1930s were particularly notorious in dooming millions to firing squads, Siberian imprisonment in a series of gulags, or starvation. While fascism was to leave some private sector activity in a "mixed economy," communism was supposed to an economy run by the state sector, with no room for the capitalist.

The bloody and highly destructive Second World War largely brought an end to the international attractiveness of the fascist model. By year-end 1945, the world was left to two dominant models of economic development: Soviet-supported Communism and U.S- backed democratic capitalism. Both Moscow and Washington supported their share of unsavory regimes, but their competing development strategies set the tone of the Cold War and the emergence of what was initially called the Third World—later termed developing or emerging markets. One significant development in Europe and even the United States was an acceptance of a larger role for the state in the economy. In Europe this was largely due to the damage caused by the war; in the United States it was pushed by the New Deal as well as by the demand for better infrastructure in a booming economy. One example of the state leading a major project in the United States was the federal interstate highway system advanced by the Eisenhower administration, and in the United Kingdom, the embrace of the National Health Care Service.

One of the more vocal voices on the role of the state in economic life was John Maynard Keynes (1883–1946), a British economist and one of the most influential voices of the twentieth century. One of Keynes's most significant contributions was the idea that free market economies did not hold all of the answers and could be a force in pushing up unemployment. Along these lines, he believed in the necessity of state intervention to moderate "boom and bust" cycles—preferably through fiscal and monetary measures but also with public works. In his classic *The General Theory of Employment, Interest and Money* (1936) he stressed the importance of an activist government economic policy, including public works to help reduce unemployment and eventually create demand: "Let us be up and doing, using our idle resource to increase our wealth. With men and plants unemployed, it is ridiculous to say that we cannot afford those new developments. It is precisely with these plants and these men that we shall afford them." His views were decidedly influenced by the harshness of economic conditions during the Great Depression. Following the Second World War, Keynesian economic policies were used in many of the advanced economies, including the United Kingdom.

In the aftermath of World War II, economic policy for most developing economy countries was founded on the idea that a large state role in the economy was the most logical approach. As the economist Lloyd G. Reynolds observed: "In most countries it was accepted with little debate that government is the main instrument for promoting economic development. The old enemy, government, has become the friend and promoter of economic progress."[10] This encompassed the government as a tax gatherer, infrastructure builder, and provider of public services.

The debate over the role of the state had a massive geographical laboratory to run its course during the second half of the twentieth century. Among the advanced economies of North America, Western Europe, and the Asia-Pacific (Japan, Australia, and New Zealand), market capitalism was well entrenched, though there were variations as to the level of state engagement. Moreover, perceptions over the level of state involvement were to change within a number of countries. In the United States this was evident in a swing away from the government being engaged in creating and maintaining a national road network and protecting the environment, under the Eisenhower and Nixon administrations, to a vilification of the government and a pronounced effort to downsize it during the Reagan-Bush I-Clinton years. Ronald Reagan, in particular, was the voice of limited government, outside of a few areas like the military. He was also a firm advocate for reducing taxes and cutting spending (though he failed on that account).

In the United States the role of the state in the economy had evolved along a different path than in Europe, Japan, or many developing economies. Whereas state intervention in the economy was represented by ownership in countries such as France, Japan, or Brazil, ownership of businesses was much more limited in the United States. In contrast to the idea of the "big state," Americans had a preference for "big business." Indeed, the large company was a major defining institution in U.S. economic development from the late nineteenth century and into the twentieth.[11] The United States was, after all, regarded as the land of entrepreneurship, innovation, risk taking, opportunity, and the "creative destruction" of the market, which meant that the idea of government-run or -owned companies had little support.[12] Rather, state involvement in the economy revolved around regulation and taxes, a mindset that was complicated by the emergence of a welfare system and entitlements in the aftermath of the Second World War. Consequently the Reagan Revolution and economic reforms that followed were geared to reduce regulation and unshackle the productive capabilities of business.

In the United Kingdom, the call to arms to limit the role of the state and to assume individual responsibility came from Baroness Margaret Thatcher (1925–2013), who was prime minister from 1979 to 1990. She had strong beliefs that the expansion of the state into many parts of British life—in particular the economy—was ultimately negative, contributing to a dysfunctional economy and a long decline in the country's standing. Thatcher's prescription for this deleterious state of affairs was a policy mix of privatization of state-owned companies, deregulation (largely aimed at the financial sector), and reduction to the power of trade unions (known to tie up the country in repeated strikes). Under her guidance, the government privatized the state's shares in North Sea oil and gas, as well as in British Petroleum, British telecom, British Gas, British Airways, British Steel, and ports and airports. Although she was forced out of office by an internal party coup (helped along by her self-righteousness, rigid nature and seeming indifference to public suffering), Thatcher left a lasting impression on the debate over the role of the state in the economy and pulled the British back in the direction of a more market-friendly system. Economists Daniel Yergin and Joseph Stanislaw observed: "She recast attitudes toward state and market, withdrew government from business, and dimmed the confidence in government knowledge. Thatcherism shifted the emphasis from state responsibility to individual responsibility and sought to give the first priority to initiative, incentives and wealth generation rather than redistribution and equality."[13]

THE SIGNIFICANCE OF TIGERS

Another important part of the story of state capitalism takes place in East Asia. What was to stir the development debate was the rise of Asia during the 1980s and 1990s. Asia emerged from the Second World War with many of its most economically advanced areas destroyed by bombing or fighting, new and inexperienced governments grappling with providing even the most basic of public services, and, in some cases, countries caught in wars for their independence and/or civil wars over political direction. India's and Pakistan's independence were accompanied by war and an uprooting movement of people, while Malaysia defeated a communist insurgency and a divorce with Singapore to which it was initially attached at independence. Indonesia was rocked by a military-communist struggle in the 1960s, while Vietnam, Cambodia, and Laos remained in the deadlock of the Cold War through the 1960s and 1970s. China underwent a civil war (1947–1949) and Communist rule, while Korea became the point of the map where the Cold War turned hot. From 1950 to 1953 North Korea, supported by the Soviet Union and China, fought it out with South Korea, backed by the United States and the United Nations. Considering the political nature of the landscape, compounded by inward-looking economic policies on the part of China and India, Asia's prospects did not look particularly encouraging.

But something important was happening in Asia, first in Japan, followed by South Korea, Taiwan, Singapore, and Hong Kong, and later by Malaysia, Indonesia, Thailand, and China. Myanmar would follow still later. For a Japan emerging from a devastating conflict and occupation, as well as the loss of its colonies (Korea, Manchuria, and Taiwan), capital was in scarce supply, factories lacked equipment (not to mention buildings in some cases), and the communications infrastructure was in disrepair. What was to emerge was a government that guided scarce capital from the financial sector to selected industries (run by the private sector) and helped by tame labor unions (who kept wages down). By the 1960s Japan was rapidly emerging as one of the world's more dynamic economies, based on export expansion. In many regards, Japan's economic approach was similar to the French *dirigisme* efforts in the late 1940s and 1950s.

Japan's success was noted throughout the rest of Asia. Although China and India remained inward-looking, with the former caught up in the highly disruptive Cultural Revolution and Red Guard Movement, Korea, Taiwan, Hong Kong, and Singapore—to varying degrees—saw the state play a role in lifting economic growth, working with local privately owned corporations, and competing in global export markets. The approach was quasi-managed, quasi-free market oriented, something that has left a lasting debate over the developmental nature of the state. To fully call the "Asian tigers" statist-driven leaves out important aspects. Asian policymakers were aware of the failures that occurred elsewhere in the Keynesian demand-management and import-substituting industrialization strategies, in both advanced and emerging economies. At the same time, these countries were sensitive to the need to make cost-efficient and competitively priced products for export.

The East Asian model that was to propel the region forward, with strong growth rates and gradually improving standards of living, allowed for a substantial state role in the economy. Markets are hardly perfect; they have a tendency to be volatile and, on occasion, can have devastating downsides. While there could be agreement with U.S. and British policymakers over a public role in infrastructure, education, basic scientific research, and national security, areas such as currency support, subsidies and protective trade policies for certain economic sectors, and preferred local business partners became more contentious over time, especially as Asian companies made gains at the expense of their American or European counterparts. Nonetheless, the East Asian model became a powerful force in any discussion about development strategies. It was also something that other Asian countries, such as India, Bangladesh, and Myanmar, took lessons from as they moved away from more inward and statist strategies. And most of all, the success of the East Asian economies flew in the face of the Marxist-Leninist school on development. What were supposed to be hapless natives, ruthlessly exploited by imperialists and their "running dog lackey" local allies, actually emerged as significant trading nations, carving out global market shares in a wide range of products and earning a degree of influence in the international system. At the same time the application of capitalist economic policies provided employment, raised taxes needed by governments for upgrading infrastructure, and, over time, pulled millions of out of extreme poverty and enlarged local middle classes. Although the tigers had their own set of challenges, the East Asian model was persuasive due to its track record of relative success.

Asian economic success reflected a process of major changes in the global economy in the late twentieth century, including a revolution in communications, computers, and the use of the Internet, biotechnology, and globalization (a breaking down of geographical borders). In the United States, deregulation of financial markets and technological innovation made the 1980s a decade of growth and allowed the Reagan administration to challenge the Soviet Union to a new weapons race over Star Wars (a missile defense system). The Soviet Union was ill-prepared for such a challenge, as the closed nature of its political-social system failed to allow the circulation of new ideas and the military-industrial complex was falling behind the West. Moreover, most Soviet citizens were increasingly aware of the discrepancy in their standard of living vis-à-vis Europeans and Americans. East Asia's success, including China's turn to market-oriented policies from 1978 on, also resonated with the Kremlin. Reagan could start a high-tech arms race and maintain the abundance of consumer goods, while the Soviets struggled with both, while China's real GDP growth was taking off. By 1991, the Soviet Union dissolved, with a number of new countries emerging from the wreckage. Significantly, the major challenge to capitalism was gone with the end of Russia's communist experiment. The path ahead was to be dominated by capitalism. It is important to emphasize that democratic capitalism emerged as the victor to the Cold War. However, in the post-Cold War era, democratic capitalism did not have the field to itself, as autocratic or quasi-authoritarian regimes embraced capitalism.

THE APEX OF ANGLO-AMERICAN CAPITALISM?

The period from the mid-1980s through the next two decades until 2007 was known as the Great Moderation. The term was originally coined by economists James Stock and Mark Watson in their 2002 paper, "Has the Business Cycle Changed and Why?"—but it was Benjamin Bernanke, then a member of the Board of Governors of the Federal Reserve, in a speech in 2004, who gave it wider use.[14] Bernanke identified the Great Moderation as the substantial reduction in the volatility of business cycle fluctuations, as reflected by major economic variables such as real GDP growth, industrial production, monthly payroll employment, and unemployment rates. The possible causes for this development are central bank independence, structural change, improved monetary policy, or simply good luck.

Indeed, growth was relatively strong through much of this period; inflation was under control, and financial markets rose. And the benefits of the Great Moderation were enjoyed by other advanced economies, including Europe, much of Asia, Latin America, and the Middle East. Even the al-Qaeda terrorist attacks on the United States in 2001 failed to puncture the Great Moderation.

The Great Moderation period also witnessed the apex of Anglo-American capitalism as a model of development. In advanced economies, this meant streamlined government and fewer regulations, especially in the financial sector. This was evident in the dismantling of Glass-Steagall in the United States, which divided commercial and investment banking activities, and the McFadden Act, which created barriers to interstate banking and was enacted to help protect local banks. Deregulation lead to a massive expansion of the use of derivatives in the financial industry, some of it needed for hedging purposes and some of it for out-and-out speculation and profit-enhancement. There was also talk about the democratization of equity, which was used to define the shift of savings of many Americans into investing in equity markets.

And the mix of technology and finance led to the creation of derivatives geared for the expending mortgage market in the United States. The confluence of low interest rates, strong economic growth, and U.S. policies regarding home ownership helped the U.S. financial sector and a group of foreign banks and hedge funds achieve record profits. The less creditworthy and more risky U.S. subprime mortgage loans in particular became attractive to package into higher-yielding derivatives, which were sold around the world to pension funds, asset managers, and sovereign wealth funds. Real estate loans also became a more significant source of business in other parts of the world, as in Ireland, the United Kingdom, and Spain.

The rise of the financial sector in the United States was evident in other ways as well. As a share of the economy, the financial sector's portion of U.S. GDP climbed from around 10 percent in 1980 to a peak of around 40 percent in 2007.[15] The expansion meant that finance was the place that many of the best and brightest turned to make their fortunes, while the rapid expansion of hedge funds and private equity funds added to the mystique of "high finance." The financial industry also gained in political influence, with major contributions filling the campaign coffers of both Democrats and Republicans. Financial capitalism benefited from globalization, as it was able to touch every aspect of economic endeavor, from housing and food to mining.

From a business perspective, financial capitalism had much to sell it, as it was a transforming force, mutating old forces into something bold, different, and capable of generating greater wealth. As the *Financial Times'* Martin Wolf observed in 2007: "Powerful arguments can be made in its favour; active financial investors swiftly identify and attack pockets of inefficiency; in doing so, they improve the efficiency of capital everywhere; they impose the disciplines of the market on incumbent management; they finance new activities and put inefficient old activities into the hands of those who can exploit them better; they create a better global ability to cope with risk; they put their capital where it will work the best anywhere in the world; and in the process, they give quite ordinary people the ability to manage their finances more successfully."[16] Wolf did voice concerns about the challenges posed by financial capitalism, but the self-assured sales job by the financial sector, along with eye-popping profits and compensation, muted most contrary views.

The rise of financial capitalism also raised the issue of the role of the state. For many in the brave new world of Schumpeter-like change, the state was an impediment and clearly behind in terms of its ability to understand the full significance of what financial capitalism was doing. Indeed, it was often easy to move ahead of regulations created for another age of finance, dominated by bricks and mortar (building/branches), customer/community service, and a safe (and boring) place to put money. Financial capitalism would eventually see the melting away of the state, except to sustain some of the basic functions of national security and uphold contract law. But the bright and shiny future outlined by financial capitalism was to demonstrate substantial flaws, as there was a fundamental incompatibility between unfettered global finance and a fragmented system of political sovereignty at the national level. Ultimately, when the bubble of financial capitalism burst, the state would be there to pick up the pieces and guarantee that what was to become the Great Recession did not become a second Great Depression.

THE REST OF THE WORLD FOLLOWS IN THE WAKE

What appeared so successful for the advanced economies was a mix of commonsense policies along classical economic lines, which became known as the Washington Consensus. The term is traced to the British economist John Williamson and describes ten relatively specific economic policy prescriptions that he considered constituted the "standard" reform package promoted for economically troubled developing economies (many of which, at the time, were in Latin America). The prescriptions encompassed policies in such areas as macroeconomic stabilization, economic opening with respect to both trade and investment, and the expansion of market forces within the domestic economy. The term stems from the use of such policies by Washington, D.C.–based institutions, including the World Bank, the International Monetary Fund, the Inter-American Development Bank, and the U.S. Treasury Department. These policies were as follows:

1. Prudent fiscal policies that seek to avoid large deficits;
2. Reduction or elimination of subsidies and rechanneling of public spending toward more pro-growth areas such as education, health care, and infrastructure;
3. Maintaining interest rates that are determined by market factors and are moderate in real terms;
4. Keeping exchange rates competitive (especially if the country is an exporter);
5. Liberalization of imports, with a particular emphasis on the elimination of quantitative restrictions (licensing, etc.);
6. Trade protection through low and relatively uniform tariffs;
7. Inward foreign direct investment, to be encouraged by liberalization of investment regulations;
8. Privatization of state-owned enterprises, as the private sector can run them better;
9. Regulations that impede market entry or restrict competition, except for those justified on safety, environmental, and consumer protection grounds, and prudential oversight of financial institutions need to be streamlined; and
10. Legal security for property rights.

Although Williamson later contended that he did not intend for his ideas to be called "the Washington Consensus," or that they were intended to give market fundamentalism a clearer menu to draw from, these principles served as a reference point for many economic policymakers in the developing world. The Washington Consensus was attractive, in that it offered commonsense ideas about economic development. Indeed, parts of the Washington Consensus were evident in Asia's economic success in the 1980s and early 1990s. Much of Latin America moved in the direction of like-minded reforms, and the former Soviet bloc moved to more market-driven systems. Southeast and East Asia hit a speed bump in 1997–98, related to the buildup of corporate debt and lack of transparency, but was able to rapidly bounce back, pushed along by structural reforms. A critical catalyst was the rise of China into the ranks of the world's leading economies. By the 1990s the Chinese industrial machine was becoming a voracious consumer of commodities, ranging from iron ore and coal to oil and gas. China's dynamic economic expansion had a ripple effect, creating greater demand for goods from economies such as Australia, Colombia, Peru, Brazil, Mongolia, South Africa, and Zambia. China's expansion also occurred simultaneously with and helped reinforce the economic surges of Brazil, Russia, India, and South Africa, which, together with China, became known as the BRICS. All five of these nations followed economic systems broadly defined as state capitalist.

The rise of emerging markets was a significant development in the late twentieth and early twenty-first century. It triggered a debate about how Asia and Latin America were achieving higher growth rates on a relatively sustainable basis. While market reforms along the lines of the Washington Consensus were very much part of the picture, the role of the state remained an important force, especially in Brazil, China, and South Africa. Moreover, the surge in financial capitalism in the United States and Europe was noticed in emerging markets. This took the form of sovereign wealth funds, such as the Hong Kong Monetary Investment Portfolio (1993), China Investment Corporation (2007), Qatar Investment Authority (2005), Russia's National Welfare Fund (2008), Kazakhstan's Samruk-Kazyna JSC (2008), and Trinidad and Tobago's Heritage and Stabilization Fund (2000). The SWFs became an important force in the globalized economy, in many regards a positive force in promoting trade and investment.

Another important development coming out of the rise of emerging markets was the growth of a middle class and the related push in urbanization. A McKinsey & Company study observed: "Emerging markets are changing where and how the world does business. For the last three decades, they have been a source of low-cost but increasingly skilled labor. Their fast-growing cities are filled with millions of new and increasingly prosperous consumers, who provide a new growth market for global corporations at a time when much of the developed world faces slower growth as a result of aging."[17] According to the World Bank, the number of people it considers middle class rose in China from 175 million in 1990 to 800 million in 2005, and in India from 150 million to 265 million over the same period.[18]

A new and unprecedented world of economic growth beckoned in 2007, in which both advanced and emerging economies appeared ready to achieve new peaks of wealth and prosperity. That was not to be. Indeed, the much vaunted Anglo-American financial and private sector–led approach, much of which was captured in the Washington Consensus, was to collide with the hard reality that such a strategy had some very serious flaws.

THE GREAT RECESSION AND REASSESSING CAPITALISM

The financial imbroglio that began in 2007 with subprime mortgages and torched global financial markets was a self-inflicted wound to market capitalism. It quickly led to considerable questioning over whether the deregulation of financial markets was a good thing, especially if the major players indulged in an orgy of leverage and used complexity to create an opaque world imbued with risk. As institutions such as Bear Stearns, Lehman Brothers, and AIG fell into difficulty, confidence in markets and institutions fled. The role of the state in the economy was quickly revisited, as it was left to the government (ironically the pro-market Republican Bush Administration) to prop up the financial system by providing massive stimulus, with help from the Federal Reserve. President Obama, who came to office in January 2008, continued and expanded those policies. Despite the propping up of the U.S. financial system, the Great Recession rippled from the financial and housing sectors into the rest of the economy. The state intervened in the face of an acute market failure. The choices for American policymakers were stark: radically cut spending and allow much of the financial sector to collapse, or pump a massive amount of liquidity into the financial system to avoid a collapse. Considering that the former had been done in the late 1930s with disastrous consequences, the latter policy won out and was implemented.

Although a depression was averted, the financial crisis triggered the worst economic recession since the 1930s. The U.S. economy contracted by 2.8 percent, the UK by 5.2 percent, and Ireland by 5.5 percent. Europe's economic engine, Germany, also contracted by 5.1 percent. The crisis rippled throughout the rest of Europe, where decades of heavy social spending, slowness to enact structural reforms, and dependence on international capital flows resulted in a number of countries—Greece, Ireland, Cyprus and Portugal—turning to the European Union and the International Monetary Fund for help. Greece's troubles began in late 2009 and continued through 2015, pushing unemployment over 20 percent and putting angry people into the street to protest the unexpected and brutal downturn in their standard of living. Questions were also raised over the viability of the Spanish and Italian economies, especially as these economies were deemed potentially too big to bail out. It was only by a concerted EU effort, greatly aided by the European Central bank and the IMF, that the situation was stabilized.

The 2008 crash and subsequent global recession raised serious questions about the future viability of the rough-and-tumble nature of Anglo-American capitalism, with its heavy reliance on the financial sector. These questions focused on the volatility in financial markets, the nature of what the gains were to society, and the rising inequality of income. They also took issue with the dimension of open political systems and the challenge posed by the political class's dependence upon moneyed interests. Indeed, the issue soon focused on who the political class represented. Was it the entrenched financial and industrial interests or the citizens who voted to put political leaders into office?[19] For the cynical it was easy to question the sincerity of liberal democracy and its relationship to corporate interests—in particular, the mavens of Wall Street.

Public resentment over the bailouts of the banks (and other institutions such as insurance giant AIG and General Motors and Chrysler) in 2008 and 2009 in the United States and the United Kingdom also brought greater attention to a widening income gap between the wealthy and less wealthy. The gap between the "working rich" and other American workers emerged as a problem in the early twenty-first century. During the 1950s and 1960s, generally strong economic growth had lifted all boats, and wealth was more evenly divided. This started to change in the 1970s but really accelerated in the 1980s, the 1990s, and the first decade of the twenty-first century, as financial capitalism gained momentum, greater efforts were made to enhance productivity, shareholders of many public companies allowed substantial pay raises to lock in "executive talent," and incentives for executive compensation increased risk taking. In 1965, the typical American chief executive officer made 24 times the annual salary of the American worker; by 2007 that differential increased to 275 times.[20] In many regards, the disparity of wealth and social inequalities in the United States reached levels not seen since the Great Depression.

What is important about income disparity is that it raises a fundamental question about the role of the company in society. This cuts across both democratic and autocratic market-oriented economies. In more open political systems the company needs a franchise with the public, which encompasses everything from providing goods and services to assuming a role of social responsibility. Following the Great Recession, there has been extensive debate over corporate social responsibility, especially as it was taxpayers' dollars that bailed out major financial institutions, and unemployment has remained high in most advanced economies. This was certainly the case in the United States, where the financial system and its new form of capitalism turned out to be have serious flaws. While it was argued by the financial industry that what was done was essential to the global economy (and much of it was and is), the highly lauded risk management of major financial players was unable to halt a series of major crises:

- The October 1987 stock market crash in the United States;
- The savings and loan crisis in the U.S. in 1989–90;
- The bursting of Japan's bubble economy in 1989–90;
- The Asian financial crisis of 1997–98;
- Long-Term Capital Management's (LTCM) collapse and Russia's debt default in 1998;
- The bursting of the dotcom bubble in 2000;
- The Worldcom and Enron scandals in 2001; and
- The Lehman crisis in 2008–09.

Considering the string of crises and rising inequalities, U.S. historian Joyce Appleby, in her *Relentless Revolution: A History of Capitalism*, observed: "Unlike their predecessors who financed railroad construction in the nineteenth century, they invested in securities they created for their customers, throwing caution to the wind in order to make loans with fewer assets as ballast."[21] The Great Recession briefly interrupted this approach, and regulatory efforts were made to reduce risk from the financial sector. However, the massive profits at financial firms continued in the post-Great Recession global economy. The distortions being created in U.S. and European societies, and the often brutal squeezing of the middle and working classes, made income inequality a major consideration, looking ahead, for both private sector–driven and state capitalist economies.

POST–GREAT RECESSION ECONOMICS

While the competition between state and private sector–led capitalism clearly dominates the policymaking environment, these competing systems must not only deal with income inequality issues but also must determine how to cope with new technology and how to achieve natural resource security. Technology was a factor in the upheaval of the Great Recession and the body blow suffered by Anglo-American capitalism. The mix of finance and technology still represents a substantial risk, in the form of high-frequency trading and flash crashes. But even without the mix of finance, technology is a game-charger in great swaths of the global economy. *The Economist* (2014) observed: "Even if new jobs and wonderful products emerge, in the short term income gaps will widen, causing huge social dislocation and perhaps even changing politics. Technology's impact will feel like a tornado, hitting the rich first, but eventually sweeping through poorer countries too. No government is prepared for it."[22] This theme was also picked up by the National Intelligence Global Trends 2030 report, which noted that "the characteristics of IT use—multiple and simultaneous action, near instantaneous responses, mass organizations across geographic boundaries and technological dependence—increases the potential for more frequent discontinuous change in the international system."[23]

Mastering new technology is an important part of how both democratic and autocratic capitalist systems will deal with change in the decades ahead. While countries like China, Russia, and Iran have mastered varying degrees of cyber warfare abilities, it is the flow of ideas and information that favors more open political systems. This is evident from the fact that Silicon Valley is located in the United States and not in Russia. All the same, technology represents challenges even in open societies, especially when seeking to discover the balance between the state authority and big data's influence on the economy and politics. Equally important in this is the issue of how technology provides an important cutting edge in how private sector–driven economies compete with state capitalism. While the level of freedom of communications in democratic political systems can be debated, the argument is starker in socio-political systems that are founded upon control of dialogue and access to ideas. The power found in social networking is difficult to turn off and runs on people's desires to be interconnected. Technology by itself is a disruptive force; technology that is difficult to control is potentially even more disruptive, especially as its user base continues to expand and censorship can be bypassed by the persistent and the tech savvy.

Natural resource security also factors heavily in economic policymaking in the early twenty-first century. A Chatham House study warned: "The world is undergoing a period of intensified resource stress, driven in part by the scale and speed of demand growth from emerging economies and a decade of tight commodity markets. Poorly designed and short-sighted policies are also making things worse, not better. Whether or not resources are actually running out, the outlook is one of supply disruptions, volatile prices, accelerated degradation and rising political tensions over resource access."[24] Those critical resources also include food and water. As the national Intelligence Council observed: "Demand for food is expected to rise at least 35 percent by 2030 while demand for water is expected to rise by 40 percent. Nearly half of the world's population will live in areas experiencing severe water stress. Fragile states in Africa and the Middle East are most at risk of experiencing food and water shortages, but China and India are also vulnerable."[25]

Once again the issue of competition between private companies and state-owned enterprises is brought into play. Chinese companies have been very evident in the process of seeking out and securing natural resources—everything from large tracts of food-producing land to oil and gas. In all fairness, China is not the only country engaged in this practice; it is mirrored by the activities of Brazilian and Russian companies in Africa. Indian companies (public and private) have also been active, as are Japanese (private) and European (mainly private). The return of natural resource politics is one of the major arenas in which private and state-oriented capitalism collides.

CONCLUSION

In the early twenty-first century, the savage bruising of free market capitalism (and its democratic components) left the field open to other ideas, the most challenging of which is state capitalism, many of its practitioners having authoritarian or hybrid forms of government (for example, democratic facades but autocratic rulers). This has created an environment in which market-oriented democracies and their private sector components find their approaches to global economics and business under siege. At the same time, the friction between private and state-owned companies augments stress levels in a global economy already facing considerable uncertainty due to differing developmental objectives with regard to national wealth generation, natural resource security, environment concerns, and ultimately power and influence in the international pecking order. This leaves the early twenty-first century a laboratory of competing ideas over development: private sector, state sector, or a mixed (balanced) approach. One of the outcomes has been trod before: the road to 1914 that pulled in competing nationalisms, sparked by an act of terrorism into a World War. The other outcome has been to seek accommodation between the different types of capitalism, which has its own set of challenges as we shall see in the following chapters.

NOTES

1. Daniel R. Fusfield, *The Age of the Economist* (Glenview, IL: Scott, Foresman and Company, 1977, Third Edition), p. 7.

2. Fusfeld, *The Age of the Economist*, p. 15.

3. Pierre Goubert, *The Course of French History* (New York: Routledge, 1988), pp. 125–126.

4. "Our Markets," www.saint-gobain.com/en/group/our-markets.

5. The leading Physiocrats were Francois Quesnay (1694–1774), a court physician to Louis XV, and Jacques Turgot (1727–1781), who was briefly minister of finance. The latter got into political trouble for pushing anti-feudal and anti-mercantilist reforms.

6. Fusfield, *The Age of the Economist*, p. 21.

7. Joyce Appleby, *The Relentless Revolution: A History of Capitalism* (New York: W. W. Norton & Company, 2010), p. 154.

8. Norman Angell, *Europe's Great Illusion* (London: Simpson, Marshall, Hamilton, Kent & Co. Ltd., 1909), pp. 44–45. This was a pamphlet, republished in book form as *The Great Illusion* in 1910.

9. For a more comprehensive look at fascism and corporatism, see Howard J. Wiarda, *Corporatism and Comparative Politics* (Armonk, NY: M. E. Sharpe, 1997) and Renzo De Felice, *Interpretations of Fascism* (Cambridge, MA: Harvard University Press, 1976).

10. Lloyd G. Reynolds, *Economic Growth in the Third World: An Introduction* (New Haven: Yale University Press, 1986), p. 109.

11. John Micklethwait and Adrian Wooldridge, *The Company: A Short History of a Revolutionary Idea* (New York: The Modern Library, 2003), p. 103. They noted: "By the outbreak of the First World War, the big company had become a defining institution in American society: the motor of one of the rapid periods of economic growth in history; a dominating figure in political life; and a decisive actor in transforming America from a society of 'island communities' into a homogenous national community. Thanks largely to its embrace of this extraordinary institution, the American century was under way."

12. Daniel Yergin and Joseph Stanislaw, *The Commanding Heights: The Battle for the World Economy* (New York: Free Press, 2002), pp. 341–342.

13. Yergin and Stanislaw, p. 104.

14.   Remarks by Governor Benjamin S. Bernanke, "The Great Moderation," at the meetings of the Eastern Economic Association, Washington, D.C., February 20, 2004.

15.   Michael Lind, *Land of Promise: An Economic History of the United States* (New York: Harper Collins Publishers, 2012), p. 440.

16.   Quoted from Dani Rodrik's weblog, June 19, 2007. Rodrik.typepad.com/dani-rodrik-weblog/2007/06/martin_wolf_mak.html.

17.   McKinsey Global Institute, "Urban World: The Shifting Business Landscape," October 2013. Richard Dobbs, Janna Remes, Sven Smit, James Manyika, Jonathan Woetzel and Yaw Agyenim-Boateng. http://www.mckinsey.com/insights/urbanization/urban_world_the_shift.

18.   Skolkovo Business School—Ernst & Young Institute for Emerging Market Studies, *Hitting the Sweet Spot: The Growth of the Middle Class in Emerging Markets* (2013), p. 4. "By the World Bank's measure of U.S.$2–13 per day, the celebrated economic growth of emerging markets nations has put millions of people into the middle class in recent years."

19.   This issue was underscored by the U.S. Supreme Court decision in April 2014 to further reduce limits on election spending, striking down a decades-old cap on the total amount any individual can contribute to U.S. federal candidates in a two-year election cycle. This echoed the 2010 Citizens United decision that struck down limits on independent campaign spending by corporations and unions. Journalist Adam Liptak further observed: "The ruling, issued near the start of a campaign season, will very likely increase the role money plays in American politics" ("Supreme Court Strikes Down Overall Political Donation Cap," *The New York Times*, April 2, 2014. www.nytimes.com/2014/04/03/us/politics/supreme-court-ruling-on-campaign-contributions.html).

20.   David Owen, "The Pay Problem: What's to be Done About CEO Compensation," *The New Yorker*, October 12, 2009, p. 58.

21.   Appleby, *The Relentless Revolution*, p. 402.

22.   "Coming to an Office Near You," *The Economist*, January 18, 2014, p. 9.

23.   National Intelligence Council, *Global Trends 2030: Alternative Worlds* (Washington, D.C., National Intelligence Council, December 2012), p. vii.

24.   Bernice Lee, Felix Preston, Jaakko Kooroshy, Rob Bailey, and Glada Lahn, *Resources Future, A Chatham House Report*, December 2012, London.

25.   National Intelligence Council, p. v.

THREE

Market Leninism at Work in China

The South China Sea emerged in the late twentieth century as a zone of overlapping maritime claims between China, Taiwan, the Philippines, Malaysia, Brunei, and Indonesia. The intensifying interest in this watery zone was the potential represented by oil and gas fields beneath the water's surface. This was amply reflected in 2014, when the state-owned CNOOC (China National Overseas Oil Corporation) temporarily installed a $1 billion deep-water rig in waters disputed with Vietnam. CNOOC suddenly found itself in the middle of the South China Sea controversy. Vietnam's response to this was an official government protest, an effort to block the waters in the disputed area, and a round of anti-Chinese riots. The last, which took Beijing by surprise, damaged Chinese businesses operating in Vietnam. CNOOC, however, remained offshore from Vietnam, protected by an armada of Chinese naval ships, increasing tensions. CNOOC brought more rigs and announced in June that it was opening nine new blocks in the South China Sea to foreign oil companies for exploration. Although COOOC eventually departed the area, the development left negative sentiment vis-à-vis China, the region's traditional hegemon.

CNOOC's involvement in China's maritime disputes raises many questions about the company and its relationship with the Chinese state. Listed on the Hong Kong and U.S. stock markets, the company's Bloomberg listing says: "CNOOC Limited, through its subsidiaries, explores, develops, produces and sells crude oil and natural gas. The Group's core operation areas are Bohai, Western South China Sea, Eastern South China Sea and East China Sea in offshore China. Internationally, the Group has oil and gas assets in Asia, Africa, North America, South America and Oceania." The company also has a market capitalization of a little over $77 billion. In many regards CNOOC's description makes it sound like a smaller version of Exxon Mobil (with a market capitalization of $442 billion), Royal Dutch PLC ($267 billion), or British Petroleum ($163 billion). Indeed, CNOOC competes in many of the same waters, territories, and markets as these private sector companies. However, there is one major difference: ownership. The major oil companies from the United States, the Netherlands, and the United Kingdom are overwhelmingly owned by private sector shareholders. The same cannot be said of CNOOC. Although the company counts the Overseas Chinese Bank, Al Rajhi Bank, Macquarie Group, and Invesco among its shareholders, the controlling majority of shares are held by the Chinese state through various entities. Moreover, the company's top management must be acceptable to—and to some extent are vetted by—the ruling political elite, the Chinese Communist Party (CCP). This is not the case with Exxon Mobil, Royal Dutch Shell, or British Petroleum. And it is questionable that any of these private sector companies would be used (or give the appearance of being used) to advance their country's foreign policy goals in a maritime dispute, as CNOOC was in 2014.

China is dependent on foreign supplies of energy, a factor that drives the country to aggressively seek new sources of oil and gas. Because of this, Chinese energy companies are actively spanning the planet to discover, help produce, and transport oil and natural gas, as well as coal, back to the homeland. Along these lines, China's companies are involved in such far-flung locations as Angola, South Sudan, and Venezuela, balancing cost-efficiencies and logistics with discreet national security interests. At the cutting edge of China's energy policy are large state-owned enterprises that include CNOOC, China National Petroleum Company (which owns Petro-China), and Sinopec (China Petroleum and Chemical Corporation). This handful of companies and others represent one dimension of China's projection of its national interest overseas. They are also large multinational businesses that seek and do make profits, deal with shareholders (to varying extents), and compete with their Western private sector competitors. The challenge that these state-owned companies face, as do policymakers around the world that deal with them, is straightforward: are they corporations pursuing objectives, or are they extensions of the interests of the Chinese state?

It is the purpose of this chapter to examine state capitalism in China, with the view that the strategy has many strong points but also some critical weak points that increasingly make the country vulnerable to a sharp economic downturn and related social upheaval. China's economy over the long term will continue to grow, but it faces major challenges along the way—the most significant of which is how it will handle such stress tests as an aging population, the restructuring of the economy from top-down investment-led growth to a greater role for the domestic economy, and how to make its financial sector less opaque and more creditworthy. At the heart of this is the CCP's role of maintaining a pact with its citizens that they forego political activity (leave that to the party) in exchange, for economic prosperity. Thus the CCP has been willing to allow citizens to enjoy economic freedom via market economics, but political activity remains under the rubric of the Leninist one-party state. Since the 1980s this system has left China in a near-perpetual mode of strong economic growth. The looming challenge is what happens when growth slows or, in a more extreme scenario, contracts? Related to this is the question of how the relationship between the party and state-owned businesses and the largest private sector companies evolves. As it is wrong to regard the CCP as a monolithic organization with all party members marching in lockstep (despite appearances), the relationship between the party and state-owned corporations is not a simple one, sometimes leading to strong differences. The sometimes ambiguous relationship between state-owned enterprises and the party complicates China's global reach. It also significantly raises serious questions over the long-term competitiveness of the Chinese model of autocratic state capitalism vis-à-vis democratic private sector–led capitalism.

THE RISE OF CHINESE STATE CAPITALISM

State capitalism has been successful in China. Real average GDP growth from 1979 to 2013 was close to 10 percent, a stunning achievement by any standard. According to the World Bank, this strong growth helped lift 500 million people out of poverty. Moreover, throughout the last three decades, China climbed from a relatively weak and struggling developing economy to become one of the world's two largest economies and a key stabilizing force to the global system in the Great Recession. China's industrial development has been and continues to be fueled by key natural resources, making it a major trade partner to a host of other counties, ranging from Argentina and Angola to Indonesia and Zambia. What happens in China has important implications for global markets, ranging from copper, oil, and coal to currencies and corporate bonds. In the early twenty-first century China has clearly re-emerged as a significant global power.

Capitalism in modern China has a varied history. The Qing dynasty (1644–1911) practiced a rudimentary form of capitalism, but the state played a dominant role in maintaining infrastructure, running imperial monopolies and controlling trade. The apogee of imperial power came with the Qianlong Emperor (r. 1735–1796), and what followed was a prolonged and economically disruptive period of internal upheaval and foreign encroachment. The dynastic political center throughout the nineteenth century was increasingly feeble and eventually unable to hold China together. In 1911, the Qing dynasty collapsed, and China entered a chaotic period dominated by warlords, a civil war between the Nationalists (Koumintang or KMT) and Communists, and in the 1930s by an aggressive Japan seeking to incorporate parts of the Asian mainland into its imperial domain. Conditions for a functioning capitalist economy were only further derailed by the advent of the Second Sino-Japanese War in 1937, and that conflict morphed into the Second World War. The resumption of the struggle between the Communists and Nationalists soon resumed, but in 1949 the Communists under the Great Helmsman, Mao Zedong, emerged victorious.

Following the Communist victory, China's experiment with capitalism was confined to what was left of the Republic of China, namely Taiwan. On the mainland, the Communists under Mao turned the economy inward, emphasized self-sufficiency, and eliminated sources of capitalist poison, such as wealthy landlords, merchants, and industrialists. The new economic system was state-controlled, marching to the order of set production targets, controlled prices, and allocated resources. Among the radical economic experiments were the shifts in the 1950s of the peasants to large communes and the infamous Backyard Furnace Campaign, which sought to transform China into of the world's leading iron producers. Unfortunately these policies led to many peasants melting their farm tools to make very poor-quality iron, which complicated food production and helped push China into a severe famine (1958–1961). This also led to a partial eclipse of Mao's power.

China's economic development was further hindered by considerable political foment. Much of this was guided by Mao, who reasserted his control during the late 1960s with the Cultural Revolution, aimed at the country's political elite, including party officials, bureaucrats, and intellectuals as well as any leftover members of the old regime. By Mao's death in 1976 the Chinese economy was inward-looking, filled with inefficiencies, and characterized by low living standards—even by standards among developing countries. The main economic actors were the centrally controlled state-owned enterprises, which generally were not competitive but offered what was often referred to as the "iron rice bowl": low pay but lifelong employment and some form of company-provided social benefits.

Prospects for the emergence of China as the world's second-largest economy with an embrace of market policies did not seem particularly positive in the immediate aftermath of Mao's death. The ultra-left clique led by Mao's widow appeared ascendant, and government policies kept the Chinese economy relatively stagnant and inefficient. Most aspects of the economy were managed by the central government, which meant there were few profit incentives for firms, workers, and farmers. At the same time, competition was hardly existent, and foreign trade and investment flows were small, deriving largely from Soviet-bloc countries. Rounding out the picture, price and production controls caused distortions throughout much of the economy.

The trajectory of China's economy radically changed in 1978, when Deng Xiao-ping, a diminutive member of the Communist Party since 1923, emerged as the dominant political figure. Unlike Mao and many other members of the party, Deng was highly pragmatic. He is well known for his comment: "It does not matter if the cat is black or white; it is a good cat as long as it catches the mouse." The implications was that certain capitalist practices had value and should be adapted to improve the Chinese economy—and, with that, the standard of living for the Chinese people. Deng had seen firsthand the damage of rigid ideological views and understood the population's desire for political and social stability.

Deng Xiao-ping's reforms liberalized the country's agricultural sector, provided incentives for a fledgling private sector, created special economic zones, and worked to attract foreign direct investment. The reforms also decentralized contracts over economic activity, allowing local businesses to make their own decisions. The results of this change were rapid economic expansion, a growing urbanization of the population, and an overall improvement in living standards. China made considerable strides away from being an agriculturally based economy toward becoming an increasingly industrial manufacturing economy. It initially had many of the natural resources to fuel industrialization, but as China moved through the 1980s, its needs for foreign inputs increased. At the same time, serious questions emerged over the effectiveness of the country's SOEs, which seemed increasingly less attuned with the greater demands for market efficiencies. By the late 1980s many of the SOEs represented a "zombie" threat, companies that had lost their economic effectiveness and were allowed to continue, propped up by state help. Privatization was not seen as an option in the 1980s, and there was a strong desire for "Reform without Losers." Nonetheless, the reforms were creating losers, and most of them were SOEs.

A major catalyst for the embrace of SOE reform was political: Tiananmen Square. In late 1980s the Chinese economy encountered a number of problems. The fast pace of economic growth was beginning to slow, inflation was becoming an issue, and the world outside China was radically changing as the Soviet Union headed into collapse and the forces of globalization were gaining ground in terms of trade, investment, and the spread of liberal democratic ideas. In 1989 these forces came into play in Beijing's Tiananmen Square, where students and workers protested corruption and called for democratic reforms. Although the party was able to rally its forces and ruthlessly suppress the protest movement, the events shook China's leadership.

Faced with a global political economy in the throes of its most significant change since the Second World War and internal rebellion at home, China's leadership moved to redefine Communism, seeking to make it more pragmatic and ultimately less rigid ideologically—at least in the economic sense. As journalist Richard McGregor observed: "Instead of trying to protect the moribund state sector which was threatening to sink the economy and the political system along with it, the party decided on a new, high risk course of action. The party resolved to ruthlessly streamline government enterprises, place the survivors atop of the commanding heights of profitable industrial economy under its control and pilot them into global business arena. Chinese leaders wanted worldly enterprises that were both Communist and commercial at the same time." [1]

China under Deng's guidance (he died in 1997) and that of his successors, Jiang Zemin (1993–2003) and Hu Jintao (2003–2013), made a great economic leap forward, and the SOEs played a role in the transformation of China. During the early part of this period, economic control of various enterprises was turned over to provincial and local governments, which were generally allowed to operate and compete on free market principles, rather than under the direction and guidance of state planning. This was to be an important development, as it pushed some state-owned enterprises to take control of their own destiny and seek to be less dependent on the state—that is, to move to become competitive.

The relationship between the state and the market underwent deeper changes in 1990s and the first decade of the twenty-first century. The main force behind this was the CCP's recognition that many SOEs were still not competitive economically and that it was not necessary to have a state company in every sector of the economy. This led to the encouragement of private sector companies, which rapidly gained ground in the economy. In the mid-1990s the government pushed in a more sustained fashion to move the larger state-owned companies into strategic sectors and consolidate their positions by acquiring smaller companies. The reform process was highly political, as the government had to balance the short-term social cost of reform against the longer-term prospect of slower growth without reform. [2] Although the number of SOEs shrank and their share of fixed income asset investment declined from 58 percent in 2004 to below 35 percent in 2012, the state remains heavily represented in strategic sectors related to energy, power generation, metals and mining, telecommunications, and transportation.[3]

The changes in China's state capitalist strategy cannot be appreciated without taking into consideration the rate of urbanization as a driving force. In 2011, 50 percent of China's population was urbanized, a radical departure from the country's agrarian past. According to World Bank projections, in 2080 China's urban area is expected to be home to close to 1 billion people—close to 70 percent of the total population. Along these lines, urbanization is seen as a central element of China's future economic expansion. The massive development of housing, shopping malls, ports, roads, airports, and mass-transit rail all require steel, copper, and other industrial inputs. According to Lou Jiwei, Chinese Minister of Finance (March 25, 2014): "Urbanization is a powerful engine of China's sustained and healthy economic growth."[4] The price tag over the 2014–2020 period is forecasted at $6.8 trillion. Linked to the growth of cities, the government also made a push to connect these urban centers by rail. By 2020 the high-speed rail network is expected to expand by about two-thirds, with the addition of another 7,000 km (4,800 miles).[5]

Related to China's urbanization is the development of a growing Chinese middle class, hungry for goods and services the likes of automobiles, public transit, and clean water. The capital invested into China's urbanization is fundamentally an effort to create a larger middle class that has a stake in the system, makes a value-added contribution to the economy's shift to services, and appreciates the role of the CCP in delivering the above. The creation of a new "Chinese dream," a more affluent China, depends on the ability to construct the necessary infrastructure.

CHINA, INC.

China's rise has led to numerous warnings of the dangers of "China, Inc.," a matrix of CCP, the national bureaucracy, state-owned enterprises, and well-connected heads of privately owned companies following the guidelines of an autocratic single-party state. According to Ted Fishman, author of *China, Inc.: How the Rise of the Next Superpower Challenges America and the World* (2006), observed: "China still only makes one-twentieth of everything produced in the world, but on the world stage it plays the role of a new factory in an old industrial town. It can spend, it can bully, it can hire and dictate wages, it can throw old-line competitors out of work. It changes the way everyone does business."[6] Simply stated, China's emergence as an economic power, constructed around and led by China, Inc., is a geo-economic game-changer.

At the top of China, Inc., are President Xi Jinping, Premier Li Keqiang, and the State Council. The dominant player is President Xi, who came to power in 2012 and quickly moved to consolidate his power. Although the president is elected by the National People's Congress for five-year terms, the decision of who becomes the top leader is a long and arduous selection process that occurs behind the doors of CCP meetings and is played out between the party's factions. There is a degree of rough-and-tumble in the process, though the rise of a Chinese leader to the presidency is usually not accompanied by widespread and lethal purges that used to occur under leaders like Mao or the Soviet Union's Joseph Stalin.

It is important to clarify that we use the term "China, Inc.," in a loose fashion. China has embraced state capitalism and is an autocratic state, but there are different and contracting views within the ruling party. There are factions that can and often do disagree with the president, though they do so at their risk. Chinese presidents have considerable power and sit at the apex of the power pyramid, but they do not always get their way. Moreover, serious policy stumbles can weaken the incumbent—to which earlier post-Mao leaders were sensitive due to concerns over being ousted. Consequently, China, Inc., is a broad construct of important political players that together share the attachment to some form of state capitalism but at times can be found as rivals.

President Xi's rise to power did involve some drama, as his faction dealt with the more populist or "New Left" wing of the CCP built up around Bo Xilai, the charismatic former Chongqing Party Secretary. Bo had created a network among the military and various populist-leaning party officials, and was seen as a possible rival to Xi. Considering the sensitivity of political transition and the major developmental challenges facing China, the overriding imperative is to maintain control. Xi was able to outmaneuver Bo, playing to the concerns of the more conservative sectors of the party. The problem for the New Left leader was a nasty scandal involving his high-profile wife in the murder of a British businessman. Bo's wife was found guilty, and he eventually was convicted of bribery, embezzlement, and abuse of power. Although President Xi operates in a different political environment than that of Russia's Vladimir Putin, he faces many of the same challenges, including a large wealth gap, collusion between government officials and business, official corruption at all levels, declining morality, and grave social inequality and injustice. As Putin did in his early period of rule, Xi needs to firm up his regime's standing among the people and restructure the economy in such a fashion as to develop a domestic sector capable of strong growth.

Xi also needs to maintain the party's centrality to the development process, keeping any potential newcomers from emerging. Bo gave him the opportunity to knock a rival out of the competition, weakened further opposition form the New Left (at least for a while), and demonstrated to the public that even party high-fliers like Bo were not above the law as far as corruption is concerned. Bo's trial was noted for its relative transparency: he was found guilty of corruption, abuse of power, and acceptance of bribes, and is serving a suspended death sentence.

Unlike Russia's autocratic state, which tends to coalesce around a powerful personality, China's autocratic system is constructed around party factions—one more market-oriented, the other more populist. Xi's faction was clearly of the former; Bo's the latter. What made Bo a challenge were his development of a national following, his media savvy, and his ability to play to social inequalities now evident in China's society—for which he advocated, as a solution, the revival of Maoist values and stronger state intervention in society and the economy. Along these lines, Bo might have sought to roll back the use of market ideas in the management of the economy.

Bo was not the only high-ranking official to fall in President Xi's anti-corruption campaign. Thousands of officials were disciplined, including Zhou Yongkang, the country's former public security minister until 2012. Zhoiu rose through the ranks of the oil industry (he became chairman of the National Petroleum Corporation in 1996), moved into important government posts (including serving as chief of the security apparatus), and became one of nine on the Politbureau Standing Committee. At the top of the political pyramid, Zhou appeared to the untouchable. He had close relationships with key security people and amassed a small fortune over his years in the service of the state. Indeed, it was his fortune that made him a target of the government's anti-corruption campaign in 2014.

Zhou's fall from grace also was a matter of power. President Xi emerged as one of his country's strongest leaders since Deng Xiaping. Bo was a threat to his power. Zhou's crime was not corruption, per se—as so many other officials have fit that description. Rather, Zhou reportedly resisted stripping Bo Xilai of his position as Chongqing's party secretary. Additionally, rumors abounded that Zhou had plotted to upend Xi's rise to power and install Bo as president.[7] Bo was ousted, and Zhou retired. A year later China launched an investigation, and Zhou was soon under a cloud. In December 2014, he was arrested and it was reported that he had been expelled from the party. More bad news for Zhou was revealed in April 2015 when he was charged with accepting bribes, abuse of power, and leaking state secrets.

Xi's anti-corruption campaign was reinforced at the Fourth Plenary Session of the 18th CCP Central Committee in October 2014. The main focus of the meeting was legal reform and "governing the country in accordance with the law." The key point of this was to institutionalize stronger oversight over officials and reduce opportunities for corruption. It also reinforced Xi's position as the dominant political force within the CCP, which dominates China, Inc., and the country. The anti-corruption theme continued to be evident in 2015.

CHINA, INC.'S, CORPORATE WORLD

In the early twenty-first century, the business core of China, Inc., is a group of companies heavily oriented toward oil and gas, coal, metals production, transportation, and infrastructure. The large state-owned banks and sovereign wealth funds round out the mix of industry and finance, presided over by a political and related business elite. At the same time, state ownership is hardly all-encompassing, as it was meant to be under communism. Large private sector companies do exist, such as Alibaba (technology), though ties between the government and business leaders are usually close. State-owned companies are less evident in such sectors as consumer goods, food processing, agriculture, textiles, or pharmaceuticals. Indeed, state-owned companies are less oriented to meet domestic demand, but heavily oriented toward acquiring inputs required to keep the country's industrial machine moving. In this, Chinese SOEs venture out into the global economy and actively compete with western and emerging markets rivals.

What brought worry about China, Inc., to private sector companies was the buying spree embarked upon in the first decade of the twenty-first century. By 2004, China consumed 40 percent of the world's coal, 25 percent of the nickel, and 14 percent of the aluminum.[8] Simply stated, China's strong economic growth gave a strong impetus to the state-owned energy and mining companies to go out into the larger global economy and seek to lock up natural resources. The Brookings Institute's Erica S. Downs observed in 2014: "A decade ago, China's state-owned energy and mining companies seemed on the verge of becoming a global juggernaut. Driven by an unexpected surge in the country's commodity demand and fueled by cheap loans from state-owned policy banks, Chinese firms went on a resource buying binge from Afghanistan to Zambia. Many outside observers, especially in the United States, fretted that 'China, Inc.' would be able to acquire anything, anywhere, and nobody could stop them."[9]

Oil was an area where the concern over China quickly became a factor. While the Asian country has substantial reserves, it became a net oil importer in the 1990s. The nation's oil consumption accounted for one-third of the world's oil consumption growth in 2014, a level that is likely to remain high over the next decade. In 1994–1998 the Chinese authorities restructured most state-owned oil and gas operations into two vertically integrated companies that possess upstream and downstream assets, China National Petroleum Corporation (CNPC) and Sinopec. A third company is CNOOC, which has a mandate for offshore oil exploration and production. CNOOC also has extended its downstream operations in China's southern province of Guangdong. A smaller trio of companies round out China's oil industry: the Sinochem Corporation, CITIC Group, and Yanchang Petroleum.

What gained Chinese oil companies considerable international attention and placed them at the heart of China, Inc.'s, perceived grab was their appetite for foreign assets. CNOOC, CNPC, and Sinopec launched expeditions into Africa, the Middle East, Central Asia, and Latin America. CNPC bought PetroKazakhstan (based in Alberta, Canada) for $4.18 billion in 2005, while Sinopec in 2010 bought nine percent of the Canadian oil sands firm Syncrude for $4.65 billion from ConocoPhillips. While CNPC bought into operations in Azerbaijan, Canada, Iran, Sudan, Syria, and Venezuela, Sinopec was active in Gabon, Sudan, Ethiopia, Cameroon, Angola, and Nigeria. The aggressive push by Chinese oil companies to gain assets, aided by financial inducements from various arms of the Chinese state, generated concern in countries such as Australia, Canada, and the United States over China, Inc.'s, perceived juggernaut in the pursuit of global energy supplies. In some circles, the surge in Chinese asset buying generated a serious of debate over China's intentions in global energy markets—a no-holds-barred grab to secure control over what were likely to be precious energy resources that would give Beijing greater leverage over the global economy.

One of the flashpoints of China, Inc.'s, energy drive came with CNOOC's attempt to purchase the U.S. company Unocal in 2005. Unocal was up for sale, and CNOOC offered its management $18.5 billion, which topped an earlier offer from Chevron Texaco. CNOOC's main interest in Unocal was not to gain a strategic hold over U.S. assets per se, but to obtain the company's Central Asia assets. CNOOC hired Goldman Sachs to advice it and was surprised to find that its offer galvanized opposition from members of the U.S. Congress. American political concerns focused on the $13 billion available from the Chinese government for the purchase. From a technical viewpoint (clearly overlaid with nationalist sentiment), many members of Congress regarded CNOOC's bid not as a free market transaction, but as a thinly veiled bid by the Chinese state to acquire U.S. energy assets. The result was that CNOOC pulled its offer for Unocal, and a lower $17.1 billion offer from Chevron Texaco was accepted. The very public rebuff by the United States to a Chinese oil company left Asian firms much more cautious in their approaches to other bids. This was evident in CNOOC's next major effort in North America, an $18.2 billion bid for the Calgary-based Nexen in 2012. Unlike with Unocal, this time the Chinese company was able to gain approval from both Canadian and U.S. regulatory authorities. CNOOC had earlier partnered with Nexen, both in Canada and in the Gulf of Mexico. At the same time, CNOOC had completed a number of smaller U.S. acquisitions, which did not generate political tensions.

While Chinese companies have moved to purchase overseas assets to enhance reserves and used joint ventures to acquire technology and experience from western companies, the involvement in countries hostile to the United States has raised questions over possible political motives on the part of Beijing. Of particular concern from the United States has been a growing cooperation between China and Russia in 2014. China has also been active in supporting the left-leaning governments in Venezuela, including extending the beleaguered Maduro administration a $4 billion loan linked to oil supplies in 2014.

The long reach of China, Inc., was hardly limited to oil and gas assets. China Minmetals, China's largest metals and mining company, was founded in 1950 and has its headquarters in Beijing. With 146,000 employees and an annual revenue of close to $27 billion, Minmetals' operations span the globe in its quest for iron, copper, zinc, and lead. The company is also involved in trading in electrical products and maintains subsidiaries in marine shipping, real estate, and finance. Some of the company's subsidiaries are listed on stock exchanges in Hong Kong and Shanghai. Like the oil and gas SOEs, Minmetals is identified as part of China's aggressive state capitalism, reaching out into the global economy and accumulating assets and market share.

Minmetals' overseas acquisitions include the Northern Peru Copper Corp. (which it operates out of Vancouver as a joint venture with Jiangxi Copper Co.) and another joint venture with U.S. Century Aluminum Corporation in Jamaica for bauxite, most of OZ Minerals (an Australian mining company in 2009), and Anvil Mining (which gave it ownership of Zairian Copper mine Kinsevere). In 2014, the Chinese mining company led a group that agreed to pay $5.85 billion for Glencore Xstrata's Las Bamabas copper projects in Peru. Minmetals also made an unsuccessful bid in 2011 for the Canadian mining company Equinox Minerals, which had extensive copper-cobalt operations in Australia, Peru, and Zambia.

Minmetals' significance is underscored by China's role in the global copper industry. The industrialization and urbanization of China requires tons of copper wires. China imports 80 percent of its copper needs, most of it accounted for by infrastructure construction. According to the World Bureau of Metals Statistics, China imported 3.2 million tons of copper metal and 10.1 million tons of copper ore and concentrate in 2013. Its consumption totaled 9.83 million tons in 2013, or 47 percent of global demand.[10]

Another major Chinese global heavyweight is Chinalco (Aluminum Corporation of China), which is narrowly focused on nonferrous metals. Founded in 2001, it is the world's second-largest alumina producer, the third-largest primary aluminum provider and the fifth-largest fabricated aluminum producer. Moreover, it has the strongest copper capabilities in China. With 66 member enterprises, Chinalco operates in more than 20 countries and has been ranked as a fortune Global 500 company. According to the company's website, its "mid- and long-term strategy is to strengthen its aluminum business, optimize its copper segment and improve the sector of rare metals . . . Chinalco will expedite the shift to the upper stream of the industrial chain and the high end of the value chain, enhance the supply for strategic mineral resources and the national defense industry, and build itself into a world-class mining company with the greatest growth potential."[11] As Chinalco expanded overseas, it gained considerable attention, some of it hostile, in its bid to gain foreign assets.

Chinalco's involvement with the global mining business cannot be fully understood without an understanding of China's need for iron ore. As China emerged as the world's major factory, its need for steel rose substantially. As demand for steel rose, China gradually outstripped what its domestic mining industry could provide in terms of iron ore. China's iron ore imports rose steadily through the 1990s. By the early 2000s, Chinese steel makers were increasingly a force in global iron ore markets, which eventually led to their demanding greater say as to prices.

The global iron ore industry was dominated by three companies: Vale, Rio Tinto, and BHP Billiton. Together these companies controlled more than 70 percent of seaborne iron trade. Before the coming of Chinese companies, their main customers (steel producers lacking iron ore mines) were located in Japan, South Korea, and Taiwan. Every year the largest iron ore company would negotiate with the largest steel producer, their chief consumer. The prices agreed between these two parties would then be accepted by the rest on both sides. The spot market was small and largely inconsequential. This was to change when Chinese companies began to be a force in the first decade of the twenty-first century. In 2005 China's Baosteel became the largest consumer and negotiator with the iron ore miners. Although this followed the past formula, the Chinese changed the way things were done the next year, when Baosteel represented a consortium of Chinese companies, which gave them more leverage in the negotiations. At the same time, a larger number of smaller Chinese steel makers opted to use the spot market, a development that reduced the significance of the negotiated prices. The Chinese government did not support this last move, seeking to limit competition among iron ore importers and injecting a degree of confusion.

Relations between the producers and Chinese consumers deteriorated, and in 2009 the former returned to negotiating with the Japanese, Korean, and European users. Although the non-Chinese companies agreed to a price, the Chinese companies still wanted a lower price. In the middle of these negotiations, it was announced on July 4, 2009, that four Shanghai-based Rio Tinto executives had been found guilty of accepting about $13.5 billion in bribes and stealing commercial secrets. This left an impression of the willingness of the Chinese government to play hardball politics vis-à-vis multinational companies, a signal to iron ore companies. The Chinese argued that the Rio Tinto case indicated that Beijing was assuming a tougher approach with foreign companies doing business in China. Professor of Law Liu Junhai, of Renmin University in Beijing, opined: "The Rio Tinto case is sending a signal to the world, that China's model of managing its financial activities has changed. In the past, we overemphasized the country's development, but didn't pay enough attention to regulation."[12]

Another interpretation of Rio Tinto case came from Jerome A. Cohen, a professor of law at New York University, who was critical of the court for holding largely closed proceedings and conducting a trial that favored the prosecution. He noted: "The question is: can we trust the facts? It's now clear the prosecution was related to the iron ore negotiations. It's O.K. to prosecute for wrongdoing. But it seems to be a selective prosecution. The case has done a lot to show the world the problem of China's justice system."[13]

The iron ore issue fit into the Rio Tinto scandal. In 2007 BHP Billiton (the world's largest mining company) landed a $127 billion bid for its rival, Rio Tinto. As McGregor observed, this was seen in China "as an unambiguous threat, because of the way it could create a near monopoly in the seaborne iron ore trade in particular."[14] In the charged environment of off-and-on negotiations, the Politburo decided to oppose the BHP Billiton bid. The instrument to stop the purchase was Chinalco, which soon purchased 9 percent of Rio Tinto at a cost of $14 billion.

Chinalco's bid failed in large part due to the blatant political heft behind it. McGregor noted: "Then there was the way Chinalco's bid had been financed. The money came from a consortium led by the China Development Bank. Initially established to fund local infrastructure projects, CDB had lofty ambitions to follow China, Inc., abroad."[15] In the middle of this, the global financial crisis hit and commodities fell. BHP Billiton pulled back from its bid, but Chinalco moved ahead, offering $19.3 billion for the company. During this time it was also leaked that Chinalco's chairman was to be appointed to the cabinet. For anyone looking for direct links between the state and the company, the chairman's promotion to a cabinet position was evidence that China, Inc., was a very real thing.

After the deal fell apart in June 2009, when well-articulated Australian concerns were raised over selling a large part of its national resources to the Chinese state, the arrest and eventual sentencing of four of Rio Tinto's China-based executives seemed very questionable. After all of this, negotiations over iron ore prices were inconclusive, and the spot market came to play a more important role, especially during the 2009–2011 price spike. Indeed, iron ore remains a very political arena in terms of prices and competition. Prices declined since 2011, with a bruising acceleration in price collapse in 2014 and in early 2015. This was partially caused by the cooling of the Chinese economy, but also by a decision by the large private sector companies—in particular, Australia's BHP, Brazil's Vale, and the UK's Rio Tinto—to overproduce with an eye to driving out of business less cost-efficient Chinese companies. Although China's state-owned companies have considerable clout and backing from the state, they do not always have things their way, especially when they play in commodity markets and face large and experienced competitors.

BEYOND OIL AND MINING

China's state capitalism is not limited to oil and mining. Chinese companies are also involved in land investment (via the China State Farm Agribusiness Corporation and the China National Agricultural Development Group), the development of water resources, and power generation. The Chinese state's active involvement in the economy is not limited to direct state ownership of companies. It maintains ownership stakes in key companies through various organizations, such as Legacy Holdings, which is partially owned by the Chinese Academy of Science. Legacy Holdings provides the state ownership in key sectors like technology, but it is indirect. Investment in technology is important, as it determines how the economy will evolve going forward, in terms of value-added enterprises, an example is Lenovo. The company manufactures and sells personal computers and handheld devices, as well as providing Internet and IT services. Lenovo represents itself as a private sector company, with shares traded on global stock exchanges. The company was founded in 1984, with its funding helped by the Chinese Academy of Science. In 2005 Lenovo acquired IBM's personal computer business. It has joint headquarters in Beijing and Morrisville, North Carolina, with research facilities in those two locations and Singapore, and production facilities in China and Japan (with a joint venture with that country's NEC). Competing in Global PC and Internet markets, Lenovo functions very much as a private sector firm. However, the Chinese company has clearly benefited from its relationship with the Chinese state—even if that relationship is indirect, through a government academic entity. As *The Economist* (2012) noted: "the Chinese Academy of Science provided it with seed money (and still owns lots of shares), and the government has repeatedly stepped in to smooth its growth not least when it acquired IBM's personal-computer division for $1.25 billion in 2004."[16] Consequently, Lenovo is a private sector company, but there remains an important relationship with the state, albeit indirectly.

Another example of the Chinese state's indirect involvement in a "private sector" technology company is Huawei, one of the country's most important multinational corporations. It is the largest telecommunications equipment producer in the world. The company's ownership, with President Ren Zhengfei and the employees believed to hold a large stake, remains opaque. Ren Zhengfei, who founded the company in 1987, was a former officer (having held the rank of major) in the People's Liberation Army (PLA) and a member of the CCP since 1978. Those ties to the CCP and PLA did not hurt Huawei. In 1996, the company was competing with foreign companies in the domestic telecommunications business, and needed funds. Upon hearing this, Vice-Premier Zhu Rongji went to Huawei with the heads of the four largest state banks and promptly made credit available.[17]

Although Huawei has business relationships with a wide range of companies around the world, including Vodafone, Motorola, and France Telecom, and has 21 R+D institutes in counties such as China, the United States, Canada, and Russia, its links to the Chinese state have raised security concern in the United States, United Kingdom, and India. In the case of the United States, Huawei came under scrutiny because of concerns that its telecommunication equipment may be designed to provide Chinese authorities with access to U.S. systems. The U.S. Congress also questioned the Chinese company's proposed merger with 3Com in 2005 and its bid for a Sprint contract in 2010. This followed a review by the U.S. Committee on Foreign Investment (CFIUS).

THE FINANCIAL ARM OF CHINA, INC.

It would be difficult to understand China's state capitalism without being aware of the role played by the country's financial institutions, in particular the four state-owned Industrial and Commercial Bank of China (ICBC), the Agricultural Bank of China (ABC), the Construction Bank of China (CCB), and the Bank of China (BOC). Each of these institutions emerged from the original mono-bank during the 1980s. Since then the "Big Four" have played a critical role in helping to pump credit into the broader economy. Initially all four banks were overstaffed, lacked skills, and suffered from the absence of a business orientation. They were also accustomed to providing easy credit to government and party officials in the local and national bureaucracies, a practice that on more than one occasion led to a build-up of bad loans and periodic corruption scandals.[18]

The state bank sector underwent a badly needed overhaul in the 2000s. Powers at the central bank (People's Bank of China—PBOC) were strengthened when it was given authority to charter banks and set up regional banks, similar to the U.S. Federal Reserve system. Along the same lines, the Big Four concentrated more control and authority in their national headquarters in Beijing. These moves reduced the influence of local party officials and bureaucrats over loan practices. The reform also had the adverse effect of aligning the banks closer to the interest of

Beijing's political elite. Economist Barry Naughton observed in 2007: "All of these changes gave the Big Four much greater autonomy, while at the same time tying their fortunes much more closely to the central government. From this time on, all important changes of the Big Four, for better or for worse, were determined from Beijing."[19] This meant something, as the Big Four accounted for 53% of total banking system assets in 2005.

No explanation of China, Inc., would be complete if it left out the China Development Bank and the Export-Import Bank of China. Founded in 1994 and headquartered in Beijing, the China Development Bank is led by a cabinet minister–level governor, under the direct jurisdiction of the State Council. The bank's mission is stated as supporting the development of the national infrastructure, basic industry, and national priority projects; promoting coordinated regional development and urbanization; and facilitating China's cross-border investment and global business cooperation.[20] The critical line in its mission statement is as follows: "It aligns its business focus with national economic strategy and allocates resources to break through China's economic and social development." Along these lines, the CDB has been highly supportive in helping Chinese companies expand into overseas markets, a development that accelerated after 2008. While U.S. and European banks retrenched in the aftermath of the financial crisis, the CDB emerged as a major lender.

The Export-Import Bank of China plays an important role in the advancement of its country's business in overseas markets, with a mandate to promote foreign trade and investment, as well as development assistance in concessional funding. Concessional lending means that funds are provided on terms more generous than those from commercial sources. While the concessional part of the bank's business is key, export credits also play a significant role.

One last institution worth noting, in terms of China, Inc.'s, financial infrastructure, is the Chinese Investment Corporation (CIC), the country's sovereign wealth fund. CIC's role in the past has been to purchase stakes in foreign resource companies. Established in 2007 with $200 billion of assets under management, CIC has grown to $515 billion.[21] The fund holds the state's stakes in China's largest banks and is an active investor in real estate, infrastructure, and agriculture, as well as U.S. Treasury bonds.

THE RISK OF CONTRADICTIONS

Chinese state capitalism has many strengths, but it also contains inherent contradictions which are increasingly problematic and which, if not addressed, have the potential to undermine China's newfound global reach. These contradictions strike at the core of the issue of just how competitive state capitalism is going to be over the long term. Although China's multinational SOEs exhibited a powerful and noticeable surge into international markets, with commodities being one of the most evident cases, the juggernaut appears to have slowed, the pace more determined by daily business concerns as opposed to geopolitical positioning, despite the 2014 involvement of CNOOC in the South China Sea. In the view of observers Elizabeth Economy and Michael Levi: "China has followed in others' footsteps by shifting from merely buying resources through trade to investing directly overseas, in doing so, it is joining other countries, not creating a new phenomenon on its own."[22] They add to this: "it remains true that many Chinese companies (particularly the larger ones) benefit from government support that most of their competitors do not possess, thus changing the world of natural resource investments."

Along these lines, two contradictions dominate: how Chinese companies must balance corporate objectives in an increasingly competitive global business landscape and how China's leadership is going to balance party dominance and rising corporate influence that may not perfectly align in terms of policy direction. The CCP wants Chinese businesses to become global heavyweights but docs not want to surrender any power outside the party-dominated channels. Most Chinese corporate leaders would probably prefer to conduct business without political interference, but the CCP—through both direct and indirect links—is reluctant to step back. The perception that Chinese state-owned companies are the spear-tip of China's geopolitical ambitions obviously does not help advance business goals, which involve market share, access to finance, and ultimately profitability.

Yet the rise of Chinese multinationals provides China with leverage in international affairs. But this is not without internal problems. The concern is that China, Inc., represents a long-term challenge to the political status quo of party control and the contradictions built into the market-Leninist system. This friction is likely to grow, especially as many of the country's new wealthy elite are linked to the party and businesses—a fact not lost on the rest of the Chinese public.

By the early twenty-first century the interests of the CCP and state-owned business had fused into a closely entwined relationship. It is important to underscore the scale of SOE clout. By 2012 the State-Owned Assets Supervision and Administration Commissions (SASAC) companies accounted for 43 percent of China's GDP.[23] Although China has a private sector with well-known companies, the top corporate formations were dominated by SOEs, which benefited from a business–government power nexus.

The ambiguity over the status of China's major state-owned enterprises creates ongoing friction between business and the state. The state, through various institutions, dominates the corporate sector for the very simple reason that the party will not tolerate any other sources of power. China's SOEs represent jobs, privilege, and a path to wealth. With that comes influence in China's economic and trade policymaking, foreign policy clout, and leverage with party members. The major business interests of SOE management coincide with those of the party, in that the corporations provide employment for party officials and their families, business profits generate revenues for the state, and overseas these companies fulfill functions that give the Chinese government advantages over other nations—gaining market share, gathering intelligence, and helping secure natural resources.

The position of state-owned enterprises, however, is complicated by a number of other factors. Companies listed on global stock exchanges are exposed to the demands of foreign shareholders, many of whom have a very different perception of transparency and disclosure. Simply stated, foreign shareholders care about the company's financial soundness, its ability to generate profits, and its respect for their rights as owners, which encompasses a clear picture of ownership and the role of the board of directors. The same can be said for holders of Chinese corporate bonds. Neither shareholders nor bond buyers in other countries care about the CCP or domestic Chinese politics, as their involvement is based on financial considerations. Foreign shareholders and bond holders are also willing to seek redress under the law. In sharp contrast, Chinese corporate managers are supposed to know where their loyalty is—the party, which, of course, represents China. To stray from this path is to run the risk of being removed from the top management positions. Thus, China's state-owned enterprises feel a pull from external business demands for greater transparency and disclosure, opposed to the requirement of loyalty to the party.

The other contradiction is that, in the overseas surge of Chinese companies, results have not always met expectations. Indeed, Chinese companies have come on the international stage late; U.S., European, and Japanese companies are already long-established in such businesses as iron ore, coal, and copper mining, as well as oil and gas. In addition Chinese companies face other relative latecomers from India, Brazil, the Republic of Korea, and Malaysia. This has meant that Chinese firms have often found themselves competing for lower-quality, high-risk projects. Veteran oil executive Fu Chengyu (formerly CEO of CNOOC and currently at the helm of Sinopec, the country's largest refiner) observed in 2004: "It's actually not easy for us to find good projects. The world oil industry has a one hundred year history. The good projects are already taken."[24] This is evident in the track record of China's oil companies investing in countries that have held somewhat dubious human rights records, as in Sudan, Libya, Iran, and Venezuela. Such investment practices also had a political dimension, in that the above-mentioned counties were generally anti-Western and, more narrowly, anti-United States, a fact that added a degree of friction into the often tetchy Beijing–Washington relationship.

Yet another dimension of investing in more high-risk project areas is the political risk. This was brought home in 2007, when Chinese oil workers were kidnapped in Nigeria and nine Chinese oil workers were killed in Ethiopia by Somali rebels. The rebels of the Ogaden National Liberation Front, numbered around 200, killed a number of Ethiopians as well. The ONLF also kidnapped seven Chinese workers and urged "all international oil companies to refrain from entering into arrangements with the Ethiopian government as it is not in effective control of the Ogaden despite the claims it makes."[25]

While Nigeria and Ethiopia were shocks to the Chinese, Libya was a rude awakening to the world's new geopolitics. Chinese companies discovered this in 2011, when Libya's autocratic Gaddafi regime collapsed, forcing 36,000 Chinese personnel to flee. Chinese state-owned companies are thought to have invested $14.2 billion in Libya from 2007 to 2013.[26] Libya was a policy test for China. China's longstanding foreign policy was based on noninterference. This allowed it to conduct business with some substantially odious regimes, as in Sudan and Zimbabwe. China had a relatively comfortable relationship with Gadaffi's Libya; but even there—despite considerable investment and buying of Libyan oil—China's role was not entirely appreciated. Iraq's problems in 2014 raised the issue of exposing Chinese workers and investments (estimated at $14.3 billion) to local political instability.

The Chinese government has been slow in responding to the risks of its citizens, the workers of state-owned companies. Although many Chinese multinationals are state-owned, and most have connection to the state in the broadest sense, providing outright military protection raises tough foreign policy questions in Beijing. As one analyst noted in 2014 in regard to Iraq:

Not only will a slowdown or halt in Iraqi oil production surely affect China and its companies, but the Chinese government faces criticism from its citizens over its inability to adequately protect them while abroad. Beijing has a difficult decision to make. It can opt to pay the economic and political cost of not begin up its military presence in the region, despite public opinion. Or it can decide to increase the presence of PLA units and perhaps establish a military outpost in Djibouti or the Seychelles. In this case, however, both the U.S. and India will be likely to see such a move as a Chinese attempt to undermine their regional influence, contributing to tensions.[27]

While political risk is a major preoccupation for China's overseas companies, poor due diligence has also played a role. One need only look as far as the Sino Iron Project in Western Australia to see evidence of this. Developed by Citic Pacific and Metallurgical Corporation of China (MCC), the project has been behind schedule and substantially over budget. Brookings Institution China expert Erica S. Dawns noted in 2014: "The project is US $6 billion over budget and four years behind schedule. Some industry experts think it may never be economically viable."[28] The management's mistakes included an unawareness of environmental challenges specific to the project site (radically different from China) and a failure to understand Australia's immigration and labor laws. The latter was hugely problematic, in that MCC had planned to use low-cost Chinese workers to develop the project, which did not happen.

The problem of balancing of corporate and party interests in an autocratic state capitalist system is not unique to China. Many of the same concerns face corporate leaders in Russia (see the following chapter), Kazakhstan, and even Malaysia and Singapore—the push-pull of state interests versus corporate interests. While Chinese corporate interests generally align with state objectives, they occasionally are at cross-purposes, which creates tensions. Directly related to this is the high level of corruption found in party ranks and their links to business interests. This, in turn, has another political dimension: how it plays out in the view of the vast majority of Chinese, who do not appreciate the easy access of high-ranking party officials to sources of wealth—something that is painfully evident in corruption scandals.

POWER POLITICS, BUSINESS AND CORRUPTION

While China, Inc., is able to bring a focus of state resources to particular sectors and challenges, it has a problematic underbelly. In particular, economic reforms are easier to pursue than political reforms, but even the former are now more complicated. China's future economic development is contingent upon how much the state will be willing to step back from its heavy involvement in the economy and whether it will allow a more private sector–led system to emerge, especially in the deepening of the domestic economy. Li and McElveen observed: "corporate and industrial interest groups have encroached on the governmental decision-making process, either by inducing policy deadlock or manipulating policies in their favor."[29] The influence of business, therefore, is evident in how China is approaching economic policies, with an overlap into the social and political fields.

President Xi's version of state capitalism, based on the restructuring of the economy, clearly has both domestic and external consequences. While there is a strong desire to make China's SOEs more competitive, and continued use of them to advance political/security goals, the shift from investment-led growth to greater domestic demand has a political element that cannot be ignored. Reforming the Chinese economy means taking on well-established entrenched interests that straddle the world of business and the party. Because the party maintains such a high level of control over any other potential centers of power, party members dominate the SOEs and even many of the large private sector companies. Thus it makes good sense for successful and up-and-coming business leaders to be CCP members. The problem is that this has created a politico-economic group with interests that put them in opposition with structural changes that President Xi is enacting.

The need of the party to maintain its dominant position in Chinese politics has traditionally resulted in periodic purges. Mao Zedong was particularly notorious for this, but Chinese politics have seen sweepings of the ranks. As earlier discussed, President Xi Jinping took aim at the cozy networks of power and wealth that established themselves in the era of "socialism with Chinese characteristics." In the Chinese leader's anti-corruption drive, a broad swath of individuals, families, factions, and societal forces that do not answer directly to him are the targets. The 2014 purge was a clear, calculated effort to eliminate potential rivals, especially those with ties to former Chinese presidents. *Financial Times* reporter Jamil Anderlini observed: "In the Chinese system, arrests like that are not accidents since everyone in the power structure is acutely aware of where invisible patronage linkages lie."[30]

The challenge represented by purges is that while they may, to some degree, placate the citizens in the street, they can also be disruptive to the smooth running of the country. For many older Chinese, such political cleansings strike a memory of Mao Zedong's Cultural Revolution, which brought the country to a standstill. The purge also extended into the ranks of military, with several top-ranking generals from the previous administration being charged with corruption and selling officer ranks. At the same time, other forces that might have sought to uncover and point to official corruption were on the receiving end of enhanced government controls and repression. This included journalists, lawyers, nongovernmental organizations, activists, and other vestiges of civil society. Anderlini observed in mid-2014: "Most telling has been the harsh prison sentenced handed down to transparency advocates for their peaceful anti-corruption campaigns and calls for party officials to disclose their assets. The message is clear: the authority to decide who is corrupt and who is not is the exclusive domain of Mr. Xi and his closest allies."[31] Considering that such purges tend to make the link between wealth and wealth-generation (being wealthy and showing it vis-à-vis the actual act of earning that wealth), China's big business, both in its private sector and in its state-owned companies, is clearly vulnerable to any politics among the country's political elite.

There is another dimension to the efforts to clean up corruption and the use of purges: President Xi clearly recognizes that China is heading into a period of substantial change in the economy. As the economy transitions from investment-led growth to domestic demand-driven expansion, there is a strong likelihood that growth will slow. Considerable attention is given to China's economic data, in particular the state of its property market, exports, manufacturing, and real GDP numbers. There is also a focus on bankruptcies, which the government has selectively allowed. All of this points to the stark fact that the Chinese economy, for all of its substantial achievements, has massive problems that must be dealt with. Some of these problems—an overextended property market, pockets of weak companies kept alive by loans, and a large and poorly regulated shadow banking system—point to the elevated risk of a financial crisis. China's debt levels are currently moderate, but a financial crisis would most likely raise them in an extreme case to over 90 percent of GDP and be a major drag on any quick recovery to strong GDP expansion.

The anti-corruption campaign allows President Xi to amass power, clamp down on any potential threats to his (and the party's) power, and shore up the party's legitimacy vis-à-vis the population, all before a potential economic storm hits the country. History remains a key factor in China; the current leadership has no desire to be caught by the loss of the Mandate of Heaven, the ability to rule during dynastic China by virtue and accomplishment. The Mandate of Heaven was often lost by emperors and their families through corruption, failure to respond to crises, and/or foreign threats. In the early twenty-first century the trigger increasingly appears to be an extended credit boom, which is slowly heading into a conclusion. This means that, at some point, the Chinese economy will hit a considerably lower pace of growth (the feared hard landing), at which point the pact between party and citizen will be tested and hard decisions will have to be made in implementing tough reforms. China's risk of political and social turmoil is rising, undermining the feared economic juggernaut, which is often perceived as seeking to obliterate the Western private sector. Chinese state-owned companies are a challenge, but they have considerable political drag that cannot be easily dismissed. China's autocratic state capitalism has its limitations, which will be more fully explored in chapter seven.

CONCLUSION

There can be no illusion that China's state capitalism is competitive with more private sector–led capitalism from the West. At the same time, China, Inc., does not live up to its reputation—at least not in the sense of being a monolithic, well-run, financially lubricated turbo-economy pushing China down the road to global domination. There is a China, Inc., in the sense that the ruling communist party dominates almost every aspect of political activity in the country, permeates the country's business sectors, and incorporates the larger state-owned companies in its strategic vision for China. Along these lines, the geopolitical objectives of China's political elite and policymakers are reflected to some degree in the increasingly strategic reach of Chinese companies. But the use of market mechanisms in economic policymaking, the encouragement of private sector companies, and the need for expertise are creating internal contradictions for China, Inc., a potentially alternative power center based on economic considerations that usually, but not always, line up with the leadership's views and imperatives. In many regards Chinese state capitalism has helped Asia's largest country return to the global stage as a power to be taken seriously. Although aspects of this are alarming to more private sector–based economies, especially considering the autocratic and often opaque nature of China's government, there are many weaknesses and contradictions that undercut Beijing's global reach and its ability to consistently project power beyond traditionally (Asia) and more narrowly defined arenas (South China Sea and East China Sea). The much-feared juggernaut of China, Inc., has limits. Indeed, those limits represent a problematic roadmap for the future, as the very nature of state capitalism carries with it a group of contradictions that have serious risks to the entirety of China's development goals.

NOTES

1. Richard McGregor, *The Party: The Secret World of China's Communist Rulers* (New York: Penguin Books, 2012), p. 37.

2. Ibid.

3. Dong Zhang and Owen Freestone, "China's Unfinished State-Owned enterprise Reforms," Economic Roundup Issue 2, 2013, Australian Government, The Treasury. http.www.treasury.gov.au/Publications AndMedia/Publication/2013.

4. Quoted from Dexter Roberts, "A $6.8 Trillion Price Tag for China's Urbanization," *Bloomberg Businessweek*, March 25, 2014. www.business week.com/articles/2014-03-25/6-dot-8-trillion.

5. James Miler, "Building The Ocean," *The Economist Special Report: China*, April 19, 2014.

6. William Grimes, "Car Clones and Other Tales of the Mighty Economic Engine Known as China," *New York Times,* February 15, 2006. www.nytimes.com/2005/02/15/books/5grim.html?_r=d.

7. Matt Schiavenza, "The Most Powerful Man in China Is About to be Purged," *The Atlantic*, April 3, 2014.

8. Alex E. Fernandez Jilberto and Barbara Hogenboom, "China's Growing Economic and Political Power: Effects on the Global South," *The Asia-Pacific Journal: Japan Focus*, December 24, 2007. Japanfocus .org/barabara-hogenboom/2611.

9. Erica S. Downs, "Whatever Became of China, Inc.?" Brookings, June 24, 2014. http://www.brookings.edu/research/articles/2014/06/11 -whatever-became-china-inc-downs.

10. Jesse Riseborough and Rebecca Penty, "Minmetals Group Buys Glencore Peru Mine for $5.85 Billion," *Bloomberg,* April 14, 2014. www .bloomberg.com/news/2014-04-12/minmetals-group-to-buy-glencore -copper-project-for-5-85-billion.html.

11. About US. http://www.chinalco.com.cn/zglyen/gywm/gsjj/A04 0101web_1.htm.

12. Quoted from David Barbaza, "China Sentences Rio Tinto Employees in Bribe Case," *The New York Times*, March 29, 2010. www.nytimes .com/2010/03/30/business/global/80riotinto.httml?pagewanted=alle_r=0.

13. Ibid.

14. McGregor, *The Party,* p. 38.

15. Ibid., p. 59.

16. *The Economist*, "State Capitalism's Global Reach: New Masters of the Universe," January 21, 2012. http://www.economist.com/node/ 21542925.

17. McGregor, *The Party*, p. 204.

18. Barry Noughton, *The Chinese Economy: Transitions and Growth* (Boston: The MIT Press, 2007), p. 456.

19. Ibid., p. 456.

20. www.cdb.com.cn/English/colum.asp?columId=99.

21. Zhang Dingmin, "China Wealth Fund CIC Posts 10.6% Return as Equity Rally," Bloomberg, July 26, 2013.

22. Elizabeth Economy and Michael Levi, *By All Means Necessary: How China's Resource Quest Is Changing the World* (New York: Oxford University Press, 2014), p. 66.

23. Cheng Li and Ryan McElveen, "Can Xi's Government Strategy Work?" *Current History* (September 2013), p. 207.

24. Quoted in Downs, "Whatever Became of China, Inc.?" Brookings, June 24, 2014.

25. "9 Chinese Workers killed in Ethiopia," *China Daily*, April 24, 2007. www.chinadaily.com.cn/chiona/2007-04/content_858956.htm.

26. From The Heritage Foundation's Global China Investment Tracker.

27. Andrea Ghiselli, "Could Iraq Be Another Libya for China?" *The Diplomat*, June 24, 2014. thcdiplomat.com/2014/06/could-Iraq-be-considered-another-Libya-China/.

28. Downs, "Whatever Became of China, Inc.?"

29. Cheng Li and Ryan McElveen, "Can Xi's Government Strategy Succeed?" *Current History* (September 2013), p. 207.

30. Jamil Anderlini, "Xi Jinping's Anti-Corruption Drive in China Takes Autocratic Turn," *Financial Times*, June 23, 2014. http://www.ft.com/intl/cms/s/0/9b645f40-fac1-11e3-8959-00144feab7de.html#axzz3SQ5Z4HPl.

31. Ibid.

FOUR

In the New Tsar's Court

In 2008 Russia won a short eight-day war against Georgia, a part of the former Soviet Union. The nation of Georgia was the birthplace of Joseph Stalin, and today the country has a population of a little under five million. As wars go, it was not much of a contest, considering Russia's overwhelming military superiority, its support in two secessionist regions (Abkhazia and South Ossetia), and the lack of allies willing to support Georgia. The United States, Georgia's main ally, was caught up in the Lehman shock and the beginnings of the Great Recession, while much of Western Europe was feeling the financial chill that was soon to lead to a major sovereign debt crisis, and the rest of the world was focused on the Beijing Olympics. In 2014, Russia annexed Crimea from another neighbor, Ukraine, demonstrating a willingness to brave economic sanctions from the West. Russia was also active in stirring up separatist sentiment in Eastern Ukraine, a region with a large Russian ethnic group. Both Georgia in 2008 and Ukraine in 2014 represented a muscular, military-laden return of Russian nationalism to the global stage. For anyone watching, the Russian-hosted Winter Olympics held in Sochi, with considerable pomp and circumstance, underscored a strong historical tradition of the late Tsarist era. The combination of political stability, years of economic expansion, and a more aggressive nationalism clearly signaled to the world that Russia was back as a great power, a move popular at home among a population still living in the shadow of the Soviet Union's faded glory as a former superpower.

While it is easy to focus on the hard power dimensions of Russian power in the early twenty-first century, there are also soft power aspects of the

Eurasian country's political economy. In particular, Russia's state capitalism is a critical component of Moscow's power, as it has provided a means to finance a rearmament program, generate economic growth necessary to provide employment and financial betterment for an aspiring Russian middle class, and enrich and empower a tight-knit leadership elite built up around Vladimir Putin. An important element of this is a handful of state-owned companies that dominate domestic markets and compete globally. Russia's state capitalism also draws upon old-line nationalism that, over time, increasingly points to greater self-sufficiency and control over innovation and modernization. Along these lines, the market is a friend—to a point—as the state reserves the option to pick and choose the winners and losers based on which company is beneficial for the government's survival. In Russia the winners are, generally speaking, linked to natural resources, in particular energy, but also technology and communications. These companies, far fewer in number in Russia than in China, represent the commanding heights of the Russian economy. However, like China, Russia's state capitalism plays by a different rulebook than Western capitalism, a fact that became increasingly evident in the 2010s as companies like Gazprom blatantly became the spear-tips of Russian foreign policy regarding Ukraine and the West. In the West, the state stands over the marketplace as a referee; in Russia (as in China) the state is an active participant vis-à-vis all actors, including the domestic private sector, foreign companies, and foreign governments beyond the Eurasian country's borders.

RUSSIA'S STATE CAPITALISM: THE FORMATIVE YEARS

Russia's state capitalism has its roots in the Soviet Union. Under the Soviet system the economy followed a plan outlined by the government, oriented toward meeting the public's basic needs, maintaining a military and security apparatus to defend the revolution—and, when possible, to export it—and creating pockets of excellence, especially in the defense industry. The banking system was guided by a mono-bank; large state-owned companies followed production targets but were not guided by profit motives; and bureaucrats were appointed to run the economy. A well-established party elite lived off the economic system, reinforcing the promotion of ideological objectives over economic efficiency. This elite was often referred to as the "nomenklatura," a select class of people built up around the party and holding key positions in running different parts of the economy. The nomenklatura system also guaranteed the development of endemic corruption, as people sought to inflate results and work around controls to enrich themselves. Not everything was bad. Some sectors did better than others. At the same time, the Soviet education system placed emphasis on math and science. Energy was one of the government's favorites, in large part for its ability to generate cash from exports. However, by the time the Soviet Union collapsed, the country lacked key pillars of capitalism, which complicated the transition: courts to enforce contracts, a clear legal code, a transparent system for making regulatory decisions that guided business, and a general business culture that emphasized entrepreneurship.

The end of the Soviet Union in 1991–1992 was a traumatic event and had radical effects in reshaping the Russian economy. These effects included the redrawing of the map, the birth of new countries (Belarus, Ukraine, and the Central Asian Republics, to name but a few), a shock introduction of capitalism, and societal upheaval. This last encompassed Russia's loss of status as a world power and the rude introduction of market forces into daily life, which often resulted in shifts away from guaranteed employment and long-term pension programs, and generated unemployment.[1] The political uncertainty that accompanied the dismemberment of the Soviet Union trickled into the socio-economic system in the form of well-connected oligarchs taking advantage of privatizations, pumping cash into the hands of favored politicians and bureaucrats, and eroding the legitimacy of the fledgling democratic state. These negative conditions were only reinforced by the rise of local criminal organizations that threatened the country's stability and made personal safety a point of concern for many Russians.

The man initially linked with Russia's transition into the post-Soviet capitalist world was Boris Yeltsin, a beefy-looking, white-haired populist politician and former communist. Yeltsin was the first president of the Russian Federation in 1991 and was re-elected in 1996. Although not fondly remembered by the Russian people, under his leadership the country embraced capitalism, opened up to the outside world, and enjoyed a period of relative press freedom. Political parties proliferated, and a civil society began to form. Although the oligarchs grabbed as much of the new economy as they could, Yeltsin's government did privatize much of the corporate sector and forced the former state giants to become more competitive. Consequently, the Yeltsin years were not entirely without some gains. Russian journalist Masha Gessen noted: "Despite an increase in inequality, a great majority of Russians had experienced overall improvement in their lives. The number of households with televisions, washing machines, and refrigerators grew, the number of privately owned cars doubled; the number of people traveling abroad as tourists nearly tripled between 1993 and 2000."[2]

The Yeltsin governments were successful in the implementation of the market into the economy, but they failed on the political front to install a long-term working democratic political system. While Yeltsin managed to stave off the Communists from returning to power via the ballot box, he failed to leave behind a fully democratic system. Indeed, the new constitution that became law in 1993 created a political system characterized by excessive presidential powers and a relatively weak legislature (the Duma). This was done to allow the president to override the Duma's power, which was heavily influenced by Communists and ultra-nationalists. At the same time, the creation of an imperial presidency paved the way for his successor, Putin, to enjoy an economy ready for a takeoff and a polity waiting for a reassuring autocrat. By 1999, Yeltsin's government was struggling, the president ill from strokes and rumored alcoholism, and the leadership, referred to as the Family, circled around him. Yeltsin's enemies, of which there were many, were looking forward to elections that they expected to win. If Yeltsin's foes were victorious, they would no doubt persecute and prosecute him. They would also go after many of those around him, for official corruption. Consequently, the Family turned to Vladimir Putin, a man who had quietly emerged out of the state's security apparatus and St. Petersburg's political scene.

Yeltsin resigned in December 1999, and Putin became acting president, which gave him an advantage over his rivals. Putin was supported by oligarch money and the security apparatus. Adroitly using the position of acting president as a springboard, he convincingly won the May 2000 presidential contest and preempted a second round. Yeltsin was to die in 2007, never having been arrested or prosecuted on corruption charges. His successor Putin would go on to shape Russia for the early twenty-first century, creating an autocratic political system comfortable in its embrace of state capitalism.

PUTIN'S RUSSIA

Putin's Russia commenced in 2000. The new leader embarked on some modest market reforms in his first term, won reelection in 2004, was barred by the constitution a third term and so became prime minister appointed by new president Dmitry Medvedev (a longtime member of his inner circle), and returned to the presidency after winning the 2012 election. In 2011, the constitution was amended to extend the presidential term from four years to six, giving Putin a mandate extending to 2018. He can also run for reelection, which would take him to 2024.

Under Putin's guiding hand, Russia shifted from a transitional democratic state into an autocratic state. In this the political model was more similar to Russia's Tsars than the Soviet dictatorship, in that Putin and his clique have little interest in returning the country to communism and are more oriented toward capitalism—albeit a form of capitalism defined by the Russian character, with a heavy emphasis on the state dominating the commanding heights. Other key characteristics of the Russian model include formal and informal rules (with the latter generally trumping the former); a promotion of personal connections over the rule of law (vis-à-vis property and contract rights); and a hierarchical chain of command extending up to the president and his closest allies, who constitute the inner "court."

Nationalism also plays an important role in defining the regime's nature. While Yeltsin was a Russian nationalist, the country's politics were largely focused on the transitional nature of the economy, attracting foreign investment and dealing with further separatist threats (as in the Caucasus). Complicating this was a strong sense of loss among many Russians for their former territories and a questioning as to Russia's place in the world. The transformation from superpower to economic problem case (reflected by the 1998 domestic default) was severe blow to the national ego. On top of that, the end of communism as the nation's ideology left a hole in the national fabric, something the weak liberal tradition (with its Western linkages) could not fill. Indeed, the relatively clannish oligarchy did much to taint the fledgling democratic order as they bought and controlled much of the media and financed liberal parties in the Duma, some of which lobbied on their behalf. Into this ideological and governance vacuum stepped Putin.

Putin tapped into many of the currents defining the Russian people: the sense of Russia as a great power, the fear of encirclement following the Soviet Union's breakup, and the need for a strong political leader capable of restoring law and order. This fit into Russian concerns about the United States' domineering role in the world, its missile defense plans, the invasion of Iraq, the expansion of NATO (the North Atlantic Treaty Organization) eastwards toward Moscow's borders, and the perceived threats of "democratic" revolutions spreading from Georgia and Ukraine to Russia. In this, Putin and those around him at the top of the political pyramid are nationalist with a sense of being under siege by a materialistic West fixated on personal success and prosperity. The German-language magazine

Spiegel Online's Jan Fleischhauer caught the nuances of how the Russian leader perceives the world: "In the view of its president, the battle Russia is waging is ideological in nature. It is a fight against the superficiality of materialism, against the decline in values, against the feminization and effeminacy of society—and against the dissolution of all traditional bonds that are part of that development. In short, against everything 'un-Russian.'"[3]

Russia also went from a more private sector–driven economy, dominated by the oligarchs, to a state capitalist regime in which the major businesses were retaken by the state but still run in a private sector fashion—usually by individuals or groups (often depicted as clans) close to Putin. Two forces in the rise of Russian state capitalism shaped how it was implemented and how economic policies evolved. The first of these was ideological. Putin and his "court" held a strong belief that while capitalism has benefits, it needs to be controlled. Along these lines, the state played an important, if not the central, role in the country's economic development. Considering the globally competitive nature of capitalism and the need to restore Russia to its superpower status, the essential economic sectors could not be left to strictly private ownership. Indeed, anything regarded as "strategic"—that is, core to the Russian economy (and hence to power projection in foreign affairs)—needed to be under the control of the state. Putin stated in 2012: "The experience of successful economic modernization in South Korea and China shows that the state has a necessary role to play. Large private capital willingly doesn't want to carry major risks."[4]

The second force favoring state capitalism was that Putin's clique needed the economic wherewithal to dominate the country's political economy. As many of Putin's supporters derived from the political sphere (dating back to close contacts in the St. Petersburg mayor's office) and/or the security services, they needed to gain economic resources, which were held by the country's powerful oligarchs. This put the state, as defined by Putin loyalists, lining up against the oligarchs, a small group of wealthy and influential individuals. This struggle did much to determine the rise of state capitalism in Russia and was played out with hardball actions, including prison and exile for those on the losing side. Putin's first attacks on the oligarchs were aimed at gaining control of the media, eventually driving out media tycoons Vladimir Gusinsky and Boris Berezvosky. The former was the owner of the Media-Most holding company, which included Most Bank, the NTV channel, the newspaper *Segodnya,* and various magazines. The latter owned a number of assets, but it was the country's main television channel that made him a target. Both men opted to leave Russia, although they maintained their opposition to Putin. Berezvosky later was found hanged in his London apartment.

The most dramatic struggle took place over the oil company Yukos, which produced 20 percent of Russia's oil and was led by oligarch Mikhail Khodorkovsky, the head of Menatep, a multi-billion financial and industrial holding company. In 2000–2003 Yukos was one of the country's most successful companies, and its success caught the attention of the new government then searching for attractive assets and seeking to reduce the power of the oligarchs. Khodorkovsky also did not help matters, in that he gave the impression that he might have his own political ambitions, to become either prime minister or president. He was public in his support for two liberal opposition parties: Yabloko and SPS, both of which competed with Kremlin-backed parties in Duma elections. At the same time, Khodorkovsky was publicly at odds with the Kremlin over the Iraq war (which he backed) and relations with Washington. Journalist Edward Lucas noted of the oligarch: "his beneficence, official and unofficial, had begun to create menacing political clout. Hundreds of members of both houses of parliament, plus senior officials and government ministers, were all heavily influenced in their decision making by the attentive generosity of Khodorkovsky."[5]

Adding to the drama of pitting one of Russia's billionaires against its president was Yukos' intention to purchase Sibneft, another oil company. If the acquisition had succeeded, it would have made Yukos the world's fourth-largest oil company. In July 2003, an ally of Khodorkovsky and a large Yukos shareholder, Platon Lebedev, was arrested on suspicion of defrauding the state of more than $280 million by illegally seizing shares in a state-owned fertilizer company in 1994. Together with the head of one of Yukos' security departments being charged with plotting a double murder in 2002, Khodorkovsky's fall from power was well in motion. *The Economist* opined at the time: "the lesson from the affair is this: mega-rich businessmen had better watch out—as should those who invest in their companies. And until political reform catches up with economic reform that will continue to be the case."[6]

The struggle between Khodorkovsky and the Russian state came to a head in 2003, when the government leveled a tax reassessment against Yukos, which ultimately added up to $27 billion. The government also froze the company's assets, making it impossible for it to sell assets to meet the tax demands. The issue ended up in court in Russia and, in 2006, with the court declaring Yukos bankrupt. The company sought to file for bankruptcy protection in the United States, accusing the Russian authorities of "an unprecedented campaign of illegal, discriminatory, and disproportionate tax claims escalating into raids and confiscations, culminating in intimidation and arrests." The effort failed, and the assets were sold at low prices to other Russian oil companies, in particular Rosneft, which was to emerge as one of the giants of Russia, Inc., under Putin. As for Khodorkovsky, he was charged and convicted of fraud and sentenced to nine years in prison. Although his term was initially extended to 2014, he was pardoned and released from prison in December 2013.

Putin's success derived from a number of factors. Many Russians equated the chaotic Yeltsin years with democracy and freewheeling market capitalism that created inequalities, corruption, and high levels of criminality. Putin came upon the scene as a "man on the white horse," a quietly strong political personality emerging out of the KGB, standing for law and order and, increasingly through the years, unsullied nationalism. He also injected a degree of populism, which was tilted against the oligarchs and aimed to develop the government's standing among the workers. He quickly reinforced his position at the apex of the political system with colleagues from the security services, developed a well-oiled propaganda machine, crushed any media beyond his control, and placed his loyalists at the helm of the country's major state-owned corporations. A key factor in this was the Kremlin's ability to co-opt members of the political community and the intellectual elite, bullying those unwilling to submit and providing largesse to populist groups that relied on the state. There was also a clandestine side of the regime that hinted of bombings conducted by government forces or assassinations (as with journalist Anna Politkovskaya in 2006). The result of this was a system defined thus by Lilia Shevtsova, of the Carnegie Endowment for International Peace: "Russia's system retains its key features: personal power, a merger between political and economic assets, neo-imperial ambitions, militarism, and reliance on a commodity economy and patron-client relations."[7]

The Putin and Medvedev years reshaped Russia's political economy away from a fledgling democratic capitalist system dominated by oligarchs, into an autocracy driven by nationalism and state control over the commanding heights of the economy. While there is awareness of a top-heavy dependency on oil and gas and the need to diversify the economy, the Russian government has a preference for "conservative modernization," pursuit of a policy of small improvements in the traditional economic structure, to preserve the country's socioeconomic stability.[8] This approach was guided by the view that large-scale economic reforms include certain risks, which can erode the legitimacy of the government, and that a narrower approach to certain sectors is more sound.

One of the important results of the Putin era is that it represented a period of political stability and economic expansion. Putin came into office at the economic low point of the Yeltsin years and was to benefit from the impact of earlier reforms and a substantial rise in oil prices. The Russian economy grew at an average of 7–8 percent a year until 2009 and, after a downturn related to the Great Recession, resumed relatively strong growth until 2014, when it was hit by a combination of lower oil prices and sanctions.

Although members of the opposition to Putin among the oligarchs and liberal elements of the country's political life have been on the receiving end of the security apparatus and suffered prison time, exile, or coercion, much of Russian society appears willing to forgo political activity for socio-economic well-being. This encompasses everything from personal safety and finding day-to-day goods in the local store, to having access to the Internet and the ability to travel. The country's middle class opted for stability and economic well-being over the hurly-burly struggles represented by liberal democracy, which was sullied by oligarch money and corruption. Moreover, if the state was willing to intervene in the economy and maintain certain companies (as in shipbuilding) that might not have been competitive with the advent of foreign competition, that was more attractive than having to deal with unemployment.

Another factor supporting Russian state capitalism was the expansion of the Russian middle class. World Bank research indicates that poverty reduction and middle-class growth in Russia were due to high growth in average incomes and consumption during the period of 2000–2010. Along these lines, the poverty rate fell from 35 percent in 2001 to 10 percent in 2010. At the same time, the middle class grew from 30 percent to 60 percent of the total population.[9]

The success of Putin's autocratic state capitalism is reflected by the lack of major political battles within Putin's court. Putin's strong hand was evident in dealing with the oligarchs and gaining control of their economic assets, starting with the media and moving on to energy. The key message that the regime conveys is that it is better to cooperate with Putin and associates than to resist. Indeed, cooperation has its rewards. The result is a lack of friction among the leadership elite. Political scientist Neil Robinson aptly observed: "Politically the result of this was greater stability. There were no elite divisions over Putin's succession in 2008 by Dmitry Medvedov, or at least none that came to the surface to disturb the electrical cycles of 2007–2008, and no such divisions appeared to significantly affect Putin's resumption of the presidency in 2011–2012."[10] The challenge for Putin will be how to control the political landscape through an economic downturn caused by sanctions linked to Moscow's aggressive approach to Crimea and Ukraine, and the sharp drop in oil prices. The autocratic state capitalist model works much more effectively in a growth environment; it struggles in an economic downturn.

RUSSIA, INC.

Prominently displayed on the Rostec website is the following mission statement: "The furtherance of state policy for industrial development and modernization." Rostec, headed by Putin confidant Sergey Chemevoz, is a massive state-owned holding company, and its mission since its creation in 2007 is to advance the cause of state capitalism in Russia. According to the Rostec website, it comprises 663 organizations that are part of 13 holding companies, 8 of which operate in the military-industrial complex. The company goes on to specify: "Strategic targets of the corporation are establishing it as a leader in the high technology machine-building market, enhancement of business value and capitalization increase of the ventures." It is all there—a bold, assertive articulation of state capitalism, and a focus on national security via technology, stated in business language concerned with value and capitalization. And Rostec is only one arm of Russia, Inc.

Russia, Inc., is composed of the mix of the government, a supportive bureaucracy, and a number of state-owned companies, largely concentrated in banking, transportation, and energy. In 2013 it was estimated that state-owned enterprises accounted for 50 percent of Russia's gross domestic product, up from 30 percent in 1999.[11] Indeed, shares of state-owned enterprises, as measured among the top ten firms in a particular country, place Russia as number three, behind the United Arab Emirates (number two) and China (number one).[12] The emphasis on the large state-owned companies has also meant that employment has increasingly been skewed toward the public sector. One reflection of this is the fact that only 25 percent of Russian employment is in small and medium-sized enterprises, compared to 50 percent on average in OECD countries.[13] Although the agricultural, retail trade, consumer services, nondefense manufacturing, mining, and insurance sectors are generally in private hands, the major strategic heights are under the government's control—even though some have private (albeit minority) ownership. Considering the dominance of natural resources—in particular natural gas and oil—it is unsurprising that the flagships of Russian state capitalism are Gazprom and Rosneft, which rank as two of the largest hydrocarbon companies in the world and are headed by longtime Putin loyalists (see Table 4.1).

Table 4.1   Russia, Inc.'s, Core Companies

Company Name	Business	Market Capitalization (US$ billions)	Percent State Ownership
Gazprom	National gas exporter, producer, and storage, as well as electric and heat energy generation	$100.4 billion	50.002%
Rosneft	Oil producer and exporter	$72 billion	69.5%
Rostec	Industrial holding company	NA	100%
Russian Railways	State monopoly railway operator; freight, passengers, and infrastructure	NA	100%
Sberbank	Russia's largest bank	$55.3 billion	50.0% + 1%

Source: Bloomberg Markets, March 2014.

The significance of Russia's oil and gas complex is impossible to overlook. The following points underscore the centrality of Roseneft and Gazprom (and other private sector oil and gas producers and exporters) to the economy:

- Russia was the world's third-largest producer of oil, after Saudi Arabia and the United States, in 2013;
- Russia is one of the largest producers of natural gas (the second-largest in 2012);
- Oil and gas revenues comprised over 70 percent of total exports in 2012;
- The Russian government receives about half of its budget revenue from oil and gas exports;
- The energy sector directly and indirectly employs millions of Russian workers.[14]

Gazprom is probably the best-known of Russian state-owned companies, as it is a hydrocarbon giant. Formerly the Soviet Ministry of Gas Industry, Gazprom was launched as a corporation in 1989. Under Yeltsin it was privatized, but it fell under the wings of Viktor Chernomydrin, Russia's prime minister (1992–1998), when the company was loosely regulated, becoming involved in tax evasion and asset stripping. When Putin came to power in 2000, Gazprom was a priority in the new leader's push to break the oligarchs' power. Chernomydrin was fired as chairman of Gazprom's board, and his allies were purged from the company. Putin brought in Dmitry Medvedev (the country's future president) and Alexei Miller, two men who had worked with him in St. Petersburg, to clean house, stop the asset stripping, and regain lost possessions. While Medvedev was to move on to other positions under Putin, Miller eventually assumed the helm of Gazprom.

Through the Putin–Medvedev years, Gazprom emerged as Russia's national champion in natural gas. It became the largest gas exporter to the European market, accounting for 30 percent of supplies to European end consumers. Gazprom holds 17 percent of global gas reserves (72 percent of Russian gas reserves) and accounts for 13 percent of global gas production. The company is also important in terms of Russian electricity generation. Through pipelines that reach from Siberian gas fields to Western Europe, Gazprom carries considerable economic heft, which it has not been afraid to use, especially with Ukraine. Europe is heavily dependent on Russian gas, with some countries, like Bulgaria, Finland, Estonia, Latvia, and Lithuania, over 75 percent dependent. Economist Marshall Goldman made the following observation of Gazprom's reach: "Should they choose to, these Gazprom functionaries could not only cut off natural gas from the furnaces and stoves of 40 percent of Germany's homes but also the natural gas that many German factories need for manufacturing a range of products from ammonia fertilizer to plastics. While Germany purchases more natural gas from Russia than any other country in Europe, all of Western Europe is now also hooked up directly or indirectly to the Gazprom pipeline."[15]

While Gazprom dominates the Russian gas industry, Rosneft is the country's oil giant, being the leader of Russia's petroleum industry and the world's largest publicly traded petroleum company. According to data from the company, its oil and gas output of 4.88 million barrels a day in 2013 was larger than either Exxon's and PetroChina's. The company's activities encompass hydrocarbon exploration and production, upstream offshore projects, hydrocarbon refining, and crude oil, gas, and product marketing in Russia and abroad. The main shareholder (69.50 percent) is OJSC Rosneftegaz, a 100 percent state-owned company. BP (British Petroleum) owns another 19.75 percent, and the remaining 10.75 percent of shares are publicly traded.

Rosneft is run by Igor Sechin, one of the key forces behind Russian state capitalism and the person who probably wields the most influence in Putin's inner court. Like Putin, Sechin believes that the collapse of the

Soviet Union was the greatest geopolitical catastrophe in the twentieth century, and that state capitalism is critical in the mission to restore the country to greatness. Sechin learned French and Portuguese at university, where he earned his Ph.D. in economics, served in the Soviet military overseas in Angola and Mozambique alongside Cuban forces, and worked in St. Petersburg during the same time as Putin. When Putin assumed the presidency in 2000, Sechin worked first as his chief of staff and then as deputy prime minister (when Putin became prime minister). Although he was made CEO of Rosneft in 2012, Sechin is regarded as one of the main forces behind the company's rise, its takeover of Yukos, and the purchase of TNK-BP assets in 2013. Sechin's influence has been important in developing the regime's approach to the economy and how Russian business (mainly state-owned companies) fits into the picture. According to Khodorvsky, "Sechin is a real oligarch, in the classic meaning of the word. He convinced Putin that state capitalism is right and is realizing his idea in practice."[16]

The combination of Gazprom and Rosneft has meant a considerable rise in Russian influence in global energy markets during the late 1990s and early twenty-first century. Russian oil and gas production stabilized and then slowly began to rebound toward Soviet levels, a considerable achievement. At the same time, both companies became integral parts of the Western Eurasian energy system. Simply stated, Russian oil and natural gas became a significant factor in powering much of Eastern and Western Europe's industrial machine—and kept the heat on during the winter. This gained even greater significance as the German government opted to rapidly phase out its nuclear power industry. Gazprom, with its strategic pipelines pumping natural gas through Ukraine into central Europe and Germany, had considerable clout. This became evident in the so-called Gas Wars between Kiev and Moscow in 2006 and 2009, and loomed as a major point of concern for European capitals in 2014, when Russia seized Crimea from Ukraine.

Related to the oil and gas nexus is the Russian state's control over the rail system through Russian Railways. *The Moscow Times'* Nathan Gray observed in 2013: "At a time of development planning and uncertainty over the country's future economic direction, the rail system retains a centrality in Russia's security and economic position."[17] Created in 2003, the company owns the world's third-longest rail network, contributed 1.7 percent of GDP in 2012, and at the time employed 1.2 million workers. The significance of this company is further emphasized by its ability to move 1 billion passengers a year and generate $4.2 billion in annual sales.

Russian Railways' website further outlines the company's place within Russia, Inc.: "Russian Railways is not only a strategic player in Russia, but is also expanding East-West & North-South Eurasian transport corridors to increases revenues and integrate Russia into the global economy." Considering Russia's geo-strategic position, the company plays an important role in linking the national economy, shipping everything from coal, iron ore, cement, and oil and oil products, to automobiles and grain. The company is headed by Putin insider Vladimir Yakunin, who knew him from their days together in St. Petersburg.

THE FINANCIAL PLUMBING OF RUSSIAN STATE CAPITALISM

Beyond the oil, gas, industrial-tech, and transportation sectors, state ownership is reinforced by control over the country's largest financial institutions. In the banking sector, the government controls Sberbank, VTB Group, and VEB. Sberbank is the country's largest bank, dominating retail deposits, banking assets, and corporate and retail loans. It is 50 percent, "plus 1 percent" owned by the Russian central bank (the Bank of Russia), and its headquarters are located in Moscow. Sberbank is also the largest bank in Eastern Europe and ranks highly in terms of asset size in all of Europe. Although the bank has its roots in Tsarist Russia, it re-emerged in 1990, when Yeltsin's government made it property of the Russian Republic and then privatized it. In 1993 the Bank of Russia acquired a majority share, which it maintains to this day. While the bank consolidated its position in domestic markets in 2011, it bought the Volksbank International AG, which gave it banking assets in Czech Republic, Slovakia, Hungary, Slovenia, Croatia, Ukraine, Serbia, and Bosnia and Herzegovina. In 2012, Sberbank also purchased banking assets in Turkey.

Sberbank is led by an individual well known to Putin, German Oskarovich Gref. The bank chief's background was very much in step with Putin's. Having worked in the Saint Petersburg City Administration and served as the First Deputy of State Property of the Russian Federation (1989–2000), Gref was appointed to the board of the Federal Commission for the Securities Market of the Russian Federation and to the board of Gazprom in 1999. Gref also served in the different cabinets of Putin, was a major advocate of joining the World Trade Organization, and created the Stabilization Fund. Although he was dismissed from his cabinet post in 2007, he was soon elected president of Sberbank, where he has proven faithful to the Kremlin.

Russia's second-largest bank is Vneshtorgbank, or VTB Group, which is 60.9 percent owned by the state. VTB was created in 1990 as a trade bank, owned by the Russian central bank and the Ministry of Finance. While it fulfilled its mandate as a trade bank, VTB morphed during 2002 to 2012 into a retail bank with foreign subsidiaries. Considering the choppy nature of Russia's economy in the early 2000s, VTB became a vehicle for the Russian state to acquire troubled banks and assume greater control over the financial sector. This greatly expanded the size of the bank and made it more central to the state's developmental goals.

Another important state-owned financial institution is Vnesheconombank, or VEB, commonly referred to as the Russian Development Bank. With roots dating back to 1922, VEB's mission is to "diversify the Russian economy, boost its competitive edge and encourage investment activity." To help in this mission, the bank has issued bonds. It is also the manager of pension savings funds for Russian citizens, which gives it considerable clout. Among its "sector priorities" are aircraft construction, the rocket and space complex, shipbuilding, electronics, and computer technologies and software. VEB constitutes an integral part of Russia, Inc., playing a role in channeling funds to areas the state wishes to develop.

Control over the country's major financial institutions is a critical element of state capitalism. Between them, Sberbank, VTB Group, and VEB dominate the country's banking industry, leaving much smaller markets to the remaining private sector institutions. At the same time, the Russian state maintains one other force important in controlling the economy: sovereign wealth funds. Like many other countries that have established such institutions, Russia followed suit with the Stablization Fund of the Russian Federation, which in 2008 was divided into two separate organizations, the Russian National Wealth Fund and the Reserve Fund. The former was initially given close to $88 billion and the latter $137 billion. Both are controlled by the Ministry of Finance. The Reserve Fund invests abroad in low-yield securities (like U.S. Treasury bonds) and is meant to be used when oil and gas incomes fall. The National Wealth Fund has a different mission, in that it is able to assume greater risk in making investments, which are meant to provide greater returns. It is also given the responsibility of supporting the Russian pension system.

ALIGNMENT OF GOVERNMENT AND CORPORATE GOALS

The collection of corporate leaders of Russia, Inc., have made their allegiance to Putin and his government. This is a mutually beneficial relationship—while the Putin team is willing to allow particular clans to grab state assets and assume control over private assets in exchange for personal loyalty to the president, both parties are seeking to gain maximum profit and guarantee their assets future protection.[18] This alignment of government and corporate goals is a cornerstone for Russia's present and potentially its long-term future. At home this pertains to generating enough wealth to satisfy the political elite (which functions like a renter class), finance the implementation of government policies (like modernizing the military), and create well-paying employment opportunities for the majority of Russians, especially a rising middle class. Abroad this alignment has translated into the state using its companies to exert influence, most notably in the case of the Ukraine in 2006 and 2009 over the price of gas.

Gazprom is the company most involved in those incidents over the flow of natural gas to the West, but the company was again pulled into Ukrainian affairs in 2013–2014, as the Putin administration played hardball with a government in Kiev that it had failed to anticipate and which it loathed. Gazprom, Europe's major supplier of natural gas, increasingly found itself on the firing line in a test of wills between the Kremlin and Western Europe and the United States. In the same sense, Gazprom found itself front and center in Putin's pivot East in the aftermath of U.S. and European sanctions related to his annexation of Crimea in March 2014.

Gazprom's position as a key force in Eurasia's energy markets is highly important for the Russian government's projection of power and influence. About one-fourth of the oil and gas used in Europe originates in Russia. At one end of the natural gas pipelines is Germany, one of Russia's most significant trade partners and an important source of foreign direct investment. Gazprom's relationship with its German customers is critical. After all, Germany is the economic locomotive that pulls the rest of Europe's economy. The mutual interest of Gazprom and its German customers came into play in 2014. Despite the deterioration in East-West relations over Russian aggression against Ukraine, Russian gas functioned to prevent a complete breakdown in relations—especially with Germany, which had worsened its energy dependence by making the fateful decision to eliminate its nuclear power facilities without other options on hand.

Russian corporate alignment with its political masters is evident in other ways, such as the use of the large state banks to purchase troubled private ones, or of the sovereign wealth funds to buy and sell U.S. Treasury bonds. The near-monopolistic control over Russian railways cuts many ways: the state is guaranteed control over internal communications (including strategic freight such as oil and grain) and can easily make use of rails for troops and military equipment, while Russian Railways' expansion into surrounding countries provides Russian national interest an easy gateway into other economies. The more important Russian Railways becomes for neighboring economies, the greater leverage can be applied by Moscow if there are disagreements. Although much of the discussion about state capitalism can be explained as an effort for the greater good of the Russian people, it is difficult to disguise the alignment of interest between political and economic elites. Simply stated, the money from state-owned enterprises provides a good life for those at the top and provides the necessary capital for national objectives as formulated by the Kremlin.

POTEMKIN VILLAGES?

The state-owned corporate phalanx evident in the Russian economy has strengths and weaknesses. In many regards, the strong hand of the government has reduced the upheaval from the period of oligarchy, streamlined certain business sectors, and helped project Russian political and economic influence beyond its borders. At the same time, heavy state involvement has had a number of downsides worth noting. These include corruption, opaque management styles and finances, entrenchment of inefficiencies, and lack of competition. An OECD report (2014) observed that the Russian business environment was challenging, and highlighted weaknesses related to the large state sector, including poor transparency and accountability, a lack of competitive neutrality vis-à-vis the private sector (i.e., the lack of a level playing field), and a slow move to a more professional management class.

The OECD was clear as to the detrimental impact of corruption on the economy. Although bribery has declined, the report noted: "particularly worrying is corruption in law enforcement, which accounted for a quarter of all corruption cases brought to the courts in 2012."[19] The report further observed: "Only 10% of entrepreneurs have never come across corruption, although the cost of bribes has apparently fallen in recent years. In a number of regions, corruption is so widespread that firms consider it a convenient alternative to legal and administrative compliance."[20] Part of the problem in eradicating corruption in business is that it has become part and parcel of the regime. This is not to argue that all Russian state employees are corrupt, but that in some cases corrupt actions have been politically motivated and come from well above the rank and file. Stated in another fashion, two sets of rules are perceived to operate, with the informal/personal connections (usually of large state-owned enterprises) trumping or using the law to serve its purposes in a warped fashion. This does little to foster a pro-business environment and functions as a deterrent to market entry and sustainable growth. It also stifles entrepreneurship.

The detrimental impact of overwhelming state involvement is evident in Russia's transportation sector. The OECD points starkly to Russia's transport bottlenecks as a major problem for the country's future economic development: "Russia ranks low in quality of transport and competitiveness." Problem areas include a poor road system (Russia ranks 136 out of 148 countries) and less-than-stellar ports and airports. As for Russian Railways, the OECD observes: "RZD maintains an effective monopoly in railway freight, being the owner of both infrastructure and all locomotives. This has resulted in the ineffective use of the available infrastructure, increasing prices, excessively long shipping times and even denial of service."[21] Furthermore, there is the issue of corruption. In 2014, a Reuters investigation revealed Russian Railways paying "billions of dollars to private contractors that disguises their ultimate owners and have little or no presence at their regional headquarters."[22] The Reuters investigation pointed to businessman Andrei Kapivin, once described by Yakunin, the CEO of Russian Railways, as an "old acquaintance" and "an unpaid adviser who understands banking well."

A long-term challenge for Russian state capitalism is going to be how to spark innovation. The combination of these factors is a less-than-perfect business environment, leaving the Russian economy, over the long term, in a condition of weaker comparative advantage. The problem is that the links between technology and the economy are to be driven by the state, using the system of state procurement and investment programs via state corporations like Rostec and military-related enterprises. Along these lines, in 2013 Putin harkened back to the Soviet era: "I propose a statistical evaluation of the level of technology in various branches of the economy to obtain an objective picture of our competitiveness. In the Soviet period such a system worked. It was liquidated, and nothing else was created. It is necessary to recreate it."[23]

What Putin proposed is state-sponsored technological innovation. Outside of the military sphere, such innovation has lagged. One only has to look back to the end of the Cold War, when the United States pushed the Star Wars Defense Initiative, based on U.S. technology (while fostering wider economic growth). The Soviet Union was not up to that struggle. Its economic system could not keep up with the huge advances in technology spearheaded in the West by the private sector. The same system that existed then is what Putin wants to revive. Economist Anders Aslund correctly notes of Putin's preference to turn the clock back, "Sorry, we have seen that show, and it was disastrous. I participated in the destruction of that system because it produced a miserably low level of technology.

The iPhone and iPad were not created by state standards but by competition in the market. Putin seems unaware both of the collapse of the Soviet economic system and why it happened."[24] The freeze in Russian–Western relations beginning in 2014 is only likely to further limit the flow of technological innovation to Russia.

What is left is an economy that remains overly dependent on the energy sector. There are three aspects of this: (1) Russian companies do not have the most up-to-date technology and equipment in oil and gas transport, exploration, and production; (2) the highly political nature of Gazprom and Rosneft makes them challenging business partners for foreign companies, some of which could offer technological assistance; and (3) Russia faces an increasingly competitive international gas and oil international market, a trend stimulated by the U.S. oil and shale gas revolution.

One of the major issues in the long term is how competitive Russian oil and gas will be in international markets. The major deal signed in 2014 between Russia and China is expected to be a major boast for Gazprom and helps reduce the company's dependence on selling to the West. China is and will be a major industrial machine, needy of energy that Russia can supply. The question, however, for Russian companies like Gazprom and Rosneft is whether they will be able to make the technological leaps that are in use in the West. It was the advent of new technology that helped spark the U.S. shale gas and oil revolution. Russia is behind in such technology, and the more American exports hit international markets, the lower prices are likely to be—which, in turn, raises major questions over Russia's oil and gas rate of returns. Lower energy prices will only underscore Russia's dependence on hydrocarbon exports and lack of economic diversification.

The pronounced downturn in international oil prices in the second half of 2014 underscored Russia's dependency on hydrocarbons, which constitute the lion's share of exports and are the major source of revenues for the Russian state. If nothing else, the heavy reliance on oil points to the pressing need to diversify the economy. Although the Putin administration has given lip service to the idea, Russia remains vulnerable to commodity price volatility. Russian businesses are keenly aware that to survive in the global economy, they need Western technology and capital. Russia, despite its willingness to taunt the West, remains a shareholder in the global economy, reluctantly or not. Consequently, the Putin years are a testing period for the Russian business sector, which is being forced to seek alternative relationships with non-Western economies and reduce its financial dependence on Western financial institutions.

THE ACHILLES HEEL: POLITICS, POLITICS, POLITICS

One of the major points of concern about Russia's experiment with state capitalism is politics. In this Russia faces three forces: pressure for ongoing growth and economic opportunity from the middle class, poor demographics that touch upon separatist tendencies within the Russian Federation, and political succession. While it is doubtful that Russia will move away from capitalism in a broadly defined sense and re-embrace communism, the structure and functions of the political system are more open to change. In many regards Putin is an enlightened autocrat, having more in common with some of the more reform-minded Tsars than with Soviet leaders. That leaves the political options open, either for a push in the direction of a more authoritarian political system, or back toward a democratic system that Russia briefly experimented with in the early Yeltsin period.

KEEPING THE MIDDLE CLASS HAPPY

The Putin government must also consider that middle-class support cannot be taken for granted. While loss of its support is not as critical as that of the security forces or Russia, Inc., it could greatly complicate control. The key issue here pertains to the economic-political pact. Indeed, the World Bank observed that the middle class expanded because of wage increases based on economic growth. The risk is that economic growth is substantially diminished because of foreign policy adventures such as annexing parts of Georgia and taking Crimea from Ukraine. The World Bank noted that the economic slowdown related to geopolitical tensions in 2014 had a consequence: "However, weaker growth prospects and stabilizing consumption at a lower rate dim the economic mobility outlook. Economic factors, such as the wage growth and access to good, productive jobs, rather than the demographic factors drove the middle class growth in Russia. However, in the current environment of a much slower economic growth and constrained fiscal resources, job creation will be an important condition for the future economic mobility, as well as for strengthening the role of labor income as the main driver of the middle income growth."[25]

The expansion of the middle class, the need for reducing the corrosive impact of corruption on the economy (not to mention society), the negative environment for entrepreneurs, and the overdependence on hydrocarbons all point to the need to develop a Russian civil society.

WAVING THE NATIONALIST FLAG

Another political weak point for the Putin regime is its increasing reliance on aggressive nationalism to fill the ideological void. The appeal to Russian greatness has a long tradition, dating back to the Tsars but was also evident in Soviet Russia. While Russia's intervention in Georgia in 2008 and its annexation of Crimea in 2014 may have appeared to be "irrational" to Western observers, Moscow's actions were logical to most Russians. Indeed, President Putin's ratings in opinion polls reached new highs. A Pew Poll in 2014 revealed roughly eight in ten Russians (83 percent) said they had confidence in President Putin to do the right thing in world affairs, up from 69% in 2012, the last time this question was asked.[26] Fully 52% said they had *a lot* of confidence in the Russian leader, compared with 37% in 2010. Additionally, roughly six in ten (61%) agree with the statement, "There are parts of neighboring countries that really belong to us." Only 28% disagreed. From the Russian perspective, the West had encroached repeatedly in what Russia regards as its sphere of influence, pushing everything from NATO and EU memberships to gay rights. Georgia and Ukraine fit in this regard, while the annexation of Crimea had an appeal from the standpoint of long historical ties and the existence of a sizable Russian population.

The significance of aggressive nationalism is that it allows the government the opportunity to push a popular agenda that focuses attention outside of the country and away from domestic problems. It also allows the Russian state to brand anyone who opposes its policies as a traitor—or, at the very least, of questionable loyalty to Mother Russia. This approach, however, carries with it a number of risks, including the need to keep the foreign affairs cauldron at a boil, keeping control of ultra-nationalists who could hijack government plans and create greater international tensions with potential blowback, and not losing control of popular demonstrations that could eventually turn on the Kremlin (especially if domestic economic grievances are allowed to become part of the action).

Nationalism also touches upon two other sensitive points in Russian society: the multicultural nature of the country and problematic demographics. Although ethnic Russians constitute a clear majority (a little over 80 percent) of the population, the rest of the population is broken down into a number of minority groups, with the Tatars making up the largest ethnic minority, at around 4 percent. The total number of ethnic groups is given at 170. Religiously, the country is predominantly Christian, mainly Russian Orthodox, though the Muslim population is around six percent of the total. It is the Muslim population that draws some Russian nationalism and racism, a situation exacerbated by the wars in Chechnya and various radical Muslim bombings. Historical factors have also added friction between Muslims and non-Muslims.

The Islamic issue factors into Russian nationalism in another way: the country's demographics are bad, especially in the ethnic Russian population. Although there has been some improvement in birth rates over the last couple of years, Russia's population has been shrinking; it went from 148 million in 1991 to an estimated 142 million in 2012. A United Nations Development Program (UNDP) study in 2008 made the following observation: "Russia has been grappling for some time with demographic developments, which must be qualified as a crisis. Short life expectancy is the main feature of this crisis, though by no means its only feature. The birth rate is too low, the population is shrinking and aging, and Russia is on the threshold of rapid loss of able-bodied population, which will be accompanied by a growing demographic burden per able-bodied individuals."[27]

The UNDP report also indicated that Russia's declining population was the result of later marriages, later average age of first childbearing, and a larger share of people living in informal unions and not having children (like more traditional families). Related to this is the problem of alcoholism, including large-scale problems with liver disease and alcohol poisoning. One study conducted by the Russian Cancer Centre in Moscow, Oxford University, and the World Health Organization International for Research on Cancer, noted that 25 percent of Russian men die before 55 years of age, and most of these deaths are attributable to alcohol.[28] The comparable figure in the UK was 7 percent. The alcohol situation has contributed to the shortened life span for Russian men, which in 2013 was 64 years—well behind the United States, Japan, and most of Europe.

The demography issue, its links to nationalism, and the rise of a Russian middle class all help determine how the economy will function in the future. The above mix will require a means to pay for greater military spending, rising health care costs, growing pension costs (related to the bulge in retirement-age people), and the revolution of rising expectations in the middle class. Along these lines, the UNDP report touched on the pressing need to have an economy that is able to maintain self-sustaining growth. The report stated in 2008, with even greater significance years later: "In coming decades Russia faces a historically unique task of supporting high economic growth rates despite a decline in population, particularly in working age groups. The labor force will decline in overall size, and the decline will be concentrated in the young end of the labor force."[29] Not stated in the study, which was focused on demographic issues, was the need for economic diversification measures, which the Putin-Medvedev-Putin turn of governments failed to do. In 2008 Russia was a petro-state; in 2014 it remained very much the same.

POLITICAL SUCCESSION

Unlike China's state capitalist experiment, Russia lacks a party well-identified with the state capitalist model that can offer a deeper bench of leadership. In Russia, Putin is the undisputed national leader, a fact that is backed by a security apparatus willing to use muscle to coerce any opposition—or, in some extreme cases, eliminate it. At the same time, this concentration of power leaves the economic policymaking environment vulnerable to Putin's long-term viability as national leader. Under the current constitutional settings, Putin can run for the presidency in 2018 and serve until 2024. However, old age or illness can create uncertainty on the leadership front, and at some point the issue of who will follow him into the Kremlin looms as a major factor. While political succession looms in China, there is a strong likelihood that the next set of that nation's leaders are in the Communist Party, serving in visible positions and being groomed for future assignments. Moreover, in China there is an established path for political succession, with clear-cut constituencies that must be addressed. This is not necessarily the case in Russia. Russia has considerable problems, but an aging autocrat and an absence of clear succession mechanisms could well lead to political upheaval, including competing coalitions of economic and political elites.

Political succession in Russia has not been an easy process. Putin benefited from Yeltsin's willingness to pass the baton to him. As Putin ages and health issues become potential problems, the onus for the inner court to look for solutions is likely to increase. Usually such periods are filled with political intrigue, jockeying for position among possible successors, and a reassessment of political actors by economic elites. Russia under Putin is not immune to this, especially as the regime strives to control the press, maintain an effective security apparatus, and marginalize any potential political rivals. The heavy reliance on Putin also factors into the legitimacy of the government: as long as the President is well-liked, governance is relatively easy. If, however, there are problems—usually involving the economy—Putin's standing will be more vulnerable, and regime legitimacy will be tested.

The political and economic landscape Russia is entering is likely to test the Kremlin's autocratic form of government. The cooling of relations with the West over Ukraine is going to have an economic cost, probably slower economic growth over the medium term. State-owned companies are decidedly on the receiving end, with one of the major issues being the ability of these companies to finance themselves through capital markets, most of which are in the West and blocked via sanctions. At the same time, the resumption of Cold War confrontation and hostility vis-à-vis the West will reduce the flow of foreign investment and technology. While this fits plans of the state to control new technology by using state-owned Rostec and the procurement from the Russian state to push technology along, the impact is more likely to be similar to what happened during the last round of the Cold War, when controls stifled the flow of information and ideas, and functioned as a major hurdle to innovation. Add to this the demographic issues of a shrinking workforce and the costs of an aging population; Russia heads into the future with some substantial disadvantages that are likely to hinder self-sustaining economic growth. These issues could also foster the type of environment in which any political loosening of controls could lead to a groundswell of popular discontent. Considering the heavy-handed nature of the government, if economic conditions deteriorate and a foreign adventure goes wrong, the durability of regime strength will be questionable, especially if Putin is ill or otherwise incapacitated.

RUSSIA AND THE NEW NORMAL

Alongside China, Russia is a core part of the New Normal of competition between democratic and autocratic capitalist states. As already demonstrated in this chapter and the one on China, state-owned enterprises have, despite their protestations to the contrary, a political component that cannot be overlooked. For example, Gazprom's control over a large portion of Western Europe's energy lifelines has obvious political significance. Rostec's heavy involvement in military projects and Russian Railways' dominance over transportation both have political components in advancing what the Kremlin wants.

Russia's system of an autocrat and his inner court at the top of the political pyramid, presiding over different clans who have taken control over the commanding heights of the economy, is found in a number of other countries that emerged from the former Soviet Union. These include the Central Asian republics, such as Kazakhstan, Tajikistan, Turkmenistan, and Uzbekistan. Azerbaijan and Belarus certainly fit along similar lines.

In each case, strong leaders have presided over the political landscape, inner courts extend the leader's power and influence into the economy via large state-owned companies, and the private sector survives in a world of informal relationships and accommodations that trump the rule of law. It was hoped that democratic forces would eventually push aside Soviet traditional autocratic structures. It would appear that the autocratic traditions were more difficult to overcome than initially expected. Furthermore, the embrace of state capitalism, especially in the takeover of the natural resources sector (oil and gas in Azerbaijan and the Central Asian republics) has provided autocrats with the economic means to survive.

The attractiveness of the Russian system is also evident in parts of Eastern Europe that are now part of the European Union. While the Kremlin is concerned about the spread of Western liberal ideas eastward into countries like Belarus, Ukraine, Moldova, and even Russia, the conservative nature of Putin's strong-handed rule has an appeal in a region that has struggled economically since 2007. While all of Eastern Europe has not been lured, there has been an erosion of democratic practices and rights in countries such as Hungary and the Czech Republic, and inter-elite struggles, as in Bulgaria and Romania. As Princeton University's Professor of Politics Jan-Werner Mueller observed in 2014, of the growing attraction in Eastern Europe of a more autocratic state capitalist approach, "something new is emerging: a form of illiberal democracy in which political parties try to capture the state for either ideological purposes or, more prosaically, economic gain. Some countries in Eastern Europe (like Hungary and Serbia) are moving toward a model of governance that resembles that of Russian President Vladimir Putin. Like Moscow, the governments of these countries are careful to maintain their democratic facades by holding regular elections, but their leaders have tried to systematically dismantle institutional checks and balances, making real turnovers in power increasingly difficult."[30]

Putin's strongman rule, with a play to more traditional values (like strong nationalism), has also gained the Russian leader a following among the Euro-skeptic right-wing parties that did well at the polls in the May 2014 Euro-Parliamentary elections. *The Economist* noted: "many are attracted by Mr. Putin's muscular assertion of national interests, his emphasis on Christian tradition, his opposition to homosexuality and the way he has brought vital economic sectors under state control."[31] The European far-right parties also like Putin's anti-Americanism and his disdain for the European Union. In many regards, Russia as well as China (with less attraction as a model in Europe) have proposed an alternative to Western democratic capitalism which has a political, economic, and ultimately, existential sense of struggle about it.

The growing discord linked to the New Normal is likely to create more discord in Europe's borderlands in the years ahead. The autocratic model is already forcing a number of countries, like Poland and the Baltic states, to adopt more defensive measures to secure their national interests vis-à-vis Russia. At the same time, Moscow is pushing hard to create a counter-bloc to the EU, in the form of the Eurasian Union, which was formally ushered into existence in June 2014, between Russia, Belarus, and Kazakhstan. A number of countries invited to join the Eurasian Union have either passed, as with Ukraine, or are hesitating, as with Armenia, Georgia, and Azerbaijan—as membership to the new bloc means potential loss of trade and investment opportunities with the West. It is likely that the pressure to choose sides will increase going forward. For Russia this is a gamble, as trade and investment possibilities with the West—including membership in the World Trade Organization—are beneficial to economic development in particular countries. Loss of trade links with the West also creates deeper dependence on Russia, much as it was during the Soviet period, which carries difficult historical memories. Additionally, many potential members of the Eurasian Union have to question what will happen in a post-Putin Russia. The record of political succession in Russia is one of uncertainty and factional infighting. Russia's current autocratic model will find this a major test, something that limits the appeal of the Eurasian Union—do other countries want to go through the travails of an intense succession struggle where the losers could end up in prison or exile? Furthermore, the economic crunch hitting Russia in 2014 and 2015 reduces the appeal of a closer embrace with Moscow, especially if it complicates relations with the West.

CONCLUSION

Russia's state capitalism has considerable strengths but also weaknesses. The "model" used by Putin and the ruling Russian elite seeks to provide order and stability at home and greater standing in the world. Both domestic and international goals are meant to be mutually reinforcing. In this system, state-owned enterprises play a highly significant role, functioning as a means of financing the ruling class and government, providing employment for an aspiring middle class, and advancing Russian national interests in the arena of foreign affairs. The handful of Russian state-owned companies are also competitive with foreign and domestic companies, as they benefit from considerable state support, a relationship that demonstrates a high level of interdependence. At the same time, the incestuous nature of the relationship has a substantial downside, encompassing cronyism, corruption, and hindrance to achieving greater efficiencies in the country's economic life. This ultimately plays against the Russian political economy as it stands, especially as outside economic competition is set to increase in the international energy field. If the Russian state is unable to deliver economic benefits to the Russian people—an ability that is likely to be challenged in the years ahead—and if other problems are not addressed, state capitalism could see dark times, and its value as a development and business model will be strongly questioned.

Of all the challenges facing Russian capitalism, the major Achilles heel is political. The autocratic nature of the political system, and its concentration of power in the hands of Putin and his inner court, raises the delicate issue of political succession and the ways in which aggressive foreign policy may result in regime isolation. If nothing else, it leaves a high degree of uncertainty with political outcomes based on one individual. Moreover, at some point the aging of the autocrat, or deterioration in his health, may open the door to potential rivals seeking to maneuver for the right moment to strike. The question also exists: If the economy slips into a deep recession, will economic interests seek to remove the national leader? In turn, would a new leader maintain the same court around him or seek to change it? While Russia's state capitalism exhibits many strengths, it suffers from critical weaknesses, both political and economic in nature, which raise considerable question over the long-range achievement of order and stability at home and competitiveness in the global economy.

NOTES

1.   Economist Marshall Goldman noted of the change from the Soviet command economy to a market-driven one, in particular regarding recessions: "Recessions had never been a problem in the days of the Soviet Union. Maintaining economic growth in the Soviet centrally planned economy era was in many ways easier to do than in it was in a market economy. Soviet central planners simply ordered factory managers to produce a certain quantity of goods without worrying whether or not there were customers for those goods. By contrast, after the move to the market economy, the Russian government and its central bankers have had to juggle a variety of indirect economic variables such as interest rates, money supply, and government expenditures as well as tax cuts and increases,

in the hope that consumers and businesses will take the bait and increase or decrease their spending in tandem with the government's objectives." *Petrostate: Putin, Power, and the New Russia* (New York: Oxford University Press, 2010), p. xi.

2. Masha Gessen, *The Man Without a Face: The Unlikely Rise of Vladimir Putin* (London: Granta, 2013), p. 14.

3. Jan Fleischhauer, "Putin's Not Post-Communist, He's Post-Fascist," *Spiegel Online International*, May 2, 2014. http:Spiegel.de/international/world/speeches-by-russian-president-putin-betray-fascist-inspiration-a-967283.html.

4. Quoted in Irinia Reznik, Stephen Bierman, and Henry Meyer, "Remaking Russia's Economy," *Bloomberg Markets*, March 2014, p. 42.

5. Edward Lucas, *The New Cold War: Putin's Russia and the Threat to the West* (New York: Palgrave Macmillan, 2009), p. 49.

6. "Khodorkovsky Cornered," *The Economist*, July 4, 2003. www.economist.cam/node/1904504.

7. Lilia Shevtsova, "The Next Russian Revolution," *Current History* (October 2012), p. 252.

8. Elena Shadrina, *Russia's State Capitalism and Energy Geopolitics of Northeast Asia*, University of Turku, Electronic Publications of Pan-European Institute, January 20, 2013.

9. World Bank website, http://data.worldbank.org/country/russian-federation.

10. Neil Robinson, "Economic and Political Hybridity: Patrimonial Capitalism in the Post-Soviet Sphere," *Journal of Eurasian Studies*, 4 (2013), p. 142.

11. Reznik, Bierman, and Meyer, "Remaking Russia's Economy," *Bloomberg*, p. 40.

12. Organisation for Economic Cooperation and Development, *OECD Economic Surveys: Russian Federation* (Paris: OECD, January 2014), p. 20.

13. Ibid.

14. Data on Russia's oil and gas industry is from the U.S. Energy Information Administration (EIA), "Russia," November 26, 2013. http://www.eia.gov/countries/cab.cfm?=RS.

15. Goldman, *Petrostate*, p. 2.

16. Reznik, Bierman, and Meyer, "Remaking Russia's Capitalism," *Bloomberg*, p. 42.

17. Nathan Gray, "Rail Still at the Heart of Russia's Economy," *The Moscow Times*, May 24, 2013. http://themoscowtimes.com/business/20130422/191459818/Rail-still-at-the-heart-of -Russia's economy.

18. Shevtsova, p. 253.

19. OECD, "Russia," p. 16.

20. OECD, "Russia," p. 16. Also see European Bank for Reconstruction and Development, "Diversifying Russia: Harnessing Regional Diversity" (London: European Bank for Reconstruction and Development, 2012).

21. Ibid, p. 23.

22. Douglas Busvive, Stephen Grey, Roman Anin, and Himonshu Ojha, "Russian Railways Paid Billions to Secretive Private Companies," *The Globe & Mail* (Toronto), May 23, 2014.

23. Quoted in Anders Aslund, "Putin's Conservative State Capitalism," *The Moscow Times*, December 18, 2013. http://www.themoscow times.com/opinion/article/putins-conservative.

24. Ibid.

25. Andrey Ostroukh and Alexander Kolyandr, "Russian Economy Faces Contraction Threat," *The Wall Street Journal*, March 27, 2014, p. A8.

26. Pew Research Global Attitudes Project, chapter 3. "Russia: Public Backs Putin, Crimea's Succession," May 8, 2014. www.pewglobal .org/2014/05/08/chapter-3-russia-public-backs-putin-crimea-succession/.

27. United Nations Development Program, *National Human Development Report: Russian Federation, 2008* (Moscow: United Nations Development Program, 2009), p. 7.

28. Tulip Mazumdar, "Vodka Blamed for High Death Rates in Russia," BBC News Health, January 31, 2014. http://www.bbc.com/news/ health-25961063.

29. United Nations Development Program, *National Human Development Report*, p. 14.

30. Jan-Werner Mueller, "Eastern Europe Goes South: Disappearing Democracy in the EU's Newest Members," *Foreign Affairs* (March/April 2014), p. 15.

31. "Why Europe's Populists and Radicals Admire Vladimir Putin," *The Economist*, April 19, 2014.

FIVE

State Capitalism, Power, and Identity in the Middle East

For almost two centuries, the Middle East was generally marginal to the global economy. This docs not discount the importance of oil and gas to the global economy, but it points to the core issue that beyond those commodities, much of the rest of the regional economy has been defined by a failure to broadly diversify and engage new industries, promote an entrepreneurial private sector, and breathe life into a moribund agricultural sector. Regional conflicts distracted from development priorities, and post-colonial attempts to achieve a measure of economic self-reliance to match political independence largely failed.[1] State-run enterprises expanded with protectionism, but their mediocre performance was blamed on ineffective management, with companies in the public sector usually run like government bureaucracies. In many cases, this legacy remains in place. However, there have been improvements and some debate as to how to improve state-owned corporate experience, which will be discussed in the chapter.

The second oil price boom, which ran from roughly 2000 to 2014, led to unprecedented growth in Saudi Arabia and the other Gulf Cooperation Council (GCC) countries (Bahrain, Qatar, Oman, Kuwait, and the United Arab Emirates—UAE). The improvement was oil-related in part, but it also occurred in non-oil activities such as construction, retail, and financial services. The United Arab Emirates, with an economy larger than that of Egypt, may be the best success story. But Saudi Arabia's economy is now the largest in the region, and Qatar is the world's richest country in terms of per capita income. These economies have growing private sectors, as well as state-run enterprises that enjoy at least some autonomy from political interference. They are also likely to weather the post-2014 lower world oil prices.

State capitalism is firmly entrenched in most Middle Eastern countries. Anyone familiar with the global oil and gas industry is aware of the power and influence of state-owned companies like Saudi Aramco, the Qatar General Petroleum Corporation, and the Kuwait Petroleum Corporation. Qatari gas fuels the industrial economies of China, Korea, and Japan, while Saudi and Kuwaiti oil is critically important to the French, Italian, and many developing countries' economies, such as those of India, South Africa, and Pakistan. At the same time, one of the world's largest airlines is Emirates, a subsidiary of the Emirates Group, which is wholly owned by the Investment Corporation of Dubai. The Abu Dhabi United Group, owned by the deputy prime minister of United Arab Emirates, owns Manchester City Football Club, while Qatar Investments Authority owns France's Paris Saint-Germain Football Club. Qatar's Al Jazeera is one of the world's largest and best-known non-Western television networks. And a group of sovereign wealth funds, including the Abu Dhabi Investment Authority, the Kuwait Investment Authority, and the Saudi Arabia Monetary Authority, hold in excess of $1 trillion in global assets. Although many of the Gulf States—Saudi Arabia, Kuwait, Qatar, Bahrain, the United Arab Emirates, and Oman—have relatively small populations, their hydrocarbon wealth has allowed them to accumulate considerable power as well as influence beyond their immediate neighborhood. The key elements to Middle Eastern state capitalism, especially in the Gulf States, are a large role for state-owned companies, autocratic political systems (generally monarchies), and more than a nod to Islam.

Part of the challenge to Western-oriented economies that are dominated by private sector companies is from Middle Eastern state-owned enterprises. The combination of oil, money, and Islam has made a powerful combination, during a period when U.S. power in the Middle East has declined. Factors at play in the region include Washington's effort to pivot away from the Middle East, the more active engagement of Iran in the region, and the more conservative bent of the Gulf States. This development is reinforced by the Sunni orientation of the Saudis in dealing with the revivalism of Shia Islam, pushed by Iran and its allies.

This chapter will focus on the importance of state capitalism in the Middle East, with emphasis on the relationship between the Gulf States and their state-owned entities to the international economy. State capitalism in the Gulf States has been successful in elevating national interests on the global stage, increasing national wealth, and helping to reinforce national identities. In other parts of the Middle East, state capitalism has been less successful. It has served as a conduit for corruption, distorted national economies, and contributed to socioeconomic inequalities. In countries such as Egypt, Libya, Tunisia, and Syria, state capitalism's problematic side was a major factor in galvanizing the forces for change reflected by the advent of the Jasmine Revolution in 2010. While state capitalism has helped pull most Gulf States' populations out of extreme poverty, corruption and the autocratic nature of the governments have also left challenging conundrums for future generations. Moreover, some of the same problems that stimulated the Jasmine Revolution in North Africa, Syria, and Yemen exist in the Gulf States, raising politically delicate issues over the reliance on security apparatus to crush everything from liberal democratic activists to Al-Qaeda cells. Indeed, the effects of the Jasmine Revolution briefly rippled into Bahrain, but a prompt Saudi-led military intervention kept the Sunni monarchy in power. The future of state capitalism in the Middle East is very much up for grabs, and considering the competitive nature of some of the region's companies and extensive holdings of its sovereign wealth funds, it is incumbent to have more than a passing awareness of them.

NATION-BUILDING AND THE STATE

The concept of the modern nation-state is relatively new in much of the Middle East. Most of the national borders in existence today are a product of the European colonial era, driven by British and French imperatives following the collapse of the Ottoman Empire in 1918. Egypt was the exception to this, in that it historically maintained greater coherence in terms of identity, helped by the central geographic nature of the Nile River and the long-term development of civilization along that body of water. As the Middle East made the shift from the colonial rule to independence in the post-Second World War period, many of the new governments created state-owned enterprises. The reasons for this were that experienced and skilled people geared for a modern economy were often in limited supply, and capital was usually scarce. In some countries, state-owned enterprises were also forced to compete with companies established by large merchant families, but close links to the government gave the former a comparative advantage. Another factor helpful to reliance on state capitalism was a post-colonial mindset. Many of these countries had fallen to Western imperialism, often through economic links to trade and oil.

Upon independence, many of the new leaders opted for the state to control the commanding heights of the economy. This allowed state-owned companies to become a means of expressing nationalism and fortifying national security.

Along these lines, state-owned companies were to be the motor for national development (often with dual industrial and social development goals), be it in the oil and gas sector or, in some cases, manufacturing. In most countries, state-owned companies benefited from special privileges and exemptions from certain regulations. Indeed, the Gulf States–based SOEs historically reaped rewards from subsidized inputs and have been exempt from some aspects of national regulations.[2] This favoritism allowed state companies to have an ongoing large role in the economic life of their countries. As Alan Richards and John Waterbury observed in their seminal study, *A Political Economy of the Middle Class* (1990): "Middle East states are big; they employ large numbers of people as civil servants, laborers, and managers—sometimes, as in the case of Egypt, as much as one half of the nonagricultural work force. These states monopolize resource: they control large investment budgets, strategic parts of the banking system, virtually all subsoil minerals, and the nation's basic infrastructure in roads, railroads, power, and port."[3] The list was comprehensive in 1990; it has shrunk somewhat across the region since then, but many of the basic elements of state dominance remain, which often blurs the role played by Middle Eastern state-owned companies and government policies.

What was the role of the private sector in the Middle East in the early independence period? In many cases the private sector was perceived as being inadequate to the challenge of national development. Considering the size and scope of development challenges, it was believed that the state was better able to mobilize the critical resources and able to plan ahead, rather than being constrained by the need for short-term profits. More critical voices emphasized the greed and the exploitative nature of the private sector, its ties to the metropole, and its tendency to export capital rather than reinvest profit.[4] Along the same lines, an unshackled private sector following the laws of supply and demand was not observed as the means to deal with equity inequality throughout the region. As Richards and Waterbury observed: "The Middle Eastern state took upon itself the challenge of moving the economy onto an industrial footing, shifting population to the urban areas, of educating and training its youth wherever they live, raising agricultural productivity to feed the nonagricultural population redistributing wealth, of building a credible military force, and doing battle with international trade and financial regimes that held them in thrall."[5] In this, local private sector companies were ultimately held as incapable of meeting these challenges, whether for lack of resources or motivation, or for ideological reasons.

While state-owned companies and related corporate entities have dominated since the 1950s, they are not without their own set of problems, corporate governance being a key issue. On one side of the equation, the opaque nature of these key companies regarding their operations and governance enabled them to enjoy favorable status with the government. The Organization for Economic Cooperation and Development (OECD) reported in 2013: "And yet, for decades, the operation and governance of key state-owned companies in the region was clouded in secrecy and while the regulatory frameworks for private companies, especially listed enterprises, have evolved rapidly over the past decade, governments have reluctant to imposes similar standards on enterprises under their ownership."[6] Considering this, the track record of SOEs has been mixed, with a number of colorful scandals and failures in their wakes. Moreover, state-owned companies in some countries have suffered from lower productivity and have struggled to compete with the private sector, making them "elephants among gazelles."[7]

The role of the SOEs began to change in the late twentieth century. While SOEs were originally viewed as a start-up development strategy, benefiting from protection often accorded to infant industries and forming part of the nation-building exercise, globalization brought home the need to compete. In the Gulf States, higher oil prices provided capital for SOEs to restructure, with the view that greater competitiveness was needed. The same OECD report cited above correctly observed: "the original vision of the role of the SOEs has changed over the years as governments, having achieved higher levels of economic development, no longer view them as a mechanism of nation-building and infant industries protection, but as a source of competitiveness. In addition to being overseen by their line ministries of sectorial regulators, SOEs in a number of countries are now also affected by policies and plans of governmental organs charged with developing a broader economic strategy for their country."[8] This trend has been more pronounced in the Gulf States than in other parts of the Middle East and North Africa. In Egypt, Tunisia, and Morocco, some degree of privatization occurred, though the process slowed in the 2010s due to social considerations related to employment concerns, and any economic restructuring that would result in higher unemployment was avoided by nervous governments with little stomach for social unrest.

In the early twenty-first century, the role of the state in the economy in the Gulf States remains significant, and some of the national champions have global clout. (More on this later.) In most countries, public sector companies are still the largest employers of local citizens. According to the International Monetary Fund report on Saudi Arabia's labor market (2013): "Government employment is an important channel for oil wealth distribution and is an attractive employment option for many Saudi workers."[9] At the same time, governments are willing to create new SOEs to reflect changing global economic conditions, to restructure older, less efficient state-owned enterprises and/or capture new technologies. One example of this was evident in Abu Dhabi's Mubadala Development Company creating Masdar in 2006 to develop renewable energy and sustainable technologies industries. Mubadala is also the holding company for ATIC, a state-owned semiconductor manufacturer. Mubadala has been very upfront about its interest in making capital-intensive long-term investments in high-tech heavy industries, with the goal of leap-frogging technology and helping to create a non-oil/gas-related economic foundation for the future.

Although the Middle East suffers from a wide range of economic challenges, a number of countries have created highly competitive state-owned companies that clearly challenge their Western private sector counterparts. One situation that emerged was of Gulf State companies looking to buy Western assets. This purchase of foreign assets included everything from London and New York real estate to key infrastructure assets and farmland. In a number of cases, the activities of Arab state-owned companies sparked concerns. In 2006 Abu Dhabi's buying spree came up against nationalistic sensitivities in the United States, when D.P. World, one of the world's largest and most successful port operators, sought to purchase several U.S. ports. The opaque and often byzantine structures of many of these companies, and the assistance from the state, leave many today questioning whether the playing field is even. In many cases it is intentionally uneven, which tends to cause a degree of friction over unfair trade. The fact that the Gulf States are autocratic governments adds an element of geopolitical risk into the equation. In the case of D.P. World, its effort to purchase U.S. ports was thwarted due to political issues raised by the U.S. Congress. An Abu Dhabi–owned entity on U.S. soil, it was asserted, would be a national security risk. Part of the reasoning was that it was not so much a company buying the ports, but rather the government of an Arab country. Not surprisingly, Abu Dhabi officials were quite angry over this kind of treatment.

Abu Dhabi was not easily dissuaded from overseas investment. The hike in oil prices in the first decade of the twenty-first century gave most of the Gulf States a huge injection of capital. In 2007, the Gulf States bought $89 billion worth of foreign firms.[10] Abu Dhabi, through its SWF, the Abu Dhabi Investment Authority (ADIA), was particularly active. ADIA was known to have provided financial support for the U.S. bank Citigroup in 2008, when other sources were scarce. While the U.S. Congress wanted to prevent D.P. World from buying U.S. ports, it was content to have ADIA's help in bailing out one of its troubled banks.

THE GULF STATES AND OIL AND GAS

The Gulf States enjoy considerable wealth and have become very global in their approach to doing business. In the early twenty-first century, these states still rely heavily on state-owned companies and related corporations (which may be partially owned by government and/or government entities). There is greater space for the private sector in countries such as Saudi Arabia, but connections to the ruling elite are common. Before proceeding further, it is important for us to provide a better understanding of Middle Eastern/Gulf state wealth: oil and gas.

Middle Eastern state capitalism is highly concentrated in the region's oil and gas industry. This is evident in Algeria, Libya, and Iraq, but even more so in the Gulf States. Saudi Arabia is the world's largest producer and exporter of oil (the only producer with significant spare capacity), and as such, it plays a systemic and stabilizing role in global oil markets.[11] There, oil accounts to 90 percent of export earnings and 80 percent of government revenues. Oil and gas have the same centrality to the economies of Kuwait, Qatar, and the United Arab Emirates. Due to oil, these countries—Saudi Arabia in particular—maintain a high level of importance to the global economy. Saudi Arabia's role as the key swing producer was emphasized by the abrupt fall in Libyan oil production in 2011, as well as at times in history such as the Gulf Wars and the Venezuelan general strike. Each time, Saudi Arabia stepped up production to make certain there was no major disruption in global oil supplies.

Saudi Arabia's modern political economy began in 1932, with the foundation of the kingdom, and has been constructed around the oil industry. Along these lines, Saudi Arabia is an autocratic state, headed by a king, who is orbited by a royal court to which all of the country's major companies, public and private, have ties. Reinforcing the royal government, which is the main allocator of oil revenues, is an efficient security apparatus. Oil was discovered in quantity in Saudi Arabia, in 1938. The initial developers were a number of foreign oil companies, including the Standard Oil of California (SoCal). The new Saudi state rapidly replaced the traditional economy, which was based on agriculture and trade. Although the initial companies conducting exploration for and export of oil were American, Saudi control was gradually asserted, especially in the 1970s with the nationalization of Saudi Aramco. This coincided with the advent of the first Saudi five-year development plan, which sought to construct a modern economy. The development of the Saudi state also had a political component, as there was a price for U.S. support of Israel, which underwent a series of wars with its Arab neighbors. The oil spikes in 1973–1974 and 1979–1980 did much to bring in a massive surge in revenues for the Saudi government, which was clearly the primary agent of economic change. At the same time, the private sector was dominated by a handful of large businesses in the service sector, mainly in construction and real estate. A critical point is that the links between the private sector and the state are strong due to the companies' dependence on government patronage and spending.

Another important and interrelated dimension of Saudi Arabia becoming a critical global player is its role as a swing producer of oil within OPEC (Organization of Petroleum Exporting Countries). OPEC was created at the Bagdad Conference in 1960 by Iran, Iraq, Kuwait, Saudi Arabia, and Venezuela. Although other members joined, such as Qatar, Indonesia, Libya, the UAE, Algeria, Nigeria, and Ecuador, OPEC did not gain political and economic significance until the 1970s. Two important developments were responsible for this. First, the relationship between the dominant international privately owned, largely Western, oil companies and local Middle East governments changed. In a number of states, either the entire oil industry or significant parts of it were nationalized. These actions were undertaken to reassert national control of this strategic sector and to reduce the economic and political clout of mainly Western energy multinationals.

The second event leading to OPEC's rise to global significance was the Arab Oil Embargo of 1973, which was a response from the Arab countries against Western support for Israel during the 1973–1974 Yom Kippur War. Although Israel was able to maintain military superiority through use of Western military equipment, the Arab oil producers found a new weapon: oil, which was a point of vulnerability for Western economies. The first development positioned states to have control over their own natural resources and benefit from price increases and revenues, and the second raised prices significantly, helping inject considerable capital into economies like those of Saudi Arabia, Kuwait, Qatar, and the UAE.

The global oil industry received another windfall when the Iranian Revolution broke out in 1979. As Iran's production declined, countries like Saudi Arabia were able to step up production and hugely benefit from the surge in oil prices. Although prices would later collapse in 1986 because of too much supply, the place of oil as the king of the Saudi economy was well established. This mass accumulation of oil wealth gave the Middle East considerable leverage in the global economy. Directors of sovereign wealth funds realized this, and they have been and continue to be active in acquiring foreign assets as well as investing in the diversification of their respective economies. The former has gained considerable attention and caused a degree of apprehension in countries around the world. The motivation on the part of Middle Eastern countries encompasses a mix of the need to deploy capital, diversify future income streams, and national security in terms of acquiring strategic assets, such as agricultural land and water rights.

While the Gulf States are in many cases "petro-states," other Middle Eastern countries that fit the oil-fueled petro-state category (in the very broadest sense) arc Algeria, Iran, Iraq, Libya, and Oman. Until the civil war in 2011, Libya was one of the major oil producers in the Middle East and North Africa, and holder of the largest proven oil reserves in Africa. The Libyan economy was heavily dependent on oil and gas exports, and the nation enjoyed a standard of living well ahead of the vast majority of African countries. Like much of the region, the oil industry was in the hands of the state-owned National Oil Company (which had a number of subsidiaries), which accounted for a little over half of the country's exports. Foreign oil companies were welcomed into the country to help develop resources, especially in the early 2000s, when relations between the Gadaffi regime and the West improved. Like many of the Gulf States, Libya had its own sovereign wealth fund. The Libyan civil war and its aftermath—an extended period of socio-political strife—has cut Libya's oil profile and raised questions over the country's future.

The other oil producers have economies dominated, to varying degrees, by state-owned companies. In Oman this is the Petroleum Development Oman (PDO), which is 60 percent owned by the government (the rest is owned by Royal Dutch Shell, Total, and Partex). In Algeria, the state dominance of the economy is reflected by the overwhelming role of the state-owned Sonatrach. Oil and gas exports account for 70 percent of budget revenues and over 90 percent of exports. Algeria's government, a quasi-authoritarian secular regime dominated by the military and headed by an elected civilian president, has sought to diversify the economy, but hydrocarbons continue to dominate.

Oil, of course, is the critical foundation of Iran's economy. Oil and gas account for the overwhelmingly largest shares of the government's revenues and the country's exports. Although a private sector exists, the state's role in the economy is clearly dominant: a large part of economic activity is centrally planned, price contracts and subsidies (especially for food) are used, and state-owned companies play a major role in a number of sectors. There is also a considerable amount of corruption, and the country's relative isolation (due to its commitment to its nuclear program) has hurt the economy. Neighboring Iraq is probably more dependent on oil, as that commodity accounts for over 90% of exports. Although production costs are low in Iraq and foreign companies have been welcome, the country's high level of political risk, which was painfully evident in 2013–15 with the rise of the Islamic State, raises questions over its ability to be a key and dependable force as a major supplier.

SAUDI ARAMCO

Key to Saudi Arabia's economic muscle is the giant state-owned Saudi Aramco (originally called the Arab-American Oil Company), which in the company's own words, ranks "first among oil companies worldwide in terms of crude oil production and exports, and natural gas liquids (LNG) exports, and are among the leading producers of natural gas. We are also among the world's leading refiners and are moving further downstream into chemicals production."[12] The company further notes that it manages conventional crude oil and condensate reserves of 260.2 billion barrels, and gas reserves of 284.8 trillion standard cubic feet. It employs 57,000 workers in 77 countries. Despite efforts to diversify the Saudi economy away from such a heavy dependence on oil and gas (moving into chemicals and agriculture, for example), the oil industry and the Saudi state are strongly entwined in the country's economic and political development. As such, Saudi Aramco is a global giant and exercises considerable influence both at home and overseas. The Baker III institute for Public Policy's Amy Myers Jaffe and Jareer Elass noted in 2007: "The Saudi state oil firm, Saudi Aramco, is undeniably the most influential oil company in the world."[13] This still holds true today. The company's core significance is how it shapes first Saudi economic development and then how it influences and competes in the global economy.

Saudi Aramco has a degree of autonomy in its operations, but real authority resides with the monarchy. Indeed, ultimate authority for all decisions related to oil rests with the king of Saudi Arabia, and the company formally has no authority or formal institutional mechanism to question the monarch's decisions. While the king's authority is supreme, key senior members of the Al-Saud household have a certain degree of sway on major decisions. Nawaf Obaid, in *The Oil Kingdom at 100: Petroleum Policymaking in Saudi Arabia*, observed: "Because oil policy has such an enormous effect on the health of the Kingdom, it is set not by the whim of any individual but instead by consensus among the influential ruling family members after considerable debate and consultation with Saudi experts." In some ways, Saudi oil policy closely resembles a family business, though the royals have placed importance on having competent managers overseeing it. There is an understanding that the company manages and generates the lion's share of wealth.

What has made Aramco stand out is the comingling of Saudi national and corporate objectives. As Jaffe and Elass observed: "Saudi Aramco's strategies and aims have been greatly tailored to meet the foreign needs of the state."[14] They note that this was the case in the 1980s, when the Saudi royal family believed an oil price war would be the most optimal means to claw back the Saudi market share from emerging oil producers (namely Norway and the United Kingdom). During the same decade, the oil company facilitated Saudi Arabia's foreign policy goals to guarantee that cash-starved Iran lacked the resources to wage a successful war against Iraq. It also pressured, through lower oil prices (and higher Saudi production), the Soviet Union following its invasion and occupation of Afghanistan. In the 1990s, company and national foreign policy goals were the same, as Aramco was a key oil source for the United States, especially in the first Persian Gulf War, which saw Iraq invade Kuwait and shut down that country's oil production.

The Saudis were also apt in understanding Asia's rise in the first decade of the twenty-first century, embracing a "look East" strategic oil policy. This was emphasized by King Abdullah's 2006 four-nation trip to China, India, Malaysia, and Pakistan. China was particularly noteworthy, considering that Saudi Arabia was then the supplier of 14 percent of the Asian country's oil imports. Saudi Arabia and China signed a number of agreements, including cooperation over oil, gas, and mineral deposits. King Abdullah stated at a press conference, "We hope this cooperation will develop even more in the future," and Saudi Foreign Minister, Prince Saud Al-Faisal, elaborated: "China is one of the most important markets for

Saudi oil and Saudi oil is one of the most important sources of energy for China."[15] Since that time, Saudi–Chinese relations have moved closer, and the Middle Eastern country remains a major energy source to the East Asian economy.

Considering the centrality of oil to Saudi Arabia's future, what happens at Aramco is key to the country's future. The Saudi oil industry has been constructed around the Ghawar Oilfield, which is one of the world's largest, but it is aging. Because of the Ghawar's significance, Saudi officials treat information about its reserves and longevity as a state secret. Information on a field-by-field production is also not readily available. In the early 2000s the opaque nature of Saudi Oil production, the aging of key fields, and an increase in demand, led to considerable discussion about "peak oil," a tipping point when the oil supply would reach its peak and thereafter decline.[16] This would produce a potentially gloomy future for Saudi Arabia, especially if its efforts to diversity from its heavy dependence on oil should fail.

The "peak oil" scenario failed to materialize in the following decade, though even Saudi officials acknowledge that at some point oil production will indeed decline. The decline scenario failed to materialize for a combination of reasons: the discovery of new fields around the world, the development of alternatives (wind, solar, and biomass), and new technology to help extract more from aging oil fields.

SABIC

Saudi Arabia's state-owned company universe is not limited to oil and gas. Saudi concerns of being overly dependent on oil led to the creation of the Saudi Basic Industries Corporation (SABIC) in 1976. Today it is the largest listed company in the Middle East, with net assets of US$90 billion as of 2013. All the same, the Saudi government holds 70 percent of ownership, with some ownership held by other Gulf States and a small group of local private investors. The company is listed as a diversified chemical company, involved in chemicals and intermediates, industrial polymers, fertilizers, and metals. According to SABIC's website, it is the world's second-largest ethylene glycol producer, third-largest polyolefin maker, and fourth-largest polypropylene maker.

SABIC's creation came about by a royal decree and was staffed and guided by a small band of youthful engineers and civil servants who were recruited selectively by the country's then–Crown Prince and later King Fahd.[17] From the very beginning, SABIC's role was to be the main agent of heavy industrialization in the country. While SABIC was initially 100 percent state-owned and supported by soft loans through the Public Investment Fund, emphasis was placed on the need to generate commercial returns. The OECD observed: "SABIC's initial management team was small, and corporate expansion proceeded only after several years of careful project studies. Its political principals insisted on SABIC operating like a private company with fully autonomous management."[18]

In the early twenty-first century, SABIC is one of the most successful and profitable Saudi companies. It is the dominant player in Saudi petrochemicals and, as already shown, a global competitor. The company accounts for a little over 70 percent of non-oil exports. At the same time, SABIC expanded its operations overseas, beginning to make foreign acquisitions in 2002. Among SABIC's overseas purchases were Dutch DSM Petrochemicals (€2.2 billion in 2002), British Huntsman Petrochemicals ($700 million in 2006), and GE Plastics ($11.6 billion in 2007). In general Saudi investment via SABIC has been welcome and caused little backlash.

SABIC is also forward-thinking. In 2014 the company's chief executive officer, Mohammed Al Mady, stated that while his firm is focusing on expanding at home, it will continue to assess opportunities abroad if they are "justified."[19] He made special note of Africa, which is seen as "a very promising market" for SABIC in the areas of fertilizers and plastics. Africa's economic progress in the early twenty-first century, married to its demographic growth and the expansion of the middle class, is attracting Middle Eastern competition along with that of many Western private sector companies.

Two things can be taken from the SABIC experience. The company's success (hand-in-hand with its professionalism) has made its approach attractive to other Gulf States. With an eye to economic diversification, a number of other countries have followed suit, with Bahrain's Alba (Aluminum Bahrain), Dubai's Dubal, Industries Qatar, and Abu Dhabi's General Holding Company. As a group, these companies have been export-oriented and profitable, enjoyed substantial managerial autonomy, and remained largely unburdened by local social obligations.[20]

The second thing to be taken from the SABIC experience is the mix of practices from the private and public sectors. The OECD indicates that SABIC's experience does have a high degree of overlap in the region, including such factors "as the support of senior political principals, special dispensations to circumvent cumbersome procedures, targeted state support coupled with a clear mandate to generate returns, meritocratic recruitment and substantial managerial autonomy."[21]

SABIC is one of state capitalism's more successful ventures. It is competitive partially because of its business culture that stressed profitability, but its links to the Saudi state are also a net positive. Along these lines, SABIC's ability to advance its interests clearly advance the kingdom's.

DUBAI, INC., AND EMIRATES

The statelet of Dubai, part of the UAE, enjoyed a spectacular rise in the 1980s and 1990s and a bruising fall from grace in 2008–2009. Unlike its rival within the UAE, Abu Dhabi, Dubai lacks the same massive reserves of oil. Instead the royal family of Dubai opted to be more entrepreneurial and make use of their location to create a major trade and financial crossroads. Dubai's beginnings as a modern state, or Dubai, Inc., can be found in the development of its port as a trading center. But first we should briefly define Dubai, Inc., as it is an important force in the Gulf States and the financial world. Jim Krane, author of *City of Gold: Dubai and the Dream of Capitalism* (2008), noted: "The system of government in Dubai and the rest of the UAE is perhaps best described as tribal autocracy. It's autocratic because a single ruler, Sheikh Mohammed in Dubai's case, holds unlimited power. It's tribal because rule is based on tribe and family with power handed down the generations."[22]

In 1963, Dubai's port status was reinforced by the dredging of the Dubai Creek. Things changed even more radically in 1966, when oil was discovered in Dubai. Although the amount of oil was far less than in neighboring Abu Dhabi, it was enough to launch the emirate into a higher level of economic development. Another factor that helped the rise of Dubai was the formation of the United Arab Emirates (UAE), which followed the announcement by the British colonial power that they were leaving. Consequently, when the British did indeed depart in 1971, the UAE came into existence. In a major positive for Dubai, the formation of the UAE forced the emirate to mend its fences with its sometimes-rival Abu Dhabi, which added a degree of political stability. Considering that Dubai's oil reserves were limited, the al-Maktoum family decided that they needed a different development strategy from the other, more hydrocarbon-wealthy Gulf States. This included the important decision in the early 1980s to upgrade the airport, allowing Dubai to become a refueling stop between Europe and Asia. What came next was a national airline, Emirates.

The creation of Emirates was a major development in airline history, as it is now ranked among the top ten carriers worldwide in terms of passenger kilometers. It is also the biggest airline in the Middle East in terms of revenue, passenger numbers, and fleet size. While Emirates is today a major player in the airline industry, it had humble beginnings. In the early 1980s, a dispute over Pakistan air flights with Gulf Air and Dubai's support for Pakistan Airlines resulted in Gulf Air cutting services to Dubai. Gulf Air was the region's main airline and was owned by the governments of Bahrain, Oman, Abu Dhabi, and Qatar. Instead of being dependent on Gulf Air and external economic actors, Dubai, Inc., opted to create its own airline, with the name Emirates, showcasing the UAE flag on the tail.

Sheik Mohammed hired Maurice Flanagan, an ex-British Airways executive who ran the Dubai National Air Travel Agency, a ticket handling and ground staff management company. Flanagan was given a mandate and cash to being the new national airlines. After several years of planning, Emirates officially began in 1985, with seed capital of $10 million. Although told that Emirates would not be given any more capital and would have to stand on its own, the fledgling airline did indeed benefit from Dubai, Inc. As journalist Jim Krane noted: "Emirates did get more subsidies. Flanagan estimates the carrier got $90 million in gifts from the royal family. That included two barely used Boeing 727s that the royal air wing handed over in 1985; payment with another aircraft purchase; and a building to house its training quarters."[23] The timing of the airline's launch and the rapid economic expansion taking place in South and Southeast Asia, all helped boost Emirates into the ranks of competitive airlines. The airline further benefited from its willingness to service destinations that others shunned, including Iran, Ethiopia, and Libya. At the same time, Dubai was able to market itself as a place where tired Europeans could have fun in the sun, an alternative to the usual southern European destinations like Greece, Spain, and Portugal. This helped further develop the country's tourist sector.

Emirates' emergence as a major global airline competitor was certainly felt by other airlines and aircraft producers. Among the former, Emirates offered tough competition and was an active force in both European and Asian Markets (including Australia). For the latter, Emirates became a much-coveted customer for AirBus and Boeing. In 2008–09, Dubai's economy was hit by a severe crisis in the form of a property market bubble bursting, but Emirates was able to ride through the crisis. Emirates has faced criticism that it benefits from state help. The company disputed the claim that it gained unfair advantages from subsidies in terms of preferential fuel cost, landing and air usage fees, or cheap labor. It pointed out that while refueling in Dubai was cheaper that in Europe, it was cheaper also for other airlines refueling in Dubai. Emirates also indicated that its funding, $26 billion over the past 15 years (from 2013) was done on a commercial basis and that it does not benefit from additional funding from the government of Dubai or related entities.[24] As for labor, Emirates indicated that it did compensate its workers well, but that unlike in Europe its workforce was not unionized, a factor that tended to raise labor costs.

Abu Dhabi is particularly active in developing strategically important government-owned companies. Their close ties to the government afford them particularly high credit ratings (in the "A" to "AA" range). In turn, international investors are quick to buy their bonds when they come to the international debt capital markets. Among the most prominent is the Abu Dhabi National Energy Company (TAQA). This is a holding company for a diversified energy group engaged in investments in oil, natural gas, power, and water operations. TAQA provides more than 95 percent of the electricity and water requires for the Emirate of Abu Dhabi.

Like TAQA, Mubadala relies on heavy support from the government of Abu Dhabi. It engages in a variety of highly diversified international investments on behalf of the Emirate, including semiconductors, aluminum, aerospace, oil and gas, real estate, and other industries. Finally, International Petroleum Investment Company (IPIC) is a holding company that is also integral to the Emirate's efforts to develop the country's hydrocarbon sector. IPIC is engaged in both upstream oil operations, petroleum refining, as well as various petrochemical subsidiaries.

These three government-owned enterprises are just the largest of several public companies in Abu Dhabi and the UAE. The United Arab Emirates, Qatar, and other statelets may have tiny populations and small geographic sizes, but they are exceptionally wealthy and aggressive about promoting their interests in the global economy. They are particularly adroit at using their government-owned companies to further their economic interests.

HIGH-FLYING QATAR

Qatar represents the new jet-setting state capitalism of the early twenty-first century. Located on a peninsula with a sole land border with Saudi Arabia, Qatar juts out into the Persian Gulf. Across from the water is Iran, which has had a less-than-friendly relationship with Saudi Arabia, a situation that has often left Qatar sitting in the middle between its two larger neighbors. Yet with a population of 1.7 million and no readily available water resources, Qatar has become a significant player in Middle Eastern politics, global finance, and the developing world. It has adroitly managed relations with both Saudi Arabia and Iran, maintained good ties to the

United States (having a major U.S. airbase), and converted its capital city of Doha into a home-away-from-home for high-ranking Hamas members. It also has diplomatic relations with Israel. Additionally, Doha is home to Al Jazeera ("the island"), the state-owned broadcasting corporation, known in the Arab world for its willingness to let different views be articulated. Qatar is also set to be the location for the 2022 soccer World Cup. Indeed, one observer noted in 2013: "Qatar has transformed itself into a global hub and a central pivot of globalization. Doha, the capital, changes by the day, featuring the latest and the best of everything in its streets and its gleaming skyscrapers. The country hosts world-class universities, a world-class museum, and a world-class airline."[25]

Qatar's political system is very similar to Dubai's and those of other Gulf States: the ruling Al Thani family, led by Sheik Tamin since 2013, runs Qatar as their own fiefdom, with members in key government and corporate posts. In many ways, Qatar is more like a corporation than a country, with decision-making power concentrated at the tip of the political pyramid. The different state-owned or state-related institutions are an extension of the Qatari monarch's rule, led by the revenue-generating Qatar General Petroleum Corporation, the SWF Qatar Investment Authority (QIA) charged with investing for the future, and the propaganda arm of the state, Al Jazeera. The last is known to provide the news generally from a liberal Arab nationalist and moderate Islamic perspective, as well as being pro-Sunni and, at times, seen as anti-American. The network has also been used to occasionally poke the more conservative governments in the region, which has more than once incurred some degree of retaliation. Nonetheless, Al Jazeera has given Qatar a voice to influence events in the Middle East and has developed a sizeable audience in the region.

The foundation of Qatar's power is its vast gas wealth. According to the IMF's 2014 Article IV report: "As the world's largest exporter of liquefied natural gas (LNG), Qatar has turned into an important global financial innovator, donor and labor importer. Growth averaged 14 percent over the past decade and GNP per capita has reached $100,000, the highest in the world."[26] Along these lines, Qatar accounts for close to a third of global LNG trade and is a key supplier for Japan, South Korea, India, and the United Kingdom. The key actor in this is the Qatar General Petroleum Corporation.

The large cash flow from natural gas sales has allowed the Qatari government to continuously post large fiscal surpluses and current account surpluses (at 32 percent in 2012). The Qatar General Petroleum Corporation's foreign investment unit, Qatar Petroleum International Ltd., has used the country's gas-generated wealth to elevate it into a major financial power. Although there are obvious limits to money as a type of power, Qatar is taken seriously around the world. The country's SWF, the Qatar Investment Authority (QIA), was founded in 2005 with a mandate from the Qatari government to manage the oil and gas surpluses, and is believed to have assets of around $170 billion. The QIA does not publish publicly available numbers, and it is not known whether or not the fund makes personal investments on the part of the royal family. Nonetheless, the QIA plays a significant role in forging the Qatari image and the role the state wants to carve out in the future. As the QIA's website states: "Qatar's goal is to become a major international center for finance and investment management, a vision shared by its government, people and institutions."[27]

QIA's focus is on purchasing assets in the United States, Europe, and Asia-Pacific, as well as to help foster, via investment in non-hydrocarbon business at home. This has led the SWF and its subsidiaries to invest in sizeable stakes in Barclays, Credit Suisse, Volkswagen Group, Harrods Group, Total, and Royal Dutch Shell. It has substantial holdings in real estate in London and owns the French football club, Paris Saint-Germain F.C. (valued at $130 million). In 2013, Qatar Holding, an indirect subsidiary of the SWF, announced it was making a $5 billion investment in petrochemical projects in Malaysia, with the goal of helping the Southeast Asian country become the region's leading petrochemical hub.[28]

There is no ambiguity about QIA being an instrument of the Qatari state. As the SWF's website states: "The QIA exists to serve the government and people of Qatar by strengthening the Qatari economy. It does this by making investments in different asset classes and geographies, thereby diversifying the economy and its financial resources."[29] Equally important, the QIA is chaired by Sheikh Tamin bin Hamad Al Thani, and the board is filled with members of the ruling family and their close supporters.

Qatar's enormous wealth is used to make Doha a player in the world. The small Persian Gulf State is active in providing economic assistance to Bahrain, Oman, and Arab countries in transition (like Morocco and Tunisia), and it has emerged an active diplomatic player in the Middle East. Under former Emir Sheikh Hamad Bin Khalifa Al Thani, Qatar supported many of the uprisings that erupted in the Jasmine Revolution. This included a very active role in Libya's overthrow of the Gadaffi regime, including the actual sending of war planes. Qatar also supported the Syrian opposition in its fight against the Assad regime.

While Qatar's active foreign policy role made Doha a friend in some quarters of the Middle East and clearly elevated the small state into a player, it also injected a degree of friction within the Gulf States and elsewhere. As Bloomberg's Robert Tuttle observed: "Those efforts, which continued under Sheik Tamin after he took over from his father in 2013, triggered backlashes. The emirate's flag was burned last year by protesters in Benghazi, Libya. Saudi Arabia and the United Arab Emirates pulled their ambassadors to protest Qatar's backing of Mohamed Morsi, the former Muslim Brotherhood president of Egypt. Relations with Egypt deteriorated after the military overthrew Morsi last year."[30] Qatar's energy wealth has elevated the country into Middle Eastern politics, but it has also demonstrated that such efforts also carry risks.

DO FREEDOM AND BREAD GO TOGETHER?

In 2013 Marwan Muasher, Vice President for studies in the Middle East Program of the Carnegie Endowment for International Peace, observed that much of the Middle East before 2011's political upheaval was guided by the view that economic reform must precede political reform—the so-called "bread before freedom" approach. The argument was that to introduce political reform was premature or dangerous before meeting a citizen's basic needs. As Muasher observed: "But that strategy, even when conducted in good faith, did not work as planned."[31] Indeed, the political aspect of Middle Eastern life remains a headache, as reflected by the Jasmine Revolution that rocked the Arab world stating in late 2010.

The Saudi state has an ideological or religious element that provides an overarching prop for the regime, in the form of Islam. As Karen House observed: "religion has been a pillar of strength, steadying the Al Saud atop the kingdom that bears their name. To this day, the monarchy justifies its rule by claiming to personify, protect and propagate the one true religion. The Saudi monarch styles himself as 'Custodian of the Two Holy Mosques,' a unique title intended to convey his spiritual leadership of all Islam."[32] Saudi Arabia's relationship with Islam, therefore, is almost all-encompassing. The county is, after all, the home of two of the most important holy places of the religion, Mecca and Medina. Indeed, Mecca, birthplace of the Prophet Mohammed, is the destination point for the faithful when they embark upon the Haj, the pilgrimage required of all Muslims who are able, at least once in their life.

Considering the origins of the Saudi state in the heartlands of the Saudi Peninsula and the long relationship of the ruling family with a more austere form of Islam (Wahhabism), there is a certain logic that the kingdom is an Islamic theocratic monarchy. Sunni Islam is the official state religion, and the vast majority of citizens are Sunnis. This has left the kingdom with a strongly conservative orientation, which favors a more autocratic political tradition, married to a perception of the world observed through an Islamic-tinted lens. This explains the suspicion of democracy at home and the willingness to support more radical Islamic groups overseas, via private charities and individuals. Part of Al-Qaeda's roots came out of Saudi Arabia, reflected by Osama bin Laden's Saudi heritage. At the same time, the often behind-the-scenes embrace of Islamic fundamentalist causes and autocratic governments has brought the Saudi and other Gulf states into a more challenged position in the aftermath of the Jasmine Revolution.

The Jasmine Revolution went through the Middle East like a storm. It toppled governments, brought people into the streets demanding change, and wreaked havoc on local economies. While Tunisia experienced a relatively bloodless uprising, Libya had a no-holds-barred bloody civil war, complete with foreign intervention (France, the UK, and Qatar), and Egypt has been embroiled in a long and complicated affair. Yemen developed into near–civil war, accompanied with societal breakdown, as Syria transformed into a bloody battleground. This was all highly disturbing for the conservative Saudi leadership.

The Saudis found themselves looking at a radically changing political landscape in the 2010–2015 period. The central government in Yemen to the south fell into civil war–like conditions and was unable to assert control over its borders. Iraq to the north was a battleground between Sunnis and Iranian-backed Shias, while Tehran was actively aiding Hezbollah, the Assad regime in Syria, and Hamas. The Saudis obviously were not comfortable with any of this. Making matters worse was the loss of longtime ally Hosni Mubarak in Egypt and the election of a Muslim Brotherhood government in his place.

What was particularly disturbing for the Saudis was the challenge that emerged in Bahrain, an island country headed by a Sunni monarchy presiding over a Shia majority, just across a causeway from Saudi Arabia. Being so much closer to the House of Saud, the political turmoil that rocked Bahrain in 2011 deeply worried Saudi leadership. Bahrain's Shia majority had staged weeks of protests against the Sunni monarchy under King Hamad bin Isa al-Khalifa. The opposition demanded economic and political reform, in the form of free electoral participation. Directly related to this was a Shia majority desire to end systemic discrimination against them, in particular in the areas of employment, economic opportunity, and property ownership. Complicating matters Iran's support of the Shiite majority; Iranians probably would have been content to see the Sunni king ousted. For the Saudis, however, Bahrain was in their backyard. Moreover, the Saudis were also concerned that a Shiite victory in Bahrain would embolden its own Shiite minority in the eastern part of the country. In March 2011, 1,200 Saudi troops and 800 from the UAE moved across the causeway and secured the Bahraini monarchy's hold on power. As longtime Saudi watcher Karen House observed: "To the Al Saud, Arab dictators come and go but dynastic monarchies are sacrosanct. Royals are beloved by their people and, of course, by Allah, both of whom they serve. Bahrain was a mirror in which this Al Saudi myth was being shattered."[33] Consequently, the Saudis were willing and able to send troops into Bahrain to prop up that country's monarchy.

The Jasmine Revolution and the ensuing political upheaval that rocked much of the Middle East failed to make inroads into the Gulf States. While the revolutionary spirit of reform was unleashed in late 2010 and 2011, capturing the imagination of millions of Arabs, it ran into a wall of arch-conservatism in the Persian Gulf. There was not to be a political spring, a shift away from authoritarianism to a more open inclusive, nonsectarian, and less ideological landscape. Indeed, the Gulf States were to lead a counter-revolution against the risk of liberal democracy. Emile Nakhleh, the former director of the Political Islam Strategic program at the U.S. Central Intelligence Agency, observed: "What brings this band of Sunni autocrats together is their visceral hatred for democracy, the total mistrust of their peoples, and an innate belief in their entitlement to rule. They have waged a ferocious global media campaign telling anyone willing to listen that their peoples are not fit for democracy, that their autocracy guarantees domestic stability and regional security, and that Western interests could be better served by dictatorship."[34] The Saudis have been the leaders in this form of governance, though Bahrain has actively supported the notion. Although the Saudi intervention into Bahrain, backed by UAE, crushed the opposition and kept the local monarchy in place, major issues still face Saudi Arabia and other Gulf State societies.

The autocratic nature of most Middle Eastern governments, but the Gulf States in particular, has put them in an awkward position vis-à-vis the West, which is liberal and democratic. This hits in two ways: one is the issue of competition in a business sense, and the other is in the buying of assets. While private sector companies rightfully see the field stacked against them in certain sectors and markets, there is usually some space that can be achieved via a joint venture or, in the oil and gas business, leasing. Some major Western energy companies are very adroit at dealing with the sometimes byzantine nature of business in the Gulf States. Nonetheless, doing business in Saudi Aramco's home turf means playing by Saudi Aramco's rules—and, by extension, the Saudi state's rule, guided by Saudi national interests as articulated by the king and his advisors. The same can be said in Qatar, the UAE, and Bahrain.

The purchase of foreign assets is another matter altogether, and this is where Western political sensitivities and Middle Eastern conservatism collide. Although the Saudis are cautious in the "splashiness" of their foreign acquisitions, other Gulf States are not. As *The Economist* observed in May 2014: "Oil-rich countries do not shy away from trophy assets. Qatar holds Harrods, 95% of London's tallest building, the Shard, and Paris Saint-Germain, France's top football club. Abu Dhabi is said to be trying to buy the Time Warner building in New York."[35]

The high profile of these acquisitions sometimes raises the issue of allowing autocratic countries to purchase landmark real estate in Western democracies. While this discord is usually not enough to disrupt such transactions, it adds an element of tension, which then draws in other points of disagreement, such as the flow of Gulf State money into the hands of radical Islamic groups who target Western or Western-aligned groups. All of this points to the changing geo-economic landscape that faces the Gulf States.

A DIFFERENT GEO-ECONOMIC CHESSBOARD

The Middle East's geo-economic chessboard has changed substantially from the late twentieth century. Although large parts of the region are conflict-laden, economically mismanaged, and struggling to maintain their very borders, the Gulf States have emerged as significant regional power brokers and important international investors. The combination of oil wealth, a relatively coherent sense of identity constructed around Islam, and some degree of political acumen have given countries such as Saudi Arabia, the UAE, and Qatar the means to project influence into the greater Middle Eastern geopolitical arena. As mentioned earlier, Saudi Arabia is willing to make use of its oil as geo-economic leverage vis-à-vis other countries, including the United States. This was evident in 2014, when Saudi oil diplomacy helped push oil prices more than 40 percent lower from June to December. This was a blow against the U.S. shale industry as well as a Saudi economic strike against Russia (for its support of Syria's Assad regime) and Iran, its Shiite rival in a new Middle Eastern cold war between Riyadh and Tehran.

Qatar is also active in Libya, Yemen, and Sudan, its funding for Islamic causes, and its purchases of foreign assets. Qatar is hardly alone in the use of its wealth in seeking to determine political outcomes. Indeed, one outcome of this changing paradigm is that Gulf State unity, once a seemingly well-accepted norm, has given way to a somewhat less coherent approach. In large part, this is due to Qatar's willingness to embrace some change in the region vis-à-vis the arch-conservatism of Saudi Arabia, the UAE, and Bahrain.

A major reason for the elevation of the Gulf States is a decline in the influence of traditional Middle Eastern powers—Egypt, Syria, Iraq, and to a lesser extent Iran—a pullback by the United States, the cautious return of Russia, and the new growing relationship with energy-hungry China. Mehran Kamrava observed: "by the 1980s and 1990s, political rhetoric and appearances could no longer mark profound institutional and infrastructural weaknesses characterizing the Egyptian, Syrian, Iraqi and Iranian politics. Youth bulges and burgeoning populations, economic underperformance and chronic inefficiency, broken infrastructures and reactive policies, all had the traditional powers of the Middle East fighting rearguard action and, in the process, losing one political, economic and ideological, and diplomatic battle after another."[36] This helped elevate the role of the Gulf States and their regional body, the Gulf Cooperation Council (GCC). All the same, unity within the GCC has been hard to maintain.

Egypt's trials and tribulations are instructive as to the frailness of Gulf States' unity. The fall of longstanding President Hosni Mubarak in 2010, his replacement by Mohamed Morsi of the Muslim Brotherhood, and the ouster of the Morsi administration by the armed forces in 2013 was accompanied by fierce diplomatic competition between Qatar and Turkey vis-à-vis Saudi Arabia and UAE. This competition was significant in two ways. First, as U.S. power and influence in Egypt proved relatively marginal, the Gulf States were able to step up with offers of substantial—and competing—financial assistance. The United States found its policies constrained by such niceties as human rights: the Gulf States could make rapid decisions and did not have to contend with public dissenting views. So as U.S. influence in Egypt waned, Gulf State influence, backed by large bankrolls, increased and is likely to remain a factor.

Diplomatic competition has also pitted Qatar (backed by Turkey) against Saudi Arabia and the UAE very openly. Qatar opted to back the Morsi government with $8 billion in assistance. This was a clear demonstration of support for a leader of an openly Islamic political party and the elected head of the most populous Arab country. To put it mildly, Qatar's engagement with the Muslim Brotherhood was not appreciated by the Saudis, who have a long history of fighting against the Egyptian group and its Saudi sympathizers. Morsi's government, however, was somewhat hamfisted in ramming policies through the legislative body. It managed to rapidly alienate the secular opposition and incurred the wrath of the military. At the same time, the economy remained highly problematic. In July 2013, the military acted, launching a coup d'état. Qatar's $8 billion investment in Egyptian political Islam was a bust. Saudi Arabia and other Gulf States stepped in with $15 billion in assistance. Seeking to mend fences, the new Egyptian government returned $2 billion to Qatar, but in keeping the rest it signaled that the local military establishment and its allies did not appreciate the Gulf State's interference on behalf of the Muslim Brotherhood.

Another aspect of the changing geo-economic landscape is the nature of the Gulf States' relationship to the United States. Significantly, the once close Saudi–U.S. relationship has been complicated by a number of factors, including the declining U.S. dependence on Saudi oil (due to shale gas and oil), a persistent streak of anti-Americanism in Saudi society (perceived as part of a clash of civilizations), and the need for Riyadh to deal with other powers such as China, India, and Pakistan.[37] This was evident in the general failure of the Obama administration and the Saudi monarchy to see eye-to-eye on a number of policy issues through the last several years. Saudi Arabia was particularly concerned with the development of the U.S. shale industry and U.S. discussions with Iran. The former struck right at the heart of the Saudi economy. In December 2014 *The Economist* noted: "Their (US shale producers) manic drilling—they have completed perhaps 20,000 new wells since 2010, more than ten times Saudi Arabia's tally—has boosted America's oil production by a third, to nearly 9m barrels a day (b/d). This is just 1m b/d short of Saudi Arabia's output. The contest between the shalemen and the sheikhs has tipped the world from a shortage of oil to a surplus."[38] In 2014, from June to December, the Saudis were happy to lead OPEC into maintaining production and bringing oil prices down by around 40 percent. The Saudi game was to drive out higher-cost producers (like many in the U.S. shale patch, Russia, and Iran) and maintain market share.

Related to foreign policy challenges vis-à-vis the United States is the struggle for power and influence between Saudi Arabia and Iran. This struggle pits the Sunni Saudis against Shia Iranians. Both countries are aggressively jockeying in the region to support friends and oust enemies. This has left the Saudis, backed by Bahrain and the UAE, to support Iraq's Sunni population, the military in Egypt, and—through unofficial channels—radical Sunni groups like the Islamic State in Iraq and Syria (ISIS). In 2013–2014 this became highly problematic as ISIS took over large swaths of Syria and then Iraq's north, and announced their intention to create a caliphate that no longer recognized international boundaries set in 1923. A major challenge facing the Gulf States is their continued dependence on oil and gas. As professor Tim Niblock and economist Monica Malik observed: "A population which lives on the proceeds of the extraction of natural resources, with only a very small part of the population employed in the production process, will not be at ease in international community. Living in a cocoon created by apparently unearned income, divorced from the problems facing other peoples, sent a population apart from the global community—creating attitudes and mentalities out of touch with international realities."[39]

For all the excitement over the power of the Gulf States and the significance of their state-owned or government-related enterprises in the commanding heights of the global economy, there is a school of thought that the Gulf States are more fragile than perceived by many analysts and that the days of the Sunni autocrats are numbered. One voice in this school is that of Christopher M. Davidson, author of *After the Sheikhs: The Coming Collapse of the Gulf Monarchies* (2013), who noted: "Indeed, a compelling argument can be made that these regimes are now, more than ever, only as strong as the weakest link in their chain. If an especially brittle monarchy succumbed to a popular revolution or fell into a state of anarchy, then a veritable 'domino effect' could unfold, as the erstwhile illusion of stability or invincibility has distinguished the Gulf monarchies from the floundering Arab republics would be swiftly dispelled. In this scenario, if one Gulf State failed, then even the wealthiest and most confident of rulers would find their positions, or at least their legitimacy, under threat."[40]

To be fair, the Gulf States and Saudi Arabia are taking small steps to address complaints that they are unaccountable and that their policy dealings are opaque. Public skepticism in these countries is putting pressure on their political leaders as never before. One consequence is that corporate governance in some state-owned enterprises, for example, is changing. For example, in recent years several Gulf countries have set up state auditing entities to combat corruption or malpractice on a national scale. The United Arab Emirates have created a State Auditing Court (SAC). Saudi Arabia has a National Commission against Corruption, and Kuwait has instituted a Public Authority for Integrity. We do not want to exaggerate the impact of these institutions. These state-owned enterprises are government-controlled, but these efforts are a step in the right direction.

The global economic environment is undergoing subtle shifts in the early twenty-first century. The headlong momentum of globalization is slowing and in some cases reversing. For the Gulf States this represents a new challenge, in that the cleavages between autocratic state capitalist economies and liberal democratic private sector economies are becoming starker. Equally important, the Gulf States' financing of radical Islamic groups could lead to economic dislocation and greater political risk; the potential "blowback" of radical Islamic groups taking aim at Gulf State monarchies is a very real threat. The meltdown in Yemen of a central government in 2015 certainly raised this question, especially as the Houthi rebels turned to Iran and al-Qaeada forces gained control of part of the country, prompting a Saudi-led coalition to intervene with air power. Equally significant is the risk that the financing of radical Sunni groups will help fuel prospects for a Sunni–Shite civil war that has the potential to engulf much of the Middle East. The Gulf States have benefited from globalization. A more pronounced reversal of globalization is likely to be felt in the boardrooms and places in Riyadh, Doha, and Dubai.

CONCLUSION

State capitalism in the Middle East has a long history, remains a critical factor in most countries, and controls the commanding economic heights, even in those places where oil is not king. For the Gulf States, oil and gas have generated considerable wealth vis-à-vis those countries in the region that lack hydrocarbon resources. That wealth has been converted from oil into other assets around the world. While Gulf State oil companies have considerable clout, their position reinforced and conveyed by OPEC membership, sovereign wealth funds make Middle East investors significant players on the geo-economic landscape. This is evident in the extensive real estate portfolios of the SWFS in London, New York, and Los Angeles, as well as their ownership of airlines, media empires, and soccer teams. Yet the autocratic nature of the Gulf States, the demographic tide of a younger and social network–connected generation, and the often corrupt nature of old regimes has made the competitive nature of Middle East state-owned companies rather more brittle than often portrayed. This also complicates the ability of national leaderships to coordinate policies and to provide mutual support in an increasingly complex world. Middle Eastern state capitalism is a challenge to Western private sector companies, but the foundations of those governments are more brittle than many expect.

NOTES

1. For a fuller discussion, see Fred Halliday, *The Middle East in International Relations: Power, Politics and Ideology*, 6th edition (Cambridge: Cambridge University Press, 2010).

2. Organization for Economic Cooperation and Development, *State-Owned Enterprises in the Middle East and North Africa: Engines of Development and Competitiveness?* (Paris: OECD, 2013), p. 12.

3. Alan Richards and John Waterbury, *A Political Economy of the Middle East: State, Class, and Economic Development* (Boulder, CO: Westview Press, 1990), p. 184.

4. Ibid., p. 186.

5. Ibid., p. 187.

6. Ibid.

7. Alissa Amico, "State-Owned Enterprises: From Elephants to Gazelles." *Executive Magazine*, March 19, 2012.

8. Organization for Economic Cooperation and Development, *State-Owned Enterprises in the Middle East and North Africa*, p. 13.

9. International Monetary Fund, *Saudi Arabia 2013, Article IV Consultation*, IMF Country Report No. 13/229 (Washington, D.C.) July 2013, p. 3.

10. Kevin Whitelaw, "Abu Dhabi's Buying Binge," *U.S. News & World Report*, June 5, 2008. www.usnews.com/news/world/articles/2008/06/05/abu-dhabis-buying-binge.

11. Ibid.

12. See www.saudiaramco.com.

13. Amy Meyers Jaffe and Jareer Elass, *Saudi Aramco: National Flagship With Global Responsibilities*, The James A. Baker III Institute for Public Policy, Rice University, March 2007, p. 11.

14. Ibid., p. 7.

15. "China, Saudis Sign Pact," *International Oil Daily*, January 24, 2006.

16. One of the best-known believers in peak oil is Mathew R. Simmons, who wrote the best-selling *Twilight in the Desert, The Coming Oil Shock and the World Economy*, (Hoboken, NJ, John Wiley and Sons, Inc. 2005).

17. OECD, *State-Owned Enterprises in the Middle East and North Africa*, p. 39.

18. Ibid.

19. Ahmed Al Omran, "SABIC Chief Optimistic on Global Petrochemical Demand," *The Wall Street Journal*, June 20, 2014, p. A12.

20. OECD, *State-Owned Enterprises in the Middle East and North Africa*, p. 42.

21. Ibid.

22. Jim Krane, *City of Gold: Dubai and the Dream of Capitalism* (New York: St. Martin's Press, 2009), p. 135.

23. Ibid., p. 107.

24. OECD, *State-Owned Enterprises in the Middle East and North Africa*, p. 82.

25. Mehran Kamrava, *Qatar: Small State, Big Politics* (Ithaca, NY: Cornell University Press, 2013), p. 1.

26. International Monetary Fund, *Qatar 2014 Article IV Consultation-Staff Report*, IMF Country Report, No. 14/108 (Washington, D.C.), May 2014, p. 1.

27. Qatar Investment Authority website, http://www.qia.qa.

28. "Qatar to Invest $5b billion in Malaysian Projects," *Investline*, 29 January 2013.

29. Qatar Investment Authority website, http://www.qia.qa.

30. Robert Tuttle, "Qatar Shifts Foreign Policy After Supporting Revolts," Bloomberg, August 13, 2014.

31. See Marwan Muasher, " Freedom and Bread Go Together," *Finance + Development*, March 2013, Vol. 50, No. 1 (IMF).

32. Karen Elliott House, *On Saudi Arabia: Its People, Past, Religion, Fault Lines—and Future*. (New York: Alfred A. Knopf, 2012), p. 4.

33. House, *On Saudi Arabia*, p. x.

34. Emile Nakhleh, "Propaganda and Power in the Middle East," *Current History*, December 2013, p. 360. Also see Toby Mathiesan, *Sectarian Gulf: Bahrain, Saudi Arabia, and Arab Spring That Wasn't*.

Mathiesan notes: "Reacting to these historical changes and demands for democracy, a fairer distribution of resources, the rule of law, Gulf ruling families and their regimes around them, resorted to old tactics of denial, repression, economic largesse, and defamation. None of the Gulf states initiated significant domestic political reforms or managed to engage the emerging youth movements in a manner that would pave the way for a stable future, while the Gulf regimes often embraced the new politics and discourse of the Arab Spring abroad, they refused to acknowledge that this new era in Arab history also had a profound impact at home" (p. ix).

35. "Saudi Arabia's Investments: Oil-Fuelled Caution," *The Economist*, May 24, 2014.

36. Kamrava, *Qatar*, p. 3. Also see Toby Matthiesen, *Sectarian Gulf: Bahrain, Saudi Arabia and the Arab Spring that Wasn't* (Stanford, CT: Stanford University Press, 2013).

37. Ibid.

38. "Sheiks v. Shale," *The Economist*, December 6, 2014, p. 17.

39. Tim Niblock and Monica Malik, *The Political Economy of Saudi Arabia* (London: Routledge, 2007), pp. 1–2.

40. Christopher M. Davidson, *After the Sheikhs: The Coming Collapse of the Gulf Monarchies* (New York: Oxford University Press, 2013), p. 2.

SIX

State Capitalism in Latin America

State-run or state-owned enterprises in Latin America have played as prominent a role as anywhere in the world. Most, if not all, Latin American countries are commodity producers, being important global forces in energy, mining, and agricultural markets. In all of these, the state has nurtured and profited from the exploitation of natural resources. But strategies to grow these enterprises have varied substantially in the region, especially in the early twenty-first century. Chile, Colombia, Mexico, Peru, and Panama have taken largely market-friendly approaches. In general, these Pacific coast countries have been the most economically successful group in the region. In contrast, the Atlantic coast countries of Argentina and Venezuela, as well as Bolivia (in the central part of South America) and Ecuador (a Pacific coast country), have adopted more populist (some would say socialist) strategies that have limited their growth prospects. Brazil and Uruguay fall somewhere in the middle. Significantly, both groups have produced a group of companies—mainly, though not exclusively, in the oil sector—that are competitive rivals with Western private sector companies in both regional and global markets. There is an additional political element to this, as some of those states that have a more clear-cut adherence to state capitalism also have more autocratic national leadership. As such, politics remain electoral but are dominated by presidents with clear authoritarian tendencies, including a willingness to step on civil rights and resort to some form of coercion. Those governments have also emerged as vocal critics of the private sector and have fed the debate about the future of capitalism.

It is the purpose of this chapter to discuss state capitalism in Latin America, a region that begins in Mexico, incorporates Central America and the Caribbean, and ends at the southern tips of Argentina and Chile. The chapter's focus is further narrowed to the emergence of key state-owned companies in Brazil, Chile, Colombia, Mexico, and Venezuela. In addition, some of the more aggressive anti–private sector and statist actions will be examined in the cases of Argentina and Bolivia. Although natural resource nationalism should not be overstated, it exists as a strong undercurrent throughout much of Latin America. Throughout much of the region's economic development, it was an agricultural and mineral warehouse for the more developed regions of the global economy, which has left a historical sense of sensitivity over who controls the strategic sectors of the local economy. It was also an important market for advanced economies' industrial goods and a place for foreign direct investment. This economic arrangement often left Latin America vulnerable to the rise and fall of global commodity prices as well as boom-bust cycles in the region. This experience remains a factor in Latin America's growing role in the global economy and how governments perceive the role of the state. As will be demonstrated, the role of the state has a mixed track record and will no doubt be further assessed in the world of lower oil prices following the 2014 hydrocarbon price crash.

A BRIEF HISTORICAL BACKGROUND

Latin America's economic development has seen considerable push-pull between the forces of state capitalism and the market. In the early independence period, obliging local elites were willing to benefit from foreign companies assuming control of key sectors.[1] Latin America enjoyed an economic takeoff in 1890–1930, to a backdrop of greater political stability, foreign investment, population increases, and infrastructure development. While commodity exports were important, there were also gains in developing local industries. However, the Great Depression of the 1930s hurt the region, raising questions over what economic and political development strategies to adopt. Along these lines, in subsequent decades, the region experimented with authoritarianism, quasi-fascism, populist, single-party, and democratic forms of government. Communism was added to the experiment with the success of the Castroite revolution in Cuba in 1959. Although efforts to expand the Cuban revolution elsewhere in the Caribbean and Latin America failed, it did point to the region's severe socio-economic inequalities and its relationship with foreign companies. This was made particularly evident by the nationalization of foreign companies in Cuba during the early 1960s, including the all-important sugar industry.

Further questions over Latin America's development strategies came in the wake of the oil price hike of 1973–1974. While this helped oil producers in Latin America, it proved problematic for many countries, such as Argentina, Brazil, Chile, the Central American republics, and many Caribbean nations such as Jamaica and the Dominican Republic. By the early 1980s, global economic conditions (such as the rise of global interest rates), the buildup of external debt, fiscal mismanagement, and a fall in oil prices took their toll on Ecuador, Mexico, Peru, and Venezuela, all of which were forced to restructure their external debt. Often brutal economic restructuring programs were accompanied by socio-political turmoil, leading some to call the 1980s the "lost decade."

In contrast to the 1980s, the 1990s and early 2000s were a period in which Latin America's commodities and markets regained their luster to the global economy. A driving force in this was China, which emerged by the early 2000s as the world's leading importer of copper, zinc, platinum, iron, and steel, and a key consumer of soy. All of this was a major positive force in increasing Latin American exports. An Organisation for Economic Cooperation and Development report in 2007 observed: "China's strong demand for raw materials is, nevertheless, good news for Latin America. From 2000 to 2005, China represented nearly 40 percent of the total growth in world oil demand. China's growing thirst for oil has been driving oil prices up and boosting trade surpluses of oil exporters such as Venezuela, Ecuador and Colombia."[2] This increased demand was also very evident with copper and other minerals in Chile and Peru. It was also during this period that Latin America became more divided into the two clusters of countries mentioned earlier.

How might we distinguish these two clusters? The more moderate of these countries have largely embraced the market. They have kept their markets open to foreign trade and investment, and in some cases, have negotiated free trade agreements with the United States and other countries (Chile and Mexico). In recent years, Brazil has opened its economy to foreign capital and maintained relatively liberal policies toward international trade.[3] For the most part, these market-friendly countries have not privatized their state-owned assets to a meaningful degree, but they have not nationalized private firms either. They tend to practice conservative monetary and fiscal policies, such that the most prominent credit ratings agencies, Moody's, Standard & Poor's, and Fitch, have elevated all of them to investment-grade status. In turn, this has reassured the international investment community that these countries are creditworthy and attractive for investment purposes.

In contrast, the more populist and nationalist Latin American countries—Venezuela and Ecuador in particular—have expanded state intervention in their economies. They have asserted greater state control over their countries' natural resources, particularly in the energy sector. In Venezuela, state control even extended into the nationalization of steel manufacturing, glass factories, telecommunications, and utilities. In Ecuador, President Rafael Correa promised to "radicalize" his "citizens' revolution" by limiting bank profits and forcing oil companies to rewrite contracts under the threat of expropriation to increase oil revenues to the state. Indeed, Correa has vowed to "transform the bourgeoisie state into a popular state."[4] Further, these countries tend to spurn free trade agreements with the west and other capitalist countries. But they have pursued trade relationships with Russia, Iran, and the People's Republic of China. Indeed, Venezuela has received considerable loans from China and Russia, a sad reflection of economic mismanagement considering the extended period of high energy prices. Also, these Latin American countries have boosted state spending on social programs—some more effectively than others, and some with clear-cut political objectives, as in Venezuela.

The most prominent government-owned enterprises in the region are petroleum companies (led by Petrobras of Brazil, Pemex of Mexico, Ecopetrol of Colombia, and PDVSA of Venezuela) or copper producers (Codelco of Chile). Much of the region's mining sector, once a mix of state-owned companies, is now largely privately held and includes such multinational giants as Teck Cominco, Southern Copper Corporation of Peru, Rio Tinto, and Baosteel. The major Latin American state-owned companies generate massive profits for each nation, employment opportunities for the best and brightest (or politically well-connected) young people, and international prestige. All of these state enterprises have thrived by selling their products to both the developed and the developing world. China has played an outsized role in investing and purchasing commodity products from Latin America. But the region is being tested in 2015.

If Latin American growth doubled in 2000–2011 to an average of over 4 percent, it is now slowing to the 2.5 percent range. Unemployment is increasing. For the market-friendly nations of the region, the situation is less worrisome. They are more productive and investment-friendly. They have implemented sound macroeconomic policies, a buildup of foreign exchange reserves, prudent fiscal policy, independent central banks, and flexible exchange rates. They also benefited from cheap and abundant inflows of foreign capital and high commodity prices. They tend to favor freer trade policies, including lower external tariffs. High growth and active redistribution policies, made possible by plentiful fiscal resources, have led to a 13 percent decline in poverty rates in Latin America, a 5 percent decline in extreme poverty rates, and the emergence of an incipient middle class.[5]

Since mid-2011, however, Latin America's growth rates have cooled. China had experienced double-digit growth from 2005 to 2013, but it has now fallen to the 7.0 percent range. In turn, it is buying fewer commodities and other products from Latin America. More recently, international financial conditions have tightened since the United States Federal Reserve announced a gradual withdrawal of monetary stimulus. As a result, international financial and capital resources may become scarcer and more expensive.

For the populist nation-states, particularly Venezuela and Argentina, the prospects are particularly grim. These countries spend more on subsidies and social welfare, while saving and investing less. They tend to cap prices, tax capital, or trade flows, which squeeze profits. Venezuela is experiencing the world's worst inflation, close to 60 percent in 2015, which has eroded consumer demand. At a time of slowing growth, their state-run enterprises are more of a "cash cow" for their governments than before. These countries, and Brazil, are spending in excess of their income and financing that excess with inflows of cheap foreign capital. But they are facing dramatic downturns in the rates of consumption, investment, and public spending that have hampered growth in the past year and will continue to do so for the foreseeable future.

The Pacific coast countries of Latin America have not rejected the state apparatus, of course. They just tend to use it more effectively as a partnership with market forces. The presence of market forces allow them to exploit new opportunities through bilateral and multilateral trade agreements. They tend to have more competition, which, in turn, requires better government regulation. Such nation-states encourage creativity and foster entrepreneurship. They promote the rule of law and protections for private property. These countries have strived to design policies or institutions that are capable of neutralizing the negative impact of external shocks on output, employment, and social welfare.

Some Latin American countries are working with private sector entities to carry out public works projects such as the constructions of highways, ports, and airports. Chile has initiated a program of allowing the private sector to build and run prisons. So far the results have been mixed. How else might the state institutions work with private sector entities for the common benefit? As summarized by Alejandro Foxley, there are at least four ways that the state might facilitate economic development:

1) Providing access to capital as a way to widen the entrepreneurial base. In much of Latin America, there is no obvious network in place to keep capital flowing to entrepreneurial enterprises.

2) Designing incentives to attract foreign direct investment in higher value-added enterprises.

3) Encouraging productive clusters of businesses in a particular niche that is underserved in the marketplace.

4) Entering into partnerships with top research centers worldwide. This would generate knowledge and ideas that might produce wealth for the country.[6]

LATIN AMERICAN ENERGY RESOURCES

Several Latin American and Caribbean nations (Venezuela, Brazil, Ecuador, Mexico, Peru, Colombia, Argentina, and Trinidad and Tobago) possess substantial oil and/or natural gas production capabilities. In fact, of the ten largest companies in Latin America, the top three are state-owned Petrobras (Brazil), Pemex (Mexico), and PDVSA (Venezuela). Ecopetrol of Colombia is ranked seventh. The remaining six companies are all private enterprises, encompassing the food, mining, and retail sectors. Consequently, it is in the energy sector that Latin American state-owned enterprises clearly dominate.

Nearly a third of the world's proven petroleum reserves are in the Americas, according to statistical reports from British Petroleum (BP). Latin America has 13.8 percent of the world's petroleum. All of these countries are dependent in part or in whole (Venezuela and Ecuador) on their energy inheritance to fund government projects and to promote national interests. Broadly speaking, we can make a clear distinction between those nations that are almost completely dependent on their oil resource (Venezuela and Ecuador), from those that enjoy a more broadly diversified economy. The former tend to be autocratic and less productive; the latter more free market–oriented and productive.

Relations between the two country clusters are often tainted by ideology, which has an adverse effect on the possibility of developing more regional cooperation on energy-related issues. Along these lines, prospects for regional cooperation were badly undermined by Bolivia's 2006 decision to nationalize its gas reserves, an action that was mainly aimed at Brazil's Petrobras and Spain's Repsol. Venezuela's Chavez also pressed hard for a continent-spanning gas pipeline to feed his country's gas through Bolivia to the Southern Cone, a plan that irritated Brazil, especially as Caracas was using petro-dollars to buy influence throughout the region. The consequence is that the reciprocal needs of producing countries and importing in the region, which could be a force for greater cooperation and regional integration, have instead turned into measures that fan nationalistic flames and cause discord and energy insecurity.

According to data from the Inter-American Development Bank (IDB), demand for energy in Latin America will grow by 75 percent between 2014 and 2030. To meet that demand, generating capacity will have to increase by 145 percent during the same period. The goal would be more easily met if all of the regional players could work together. But cooperation is not a policy priority at present. Further, Latin America tends to use its energy inefficiently. Regional energy demand is very high relative to the rate of economic growth.

If energy demand is growing rapidly in Latin America, so is the propensity of several of its governments to manipulate energy resources for their own partisan purposes. Government-owned energy monopolies are particularly vulnerable to mismanagement and corruption. Over time, these companies, with Venezuela's state-owned monopoly PDVSA a prime example, can become susceptible to undue political intervention, resulting in declining productivity. Roger F. Noriega and Felipe Trigos of the American Enterprise Institute observed: "Professional management, transparency, free competition with private companies and openness to foreign capital and technology can help state-owned energy companies maximize their potential and deliver optimal long-term dividends for their nations."[7] Failure to maintain awareness of and access to the newest technology and best ideas makes it difficult for some state-owned companies to keep up.

In all fairness, keeping up with foreign technology is easier said than done. Every government-owned energy company could be adversely affected by government regulation, taxation, and interference. But populist-leaning governments in Latin America in Venezuela, Argentina, and Ecuador, among others, are particularly guilty of this. Throughout Latin America's history, oil and its byproducts have been valued as sovereign patrimony. The involvement of foreign companies and investors in the resources industry always stirs some level of nationalist debate. Typically, populist political leaders blame foreign investment and capitalism for every economic reversal. However, these arguments have been less compelling since about the year 2000, as state-run oil companies have failed to deliver great riches to the people despite historically high oil prices and the discovery of vast oil deposits. Government interference and barriers to international capital and technology have inhibited the growth of a strategic industry. As Noriega and Trigos note, "government policies based on nationalism rather than on free market principles are a recipe for failure."[8]

Over time, hybrid solutions have been proposed, whereby some private capital, companies, and competition have been encouraged alongside a state-run enterprise. The effort in Mexico to allow joint ventures between PEMEX and private sector entities in 2014 is a recent example. But policymakers should be vigilant. As long as the state has a direct state in a national oil company, over-taxation, politicization, and corruption can hamper the companies' ability to compete.

Since 2009, oil exports from Mexico, Ecuador, Argentina, and Venezuela have declined, as have natural gas exports from Bolivia. Part of the reason for the decline is geological change. But another culprit is the level of resource nationalism that can be found in these countries' energy policies. In particular, these countries have used their energy bounty to reward the politically connected with employment and government contracts.

In much of Latin America, the public is sensitive to who controls their oil companies. It could be said without too much argument that many Latin Americans see ownership of their oil and gas companies as part of their economic heritage. This explains in part the reluctance of governments in Argentina, Brazil, Colombia, and Mexico to fully walk away from the sector. The case of Bolivia is instructive in this, as the country sits on the second-largest oil reserves in Latin America, after Venezuela. Although Bolivia's economy was long driven by mining—tin during much of the twentieth century and into the twenty-first—natural gas became the magnate for foreign investment. In 1996 the Bolivian government privatized the natural gas sector, which brought a considerable inflow of capital into the country and created jobs. However, the control over such a key resource in foreign hands did not sit well with many Bolivians. In the last years of the 1990s and early 2000s, it became a loaded political issue. In 2006, the populist government of Evo Morales renationalized the industry and recreated the national energy company. Although this action hit Brazil's Petrobras and Spain's Repsol, it was very popular in Bolivia. It was also a major help in the government's finances, allowing it to pay out more in terms of badly needed social services.

At the same time, Bolivia's gas industry is lagging in technology to upgrade its infrastructure. Considering that relations with more capitalist countries, like the United States, Spain, and even Brazil are not warm, Bolivia has been quite content to seek technological assistance from Russia. Indeed, President Morales stated in 2013 on a trip to Moscow: "We want Russia to resume its technological exports to Latin America and the Caribbean. We want to learn from you, to work together and cooperate in investment, in order to diversify our investments and our market. We cannot depend entirely on the U.S. market, as some countries in Latin America do. We cannot rely entirely on the European or the Asian market. We want to have diverse markets."[9] While that makes economic sense in theory, there are practical matters to consider: Russia itself lacks the most up-to-date technology for gas extraction. How will Bolivia export its gas, and at what cost?

Argentina is another case of renationalization. Long dominated by bloated and inefficient state-owned companies as an offshoot of the populist Peron years (the 1940s and 1950s, and briefly in the 1970s), the Menem administration in the 1990s did much to privatize the state sector, including YPF, the state-owned oil company. In 1993 YPF was sold off the public books, and in 1999 it fell under the control of Spain's Repsol. In 2012 Argentina's Fernandez government decided to renationalize YPF, against the wishes of Repsol. This sparked a bitter legal battle, which ended with Argentina paying Repsol $5 billion in government bonds to settle the matter and remove legal questions over YPF assets, enabling it to lure more foreign investment needed to further develop the sector. Argentina's action, seen against a backdrop of declining economic futures and fiscal pressures at home, created a major diplomatic row with Spain and other members of the European Union who regarded the renationalism as protectionist and damaging to the country's attractiveness to foreign investment. Although the action gave a little boost to President Christina Fernandez's popularity, the positive impact was short-lived, as her overall economic mismanagement and erratic actions in other arenas left her with little long-term gain.

The challenge in Latin America going forward is how to manage state-owned energy companies. In this there are some well-defined differences between the experiences of Brazil, Mexico, Venezuela, and Colombia. There is a sliding scale in terms of what is important: cost-efficiency, profitability, and ability to compete in the global arena, or making oil and gas companies an extension of foreign policy objectives, unaccountable cash cows for state sector largesse, and a place to employ cronies.

BRAZIL AND PETROBRAS

Brazil is a giant in Latin America. It has the largest population and occupies approximately half of the South American continent. Brazil's relative economic strength or weakness has tremendous implications for the economic health of the continent. The largest government-owned agency in the region is Petrobras (Petroleo Brasileiro), Brazil's national oil company, established in 1953, which benefits from 65.4 percent government ownership. (The remainder is privately held.) By most standard measures, Petrobras has been highly successful. It is professionally managed, employs state-of-the-art technology, and is usually quite profitable. It is active in 23 countries in the exploration, refining, distribution, and sale of gas and energy, as well as petrochemicals, biofuels, and electricity. It is the world's eighth-largest corporation. But as with most government-owned enterprises worldwide, profitability is not necessarily the first priority. Instead, Petrobras must serve the political interests of the government as well.

The Brazilian government has significant influence on Petrobras' investments, fuel pricing policy, dividends, and management appointments. Brazil's government holds 7 out of 10 seats on the board and 61 percent of voting shares. Consequently, Petrobras, like government-owned energy companies throughout the region, is expected to provide a substantial portion of its profits for government purposes. It must be a "cash cow" for the government and provide funding for social programs and to help balance the government's budget. There is nothing inherently wrong about this. It is to be expected that governments in developing economies would exploit their most successful agencies. The downside of this is that governments are inclined to interfere in the activities of the company by influencing their strategic choices, but this interference grew exponentially and resulted in the *lava Jato* (car wash) scandal, the single biggest scandal in modern Brazilian history. We will return to this topic subsequently.[10]

In recent years, Brazil's economic growth has slowed to a modest rate of about 2 percent. This is not nearly enough for a country with a fast-growing population and a rising unemployment rate. Brazil's infrastructure needs are vast: it needs roads, schools, and public facilities of every sort. Brazil's domestic debt load is growing rapidly and is attracting scrutiny from international investors. Brazil's middle class has also grown rapidly, and the past ten years have witnessed tremendous progress in lifting millions of poor people into the ranks of the middle class. These people have high economic expectations for themselves and for their children, but economic stagnation has led to growing levels of dissatisfaction.

One obvious remedy for this predicament is higher levels of international and domestic investment. But incumbent President Dilma Rousseff has been less than successful in reassuring the investor community that Brazil's economic challenges are being successfully addressed. Further, her government has prevented Petrobras from raising petroleum prices to align with world prices. By keeping gas prices low, the Rousseff government hoped to attract domestic electoral support. In addition, the Brazilian government seems to be interfering in Petrobras' activities more than in the past.

Federal policymakers have imposed a "nationalistic mandate to buy oil platforms and other equipment from Brazilian companies, which has triggered a soaring debt, major project delays, and fields that are yielding less oil."[11] Petrobras is required by the government to favor domestic suppliers—despite doubts about the company's ability to produce goods and services in accordance with deadlines and strict industry standards. As recently as 2009, Petrobras was a net exporter of oil and gas. It now loses money by buying gas at international prices and then selling it domesti cally at subsidized prices. These gasoline subsidies are intended to contain inflation (currently 6 percent) and to placate voters. But they are reducing Petrobras' finances. Investors took notice. Between 2010 and 2013, Petrobras' equity shares lost 50% of their value.

In recent years, the Brazilian government could point to the dynamism of Petrobras as an example of a world-class government-owned company. In truth, Petrobras remains a reasonably well-managed and profitable company. But 2013–2014 were challenging years. The company experienced sharply reduced growth as it struggled to raise $237 billion to exploit deep-water reservoirs offshore. Also, the company experienced exchange-rate losses. Petrobras took on more debt: in May 2013 alone, it raised approximately $11 billion in the international debt capital markets to provide funding for various projects. Indeed, Petrobras was one of the largest issuers of external debt in the international debt capital markets in 2012–2014. The increase in company debt is concerning, and partly as a result the credit-rating agency Moody's downgraded Petrobras.

Not only is Petrobras less an investor favorite because of losses and a weakening fiscal performance, but in 2014 the company was engulfed in scandal. As of May 2015, the company was reeling from the "car wash" scandal. Essentially, many senior Petrobras executives had accepted bribes from major construction companies to steer government business their way. In turn, the money found its way into the coffers of the governing PT party. The president of Brazil, Dilma Rousseff, had once been the chairwoman of Petrobras. Although there had been rumors of impeaching the president as a result, there was no evidence of wrongdoing. However, several members of the Brazilian Congress, senior Petrobras employees, and construction company executives were investigated and subsequently indicted on bribery and corruption charges.

The scale of the scandal was of such scope that the government was compelled to act. Many fixed-income investors sold their Petrobras bonds. The credit-ratings agencies downgraded their ratings of the Petrobras credit to barely investment grade, in the case of Fitch Ratings and Standard & Poor's, and to junk in the case of Moody's. The rational of all of the agencies was that Petrobras faced both weaker fundamentals and liquidity concerns. In turn, Petrobras's cost of borrowing on the international capital markets increased so dramatically that the company, which had been one of the most frequent debt issuers, announced that they would stay out of the markets indefinitely. The CEO was replaced in February 2015 and replaced by the former head of state-controlled Banco de Brasil. Almost the entire leadership team of Petrobras was also replaced, whether they were implicated in the scandal or not.

The reputation of this formerly proud company had fallen to new lows. But the culture of corruption had been exposed as never before. New reforms were promised and quickly implemented. Transparency in all business activities would now be mandatory. Accounting practices would be revised. The perpetrators of this crime would be punished. Public servants would be held to new standards of honesty and efficiency. Of course, it is early, and a culture of corruption and cozy ties between the public and private sector are not so easily overturned. Nevertheless, as of May 2015, much has changed for the better in how the Brazilian government seems to do business. Further, Petrobras retains the support of the Brazilian sovereign, and that is a great advantage.

Petrobras is worthy of attention because it is arguably the most successful of all government-owned companies in Latin America. It has partnered with more than 120 universities and research centers worldwide to boost its R&D capability. As of February 2015, Petrobras was implementing and/or evaluating almost $65 billion worth of downstream projects. The company's substantial reserve base and its dominance in the Brazilian oil industry remain tremendous strengths. It enjoys world-scale integrated operations. Most notably, Petrobras is the most important company in

Brazil and is likely to enjoy government support no matter what challenges it faces. But this government support is a two-edged sword. It ensures that the company will survive for the foreseeable future. But it also ensures that company goals will always be vulnerable to the whims of government ministers. And there is something more in the case of Petrobras. The company has come under unique domestic and international scrutiny for its corrupt business practices. Perhaps a lesson here is that even the most powerful state-run enterprise is vulnerable if its worst abuses are exposed. Petrobras is a test case. Perhaps there are limits to officially sanctioned corruption if enough eyes (or the international debt capital markets) are paying attention.

MEXICO AND PEMEX

If Petrobras had one been regarded as the best-managed publically owned petroleum company in Latin America, then Pemex (Petroleos Mexicanos) has always been more of a mixed bag. As with Brazil's Petrobras, Pemex has been a source of tremendous revenue for the Mexican government. To a greater degree than in Brazil, Pemex has been widely regarded as part of the Mexican people's birthright. Since the company's establishment in 1938, the Mexican state has held complete control over Pemex's subsurface resources and byproducts. Nationalist politicians have manipulated this mandate for their own partisan purposes. As a consequence, to change the Pemex central purpose would require a change in the Federal Constitution of the country. But that is exactly what Mexico is now doing. Pemex will remain 100 percent owned by the people of Mexico. But for the first time in 76 years, Pemex is able to engage in joint ventures with other oil producers. Mexican oil and gas fields are now open to foreign and private investment. The energy reform mandate includes privatizing national oil production. As a consequence, Pemex will be able to harness the technology and know-how required to engage in much-needed deepwater exploration.

Pemex has always functioned as an arm of the state. It is the biggest Mexican company, the seventh-largest oil producer in the world, and the country's largest taxpayer. In terms of its potential, Mexico has reserves of almost 200 billion barrels of oil. In recent years, Pemex's profitability has been poor. As of the final quarter of 2013, 50 percent of its revenues (US $31.3 billion) had been taxed by the Mexican government, which uses the state-owned company to fund a third of its budget. Pemex has seen slowing levels of productivity (6.6 percent from 2009 to 2013), insufficient refining capacity to satisfy internal consumption, but a 5% increase in its workforce. Pemex may be the only energy company in the world to increase its workforce when its production was declining. Further, the largest existing oil field, Cantarell, is close to exhaustion with current technology.

Pemex is in great need of capital and technology from private companies to unlock the potential of Mexico's shale gas deposits and pre-salt oil wells. Given the 50 percent of Pemex revenues taxed by the government, the company has been able to invest only 9.6 percent of its revenue to fund all of its essential exploratory and production activities. The opening of Mexico's energy industry would bring in up to $30 billion of foreign investment annually and create as many as two million jobs.[12] For example, Chevron Corp., Exxon Mobil Corp, and Royal Dutch Shell are poised to gain access to untapped Mexican oil reserves that Pemex says could total 113 billion barrels. Approximately 26.6 billion of that is in the deep waters of the Gulf of Mexico. At current prices (as of August 2014), the reserves are worth $11 trillion.

Mexican President Enrique Pena Nieto has worked to bring the three major Mexican political parties (the ruling Partido Revolucionario Institutivo or PRI, the National Action Party or PAN, and the Partido de la Revolucion Democratica or PRD) together to support energy reform, encompassing hydrocarbons and electricity, and the resulting constitutional amendment. The bill passed Congress in December 2013, though without the support of the PRD, which sought to halt it. Petrobras would be the model of an agreement whereby there would be new opportunities for exploration, refinement, and storage to private investors. A special report by Latin American Newsletters noted of the reform measures: "It laid down the rules under which Pemex will cease to be a politically-controlled cash cow for the public purse and operate autonomously like any other company, free to form partnerships with private firms, allowing private firms also to compete for the exploration and development of oil and gas fields."[13] Additionally, three new refineries would be built over the next twelve years.

Thus far, the energy reforms have been welcomed by the debt and equity markets. The reforms may also mean that Pemex's financing activities will become less about the capital markets. Instead, the company will team up with others to finance new projects. This is not to say that Pemex will suddenly enjoy great riches. Problems include human resources issues, as Pemex is overstaffed with unskilled workers whose jobs are guaranteed for life, and understaffed with engineers and other skilled laborers. It is a very bureaucratic company that has long operated like a government office and not like an international oil company. Also, few Mexican universities train students in oil production, petrochemicals, chemical engineering, or physics. Probably more challenging is a culture of corruption in the energy industry that will have to be addressed. Further, there are staggering pension liabilities, of which only eight percent are fully funded.

Energy reform will not bring miracles. But if managed carefully, it can produce far greater efficiencies and productivity in the next few years. It will be a signal that Mexico' political parties can rise above their partisan differences to promote the national interest. It could be a signal that state-run enterprises held captive by inefficient government interests can be allowed to adapt to market forces while not losing their national character. It is a great experiment indeed.

VENEZUELA AND PDVSA

Oil has long been part of the Venezuelan economy. Substantial amounts of oil were found in the early twentieth century around Lake Maracaibo in the western part of the country. The industry was initially dominated by American companies, but was nationalized during the 1970s, and PDVSA (Petróleos de Venezuela, S.A.) was formed in 1975. Venezuela was one of the original OPEC members, indicating the significance of that sector to its economy as well as the world's. The oil sector also changed the economy, which was earlier more dependent on agricultural goods. Over time, oil came to dominate all other sectors, becoming by far the major export and the key factor in government finances. It also made Venezuela one of the wealthiest countries in Latin America and helped stimulate strong growth rates.

Through much of the second half of the twentieth century, PDVSA was widely regarded as one of the best-managed and most profitable petroleum companies in South America. This was reasonable, considering oil centrality to the nation's economic life. Significantly, the company had a reputation as being highly professional and able to compete effectively against private sector companies. Indeed, the state-owned oil company was Venezuela's major economic engine, even after international oil prices fell in the 1980s and Venezuela struggled through a profound economic downturn. During that period, PDVSA kept Venezuela afloat. That was to change when President Hugo Chavez came into office in 1993.

Leftist President Hugo Chavez feared opposition sympathizers working for PDVSA. From the time of his election in 1998, he demanded political allegiance from the PDVSA staff as a condition for retaining their jobs.

Those who would not pledge fealty to the government's leftist agenda were vulnerable to dismissal. In 2003 striking workers paid the price for their insolence to Chavez, as he fired almost half of the oil company's workforce: 18,000 technicians and middle managers lost their jobs and were banned from jobs in any company doing business with the oil company. As *The Economist* noted of Chavez's large-scale firing: "At the stroke of a pen, Venezuela lost its oil intelligentsia. It was a blow from which PDVSA has never recovered. The firm's oil production has since stagnated, despite a big run-up in prices."[14]

Not only were seasoned employees removed, so was their valuable institutional memory and competence. In their place were installed less-experienced engineers and technicians, notable for their support of President Chavez. Chavez used a large swath of PDVSA's revenues to fund an ambitious international agenda. PDVSA's productivity soon fell, and morale plummeted. One of the best-run state enterprises was transformed into one of the worst.

As of 2014, PDVSA is a thoroughly politicized institution. The company runs a food distribution network, supports various political initiatives domestically and internationally, and promotes the Chavista revolution. Venezuelan oil is made available to close ally Cuba at exceptionally favorable rates. PDVSA has formed partnerships with companies controlled by China, Russia, and Iran—partnerships that have given these countries a stake in Venezuela's rich oil and gas fields. In 2014, PDVSA appealed to Russia and China for over $10 billion in private financing to reinvest and increase crude production, and to expand existing infrastructure in both the Western and Orinoco region. Still the company is struggling to pay providers.

Although new reserves of heavy crude oil have been discovered that would make Venezuela one of the world's top three oil producers, the country is losing ground because of policies that discourage international investment in its oil sector. Consequently, the U.S. Energy Information Administration has reported that overall oil production levels have declined by approximately one-quarter between the years 2001–2012. In that same period, net oil exports have also declined (U.S. Energy Administration, Venezuela, October 3, 2012). Further, although PDVSA's oil production is declining, the company had doubled its workforce between the years 2003–2012, to 110,000 people.

President Chavez died of cancer in 2013. He was followed in office by his vice president and ideological ally, Nicolas Maduro, who lacked Chavez's charisma and street smarts. A former bus driver and union activist, Maduro has little understanding of economics, is suspicious of foreign investment, and leans heavily on Cuban security and advisers. To make ends meet, he has borrowed heavily from China in exchange for oil. He has also appointed party cronies to senior positions, and corruption remains pervasive. Entrenched interests have consistently blocked reforms, such as removing a domestic petrol subsidy that would be a major help in righting the fiscal house. Such a move, however, would counter the interest of government insiders, including senior military officers who are thought to support the government in return for cheap petrol that allegedly fuels a contraband trade worth some $4 billion a year.[15]

During the Chavez-Maduro years, Venezuela's oil production continues to fall, and profits have dropped, although accurate numbers are difficult to come by. Additional problems include an increase in accidents and the stretched nature of the workforce in terms of experienced personnel. Moreover, many ex-PDVSA workers left the country, helping oil booms in Canada, the United States, Mexico, Central Asia, Malaysia, and the Persian Gulf. Political decisions have hurt the professional nature of the company's business. Many Venezuelan oil worker exiles also headed next door to Colombia, which has been enjoying its own economic boom and a considerable improvement in political stability and personal safety— unlike their homeland.[16]

How does Venezuela's state-owned oil company compare to those of Brazil and Mexico? Petrobras, Pemex, and PDVSA are the most prominent petroleum companies in Latin America. All are government owned and managed. But each is operated quite differently. Historically, Petrobras enjoyed relative freedom to make its most important strategic decisions. That has been less true since Dilma Roussef became president of Brazil, but she faces meaningful political opposition to her plans to use Petrobras for partisan purposes. The 2015 scandal makes the need of a more autonomous management all the more critical. Pemex has long been a cash cow for Mexican political leaders, but energy reform will lead to joint ventures with private sector enterprises. In turn, this should lead to greater efficiency and productivity. PDVSA is the worst off. The leftist government of Venezuela retains a firm hold on this national jewel, and profitability and productivity suffer as a consequence.

It is not reasonable to expect any of these companies to be privatized in the foreseeable future, but state-run energy companies can be successful for sustained periods. To do so they need professional management, financial transparency, free competition with private companies, and openness to foreign capital and technology. With these attributes, they might maximize their potential and deliver optimal long-term dividends to their populations. It is evident that too close a relationship between companies and the government makes it very tempting to abuse the privilege of inside knowledge and easy access to funds. Although these companies have gained global influence, they suffer from inefficiencies and political interference, and when oil prices fall, their ability to maneuver is more limited due to these political linkages. In the last regard, large private sector multinational corporations have a competitive advantage, in that they are often not considered to be part of a social welfare program and can turn faster to make adjustments to changing markets.

COLOMBIA AND ECOPETROL

Established in 1921, Ecopetrol is the national oil company of Colombia, which owns 88.5 percent of the company though shares held by the Ministry of Finance. It is the fourth-largest oil and natural gas producer in Latin America and has been a model of successful oil liberalization. Production of petroleum has almost doubled from 2006 to 2014, and as of August 2014 the company is responsible for 64 percent of total Colombian oil production. Ecopetrol faces few of the regulatory hurdles and local content requirements that Petrobras must deal with. Ecopetrol is not captive to competing partisan political forces, as Pemex had been until recently. Ecopetrol's profits are not appropriated by a tough authoritarian government for ideological purposes, as PDVSA's are. Instead, Colombia tends to manage Ecopetrol at arm's length. The government allows Ecopetrol's managers to run the company in a professional manner.

Ecopetrol is smaller than Petrobras, Pemex, and PDVSA. Nonetheless, it is a mid-sized integrated oil company and Colombia's largest petrochemical producer. In 2014, Ecopetrol indicated that it is exploring unconventional shale gas and coal bed methane opportunities. To do this, Colombia is attracting international partners, including ExxonMobil and ConocoPhillips. Unlike Pemex and PDVSA, but similar to Petrobras, Ecopetrol has long sought partnerships with public and private sector oil industry partners. This has certainly helped the company grow and improve in terms of its use of technology.

To the extent that Ecopetrol faces major challenges, they tend to be associated with terrorist attacks on its infrastructure. FARC guerrillas have periodically bombed Ecopetrol's facilities, including pipelines and compression stations. These attacks have negatively affected oil production and sales. However, the Colombian government is engaged in various peace negotiations with these terrorist organizations and, if successfully concluded, these should reduce the threat to Ecopetrol's interests. Overall, Ecopetrol continues as one of Latin America's model government-owned oil companies. It also responded quickly to plunging oil prices in 2014, cutting capital expenditures with a view that it will take some time for markets to find a new equilibrium.

CHILE AND CODELCO

Latin America is not the domain only of oil companies. While petroleum tends to be the most lucrative and publicized commodity in the region, copper is another major export. The richest country in all of Latin America, Chile depends on copper as its most important commodity export by far. The Corporacion Nacional del Cobre (Codelco) is an exceptionally well-managed, profitable state-run enterprise. Established in 1976, Codelco is 100 percent owned by Chile, the world's largest copper producer, with a 10 percent share of world output (approximately 1.79 million metric tons for the twelve months ending March 31, 2014). Codelco is involved in every aspect of copper production including research, exploration, acquisition, and development.

Historically, Codelco has been given a great deal of operational independence by the Chilean government. Further, it is one of the most efficiently run government-owned enterprises in the region. As of September 2014, Codelco's direct cash costs were about 8 percent lower than one year earlier. It has copper reserves of approximately 75 years at current production levels. As of September 2014, the company is in the midst of revamping older copper mines to keep them competitive. To that end it will receive $5 billion dollars from the government over five years and issue its own debt in the international debt capital markets. Codelco is a frequent issuer in the capital markets, and benefits from a credit rating in the A+ range that allows it to keep its borrowing costs low.

However, Codelco is facing increasing cost pressures, and earnings have been declining in 2015. The company also faces managerial challenges such that its Chief Executive Officer, Thomas Keller, was asked to resign in June 2014 because of his unyielding approach to cutting costs and preventing an output slide. His efforts met opposition from his Codelco Board members, and particularly union leaders, who challenged Keller's efforts to increase productivity. Also, workers struck in April and September of 2013 for greater job security.

These challenges suggest that Chile's new government under President Michelle Batchelet may have priorities that differ from those of Codelco's leadership. Chile's growth rates have begun to slow, as have growth rates throughout Latin America. If Codelco ex-CEO Keller had hoped to invest as much as $20 billion in the current decade in an effort to sustain copper output and improve profitability, the Batchelet government insists on constraining that funding. In the president's view, taxes on Codelco and other enterprises must rise to fund social programs. She insists that the social safety net must be expanded in tough economic times.

Codelco remains a profitable, well-managed company and a standout among other Latin American state-run enterprises. But it has to adjust to changing economic and political circumstances as well. The company's profitability is a desirable outcome. But that goal is secondary to supporting a broad social safety net, especially in times of economic reversals. Even a model company like Codelco remains a creature of the state. In tough times, its independence can and will be curtailed. The upcoming years could represent another major challenge, in that copper prices could see an extended down period related to slower economic growth in the world's major user, China.

LATIN AMERICA AND THE CHANGING GEO-ECONOMIC LANDSCAPE

The global geo-economic landscape is changing in the early twenty-first century, a development that concerns Latin American countries and their state-owned enterprises. Three factors stand out as the region faces the upcoming decades: ongoing heavy reliance on commodities in many countries, the related and growing importance of China as a trade partner and source of investment, and questions about the role of the state in the economy. These serve as a backdrop to the political alignments that tie the region's populist autocratic-leaning countries to their counterparts internationally, including China, Russia, and even Qatar and Iran. To be fair, the role of the state in the economy is a role in more democratic countries, including Brazil and Mexico. However, the quasi-autocratic states like Venezuela and Ecuador have demonstrated a sharper edge in protecting strategic sectors from foreign investors. Will Chinese investment save Venezuela's populist economic experiment? Does China want to finance an inept government that is increasingly running into political instability?

But for Latin America and its state-owned companies, the issue of what comes next after the commodity boom probably looms the largest and could well be the single most critical factor in deciding the merits or detriments of the state capitalist model. Latin America does have some time to adjust. According to the World Bank, the investment rate in the region was around 25 percent of GDP in 2014, roughly the same level as Southeast Asia.[17] Equally important, many countries have reduced their outstanding debt levels and built up their foreign exchange reserves. They also maintain the ability to depreciate their currencies if need be. But that is where the danger looms. Currency depreciation could occur at a time when international interest rates begin to climb back, making it more onerous to pay back debt with a devaluing currency. Along these lines, there is a large amount of corporate debt (some of it from state-owned companies), including $200 billion from Brazil, Mexico, Colombia, Chile, and Peru.

Related to this is the issue of productivity. For Latin America to stay competitive, especially if China's growth and demand should cool, the region will need to squeeze more competitiveness out of its labor markets. This means reform, including education, infrastructure, and greater flexibility in the workplace. This also means reducing barriers to making large informal sectors of Latin American economies part of the mainstream, which would entail another set of reforms pertaining to taxation, permits, and licensing. State-owned economies must be included in these reforms, as they remain sizeable employers and key components to state finances, as well as being the potential spear-point for the introduction of new technology. Reforms are difficult, but lack of reform is worse, something that is evident in the declining operational abilities of a company like PDVSA. Latin America has made considerable gains in the past two decades, developing a growing middle class and supporting a number of world-class companies (some of which are state-owned). The global geopolitical landscape has changed, and there are alternatives to Western democratic capitalist models to look to for help. The issue is increasingly going to be which offers the best ideas for the long term—something that has yet to be fully ascertained by many. Yet the flow of ideas and technology does better in an open environment, a factor that limits even the most robust autocratic state capitalist models.

CONCLUSION

In this chapter, we have focused almost exclusively on government-owned petroleum companies. Attention to the oil industry is important to highlight, because it tends to be the most profitable economic sector and subject to the most government attention. But Chile's Codelco, a publically owned copper company, is one of the most prominent players in the minerals industry. There are other regional enterprises in the commodities and manufacturing industry that also play an outsize role in their nation's economy. The most successful government-owned enterprises also tend to be those that enjoy the most autonomy from the partisan interests of public officials. This should not be a surprise. But as with state-run enterprises in other regions, they are at an inherent disadvantage in terms of growth opportunities. They must always put the national interest, or the interests of particular political forces, ahead of profit. This is a two-edged sword. On the one hand, they are not subject to the vagaries of the marketplace. They won't disappear when times get especially tough. But they also may not have access to the latest research and development tools. Technological change will happen more slowly. And most importantly, when times are good and revenues are high, state-run enterprises must share large portions of their wealth with their masters in the public sector. This is not a challenge faced by private sector, for-profit enterprises.

NOTES

1. For a more fulsome discussion on Latin America's early economic development, see Victor Bulmer-Thomas, *The Economic History of Latin America Since Independence* (New York: Cambridge University Press, 2014), chapters 1 & 2.

2. Javier Santiso, editor, *The Visible Hand of China in Latin America* (Paris: Organisation for Economic Cooperation and Development, Development Centre Studies, 2007), p. 11.

3. For a fuller discussion, see Jorge G. Castaneda, "Latin America's Left Turn," *Foreign Affairs* 85 (May 2006), pp. 28–43.

4. Nathan Gill, "Socialist Correa Seeking to Boost Capital Markets in Ecuador," *Bloomberg*, April 19, 2013.

5. World Bank, Washington, D.C., 2013.

6. Alejandro Foxley, "Market Versus State: Post-Crisis Economics in Latin America," Carnegie Endowment for International Peace (Washington, D.C.: 2010), pp. 25–26.

7. Roger F. Noriega and Felipe Trigos, of the American Enterprise Institute, "Latin American Energy Monopolies: Boom or Bust?" (American Enterprise Institute, Washington, D.C.: July 31, 2013), p. 2.

8. Ibid.

9. "Bolivia Awaits Russia's Technology and Energy—Morales to RT," RT (Moscow), July 3, 2013. http://rt.com/business/bolivia-morales -russia-energy-investments-599/.

10. For further reference to the Petrobras scandal, see "Petrobras: Deep under Water," *The Economist* (April 25, 2015) and "Corruption Scandal Leads to a Big Loss for Petrobras," *New York Times* (April 22, 2015).

11. Joe Leahy, "Brazil: The Creaking Champions," *Financial Times*, April 21, 2013.

12. Adam Williams, "Not Quite a Revolution," *Bloomberg Markets Magazine* (June 2014), pp. 80–84.

13. "Mexico's Oil Future After the Reforms," Special Insight Paper, Latin American Newsletters, (London) August 2014, p. 1.

14. "Venezuela's Oil Diaspora: Brain Hemorrhage," *The Economist*, July 19, 2014, p. 31.

15. Andres Schipani and John Paul Rathbone, "Venezuela Loses faith in Socialist Government," *Financial Times*, December 11, 2014.

16. Ibid. As *The Economist* noted: "No country has benefited more from the Venezuelan exodus, however, than one next door. Colombia's oil output was declining at the time of the purge, falling from 687,000 barrels a day (b/d) in 2000 to 526,000 five years later. Today, average daily production stands at around 1m b/d. Much of this renaissance is thanks to the Venezuelans."

17. "Latin America's Economies: Life after the Commodity Boom," *The Economist*, March 29, 2014, p. 35.

SEVEN

The Limits of State Capitalism

State capitalism is and will be an important force in the twenty-first century, but it is questionable whether this model of development, especially its more autocratic form, will easily triumph over more free market–oriented and democratic experiments. Democratic capitalist economies have major problems. At the same time, they have proven to be highly adaptable to demographic, technological, and societal changes—some of these potentially highly disruptive in nature. States will have to make significant changes in the twenty-first century to remain ahead of the rest of the global economy. However, the geopolitical landscape for autocratic state capitalist countries is more daunting, considering the often opaque nature of decision-making and the dangerous and easy slide away from meritocracy to crony capitalism. And crony capitalism often begets societal discontent, political decay, and ultimately, rebellion. Additionally, most of these states must confront the often thorny issue of political succession.

It is the purpose of this chapter to examine the limits of autocratic state capitalism. On the domestic side are such challenges as employment creation, public safety, acceptable health standards, the rights of women and minorities, official corruption, and income inequalities. All of these point back to the key issue of the legitimacy of the state (be it autocratic or democratic). The external challenges in many areas easily overlap with the domestic and include the ability to attract foreign direct investment, access to cutting-edge technology, and competitiveness of local businesses in their home markets as well as competitiveness overseas. The comingling of political and business interests is likely to weigh more heavily on state capitalist regimes as the twenty-first century moves along and demands for greater disclosure and better governance become stronger. The twenty-first century is going to see massive transformations from the twentieth century, a development that is demanding states to adapt or fail. And, as history demonstrates, states can and do fail.

Based on the previous chapters, we see that there are three key areas that represent major potential limits to state-capitalist states. These are how governments process change, which encompasses such issues as technology, demographics, and natural resource management; how they contend with income inequality (a major source of societal stress); and how they earn and maintain legitimacy in the eyes of their citizens. The last includes how the state handles all of the above challenges, many of which call into question institutional reliability and adaptability as well as political succession. All three overlap and impact each other, and as a package they dominate the future of state capitalism and, by extension, the rest of the twenty-first century.

PROCESSING CHANGE

It is a given that all countries and their societies change, as the world is not standing still. Technology is causing business to change, people's daily life habits to adapt, and governments to adjust their approach in defining policy goals. Changes in climate patterns, the impact of pollution, and the levels of the oceans also need to be taken into consideration. While issues of technology and climate are important, it is people who provide the foundation for the state. Consequently, demographics represent one of the most difficult challenges for state capitalism. Western democratic capitalist states face the same problem but are better equipped for aging populations in terms of health care, housing, and quality of life.

DEMOGRAPHICS

Although serious problems exist in the democratic West in terms of the cost of pensions and other social outlays (as they require serious reform and greater cost-efficiency), countries such as China, Russia, and even more democratic states like India, South Africa, and Brazil, confront major challenges regarding their national demographics. Indeed, they are likely to hit in three ways: the eventual graying of their own workforces, sociopolitical unrest related to poor conditions for the aging, and a slowing of global growth prospects. The issue of aging is not likely to go away anytime soon. As Moody's Investors Service stated in a 2014 study: "The unprecedented pace of aging will impose a demographic tax that will slow economic growth over the next 20 years in both developed and emerging market economies, as working-age populations shrink and household savings rates decline."[1] The rating agency also noted "that by next year (2015), over 60% of Moody's-rated countries will be aging, with more than 7% of their population aged 65 or over. By 2020, super-aged societies (populations with more than 20% elderly) will increase to 13 globally from three today (i.e., Italy, Germany and Japan). By 2030, 34 countries will be super-aged." That includes Russia, China, and even Brazil.

The demographic issue calls for policy reforms over the medium term that seek to improve labor participation rates (i.e., include more women and retooling of workers), streamline immigration, and improve financial flows. A number of countries must also take into consideration the additional challenge of climate change (increasingly evident in parts of the Middle East and North Africa, in affecting food and water supplies). These represent major challenges, especially in countries where political institutions are weak. The Moody's report also noted that in the "long term, innovation and technological progress that improves productivity have the potential to lessen the forecasted dampening effects of the rapid demographic changes."

The issue of aging is a factor in China and Russia. According to the 2010 census, there were 178 million citizens who were 60 years or older in China, making up to 14.9 percent of its total population. United Nations data also indicates that the population will begin to shrink by 2030; by 2050 the number of Chinese over 60 years of age could grow to 437 million.[2] United Nations data further observed that China's fertility rate of 1.66 per woman compares badly with the 2.1 level needed to sustain population levels.

Another factor casting a shadow over China's demographic challenge is that the country's one-child policy has resulted in a generation of couples taking care of four parents. This is a significant test for China's traditional home care model, one that evolved from a more rural society where extended families shared the responsibilities of the aging segments of the population. That included elderly members of the family helping in child care. The state's emphasis on a more urban China also plays a role in this. Chinese authorities are aware of the issue, but this is not going to be an easy problem to overcome, considering the policy direction to modernize and urbanize China. The government also shifted away from its single-child policy, but the ramifications of such a policy will take decades to rectify.

One of the major concerns in China's struggle with population growth is the high cost of raising children. The government relaxed its policies on having more than one child, but adding a second child comes with its own set of problems, such as working parents, child care, and overall rising food and living costs. One professional woman, Sun Qing, interviewed by Bloomberg in 2014, observed of the high costs of having a second child: "The cost is a top consideration. My four-year-old daughter is heading to school and that will mean extra classes and higher spending. A nanny is too expensive so the grandparents look after her. They are 70 and I don't think they can handle a second child."[3]

There is one other factor facing China in its ability to handle the process of change on the demographic front: wage inflation. China is already facing wage inflation; as the economy has undergone profound transformations from agriculture to manufacturing, wages have gone up. This is eroding some of China's competitiveness. The demographic aspect throws another pressure into wages and competition—a pressure that may or may not be answered by state capitalism. In the years ahead there will be fewer workers, and only so many can be sent to Sri Lanka, Ethiopia, and Mozambique. As Hong Kong–based market strategist Hao Hang noted: "With a rapidly aging population and declining birth rate, even relaxing the birth-control act now won't help reverse the trend any time soon. China will be dealing with wage pressure soon."[4]

Russia has an even more significant problem with its demographic challenge, despite its government data indicating that it halted a decline in the population in 2013–2014. However, the population numbers remain questionable, with the number probably above 140 million (lower according to the U.S. Central Intelligence Agency, at 138 million in 2011). It is also speculated that the uptick in population is a result of immigration of ethnic Russians to the motherland from parts of the former Soviet Union.

What is not questionable is that the Russian state presides over a population with poor future growth prospects. As security analyst Ilan Berman noted: "The cause of Russia's illness includes low birth rates, meager life expectancy, a culture of abortion, the collapse of the Russian family, and an escalating AIDS epidemic. The results are nothing short of catastrophic; at its current rate of decline, the population of the Russian Federation could plummet to just over one hundred million souls by the middle of this century."[5] Despite advances in the standard of living, in particular during the Putin-Medvedev years, substantial questions exist as to tackling key issues pertaining to public health, an aging population, and a poor social security apparatus. Even if the population is stabilizing, the inability of the state to meet these challenges raises questions over the attractiveness of the autocratic capitalist model over the long term. This becomes an even more charged issue when we consider the willingness to allow opposing or critical voices. Add income inequality and high levels of crony capitalism—the remaining fig-leaf of legitimacy is nationalism, preferably one that is aggressive and high-profile.

Nationalism was clearly a factor in Russia's short-lived war with Georgia in 2008 and its annexation of Crimea and support for a breakaway state in eastern Ukraine in 2014. There is a calculated trade-off between surrendering political rights at home for an activist state willing to provide (as much as it can) consumer largesse and a recapturing of nationalist pride that Russia is again taken seriously on the world stage. For Russia's leadership, the potential anchoring of Ukraine in the Western orbit, by possible memberships in the European Union and NATO, would be taken as a defeat in the Eurasian geopolitical game, with negative repercussions at home. Due to this geopolitical tussle, Russia was hit by Western sanctions that hurt its economy and reduced the flow of badly needed technology and capital. None of this helps on the demographic front; if anything, it detracts from it on the policy side, and the consequences of Putin's adventures in Crimea and Ukraine have hurt the economy and ultimately the lifestyle of many Russians, diminishing reasons for bringing children into the world.

The demographic challenge is not limited to China and Russia. It also affects the political and economic dynamics at play in much of the Middle East and Latin America. In the case of the Middle East, veteran journalist David Brooks observed in 2012: "Morocco, Syria and Saudi Arabia have seen fertility-rate declines of nearly 60 percent, and in Iran it's more than 70 percent. These are among the fastest declines in recorded history."[6] Questions over the future, such as political uncertainty and tough economic times, and limited opportunities, also factor large in this group of autocratic countries.

TECHNOLOGY

While demographic problems point to the limitations of autocratic state capitalist countries, the issue of technology looms large in the twenty-first century. To put it mildly, technology has climbed into nearly every nook and cranny of daily life for a large number of people on the planet. Many may be unaware of the depth of the impact. It cuts across political systems, national boundaries, and ethnic and religious divisions. Technology can leap over entire countries in a single bound, and it is a major force in shaping the global economy and the pecking order of power. This is not lost on the United States, Russia, China, Japan, India, or Europe. Consequently, the ability to process new technology is a major issue in how the world is being shaped and raises many questions about the capacity of autocratic state capitalist countries to keep up.

While technology is very much part of state capitalist economic models, the challenge to maximize such forces as "big data" is profound in countries like China and Russia. China is boosting its investment in and increasing its focus on technology. The success of the Alibaba Group, China's e-commerce giant, in launching a $21 billion global stock initial public offering in 2014 reflects the fact that Chinese technology is taken seriously. Alibaba's public raising of shares in the United States (320 million American depositary shares), made it larger than 90 percent of the Standard & Poor's 500 Index companies.[7] Nonetheless, the fundamental issue is ultimately one of control, which was repeatedly made clear during the Alibaba roadshow, as global investors wanted to understand the relationship between the "private sector" company and the government. Considering China's autocratic nature, the question has to be asked: just how much autonomy does Alibaba's management have vis-à-vis the CCP and the Chinese state? Taking this one step further, from a geopolitical view, does Alibaba represent another element of the Chinese power? Although Alibaba's chief operating officer Jack Ma has sought to discuss any such official links, in a world of rising geopolitical traditions, doubts will remain.

For technology—big data in particular—to work, there needs to be a free flow of information and ideas. As Viktor Mayer-Schonberger and Kenneth Cukier observed in their book *Big Data*, "Big data is all about seeing and understanding the relations within and among pieces of information that, until very recently, we struggled to fully grasp."[8] Along these lines, big data has three very significant components that impact the role of the state: (1) the ability to analyze and gather vast amounts of data on a particular topic; (2) willingness to embrace data's real-world messiness rather than privileged exactitude; and (3) growing respect for correlations rather than a continuing quest for elusive causality. This mix decidedly has business implications that people around the world grasp. China understands this, and so does Russia. But the question lingers: do autocratic political systems based on control of information do well in areas that rely on sharing as a means of economic advancement? There are no easy answers to this, but the issue is going to become an increasing challenge to the autocratic state capitalist nations if they fail to deliver. If nothing else, this was the message that came from the Middle East's Jasmine Revolution: the young and interconnected are part of an important political dynamic that is less tolerant of brittle and unresponsive political systems incapable of delivering the long-promised economic goodies. Technology in many ways creates a flow of ideas, not necessarily wanted by governments, but persistent in their penetration.

MANAGEMENT OF RESOURCES

The other tectonic change–inducing area is the management of resources. Although this has been disputed by some as sensationalistic and overstated, resources such as food, water, and energy will be important. Demand for these resources will increase, and their availability will be a force of change. This is even more the case when climate change is added to the mix, a factor that is already changing weather patterns, creating greater extremes in cold and hot periods and wetter and drier periods. A point of concern will be the decline in precipitation in the Middle East and North Africa, Central Asia, southern Europe, southern Africa, and the U.S. Southwest. According to a study from the National Intelligence Council, *Global Trends 2030: Alternative Worlds*: "We are not necessarily headed into a world scarcities, but policymakers and their private sector partners will need to be proactive to avoid such a future. Many countries probably won't have the wherewithal to avoid food and water shortages without massive help from outside."[9]

Water is already a major issue in many countries, including China and much of the Middle East. In the latter case, historical, psychological, and political barriers have impeded cooperation and deadlocked diplomacy. The risk is growing that nations in the region are sliding toward conflict over water, as countries increasingly are forced to find a new approach to safeguard this diminishing resource. While representing 5 percent of the total world population, the Middle East and North Africa contains less than 1 percent of global water resources. With population increases through the twentieth and early twenty-first centuries, the demand for water has only grown, and the region has become increasingly dependent on external sources in the form of imported food crops. The number of water-scarce countries in the Middle East and North Africa has risen from 3 in 1955 (Bahrain, Jordan, and Kuwait) to over 12 in 2010, with more to follow by 2025. As the World Bank noted:

The situation is likely to get worse. Per capita water availability will fall by half by 2050, with serious consequences for the region's already-stressed aquifers and natural hydrological systems. As the region's economies and population structures change over the next few decades, demands for water supply and irrigation services will change accordingly, as will the need to address industrial and urban pollution. Some 60 percent of the region's water flows across international borders, further complicating the resource management challenge. This will be compounded if rainfall patterns, as predicted, shift as a result of climate change.[10]

This becomes even more the case when we factor in other societal issues, such as income inequality and the lack of a level playing field for individuals and businesses. Indeed, many of the same issues are evident in China in terms of potable water, which has been complicated by extensive pollution of the country's rivers. Some of these problems point back to the cozy relationship between polluting businesses and party officials. Despite a history of toxic spills of chemicals and mineral waste into waterways, the problem persists in many parts of the country. This also functions, as it does in many of the Middle Eastern countries, to erode the government's legitimacy in the eyes of its citizens.

Directly related to the issue of adequate water supplies is food security. For all of the problems in Western liberal democracies, they have developed highly efficient means of agricultural production, storage, and distribution. This is not to argue that Western (and for that matter Japanese) agricultural policies are perfect, but they are superior to food security systems found in most autocratic state capitalist countries, including China, Saudi Arabia, and the Gulf states. (Russia benefits from being a major grain producer.) This is certainly the case in China, which is watching an ongoing erosion in food security.

The food security issue in China touches upon many of the dilemmas inherent in state capitalism—and the danger of slipping into crony capitalism. China has sought to grow most of its own food and has developed a more competitive agricultural system than what was in existence during most of the twentieth century. The problem is that the Chinese population has grown (more mouths to feed), its diet is changing away from grains and more to proteins, and pollution is shrinking the availability of fertile land. Because of these factors, China's ability to feed its population is shrinking, and its dependence on imports for wheat, corn, and rice is expected to increase in the years to come.

For China to rectify its food production problem, it needs to deal with pollution. The emphasis in China has been on achieving economic growth, to the detriment of all other factors. This has created a situation in which

China's chemical industry has operated with few constraints (at least, few laws that are enforced), and electrical power has relied heavily on coal-fired power plants. The result has been dangerous chemicals released into the country's waterways, and the land absorbing cadmium, lead, mercury, and arsenic—none of which are helpful to producing healthy food. There is also a crony capital angle in this, as local authorities, who have much to gain from local industry, have often opted not to enforce anti-pollution laws. The World Policy Institute's Keshar Petal observed: "For many provincial and regional officials, ignoring environmental edicts means augmenting personal wealth. Though the central government has managed to establish requirements for new coal-fired power plants, it has been ineffective in implementing these requirements. Mayors in coal towns have largely ignored the regulations, choosing graft over governance."[11]

The food security issue is not limited to China. One of the major forces behind the Jasmine Revolution that swept the Middle East in 2010–2012 was the fact that governments, such as those in Tunisia, Egypt, and Libya, were hit by food insecurity concerns, and their crony capitalist nature left them open to public discontent, carried to people by social media. The food issue has not gone away and is increasingly a point of concern. According to the World Bank in 2014, one in nine people suffer from chronic hunger, more than 1 billion are undernourished, and 3.1 million children die every year due to hunger and malnutrition. While most of the autocratic state capitalist countries discussed in this book have made considerable strides addressing their citizens' nutritional needs, these same countries face considerable competition for food supplies in the upcoming decades. This becomes even more problematic when combined with the water issue.

THE CHALLENGE OF INCOME INEQUALITY

While considerable attention is given to income inequality in the United States (and rightfully so), the gap between China's rich and poor is the world's most significant—at least when using the metric known as the Gini coefficient. That metric would be zero in a society in which all income is equally distributed, while a score of one would indicate that all wealth is concentrated into the hands of a single person. In a University of Michigan study, it was demonstrated that income inequality has been rising rapidly in China and surpassed the United States by a large margin. Indeed, the study found that income inequality in China is among the highest in the world, especially in comparison to countries with comparable or higher standards of living.[12] This raises historical memories of

Tiananmen Square, a traumatic event that shook the nation's leadership and has remained a factor in the country's approach to development issues ever since.

In the run-up to 1989, urban workers began to have doubts about the gains of reforms in the face of inflationary pressures and official corruption. At the same time, the gaps between the countryside and cities were increasingly evident. All of this led to questions about price stability and social security, as well as who was benefiting from Chinese economic restructuring. In his *The End of the Chinese Dream*, Gerard Lemos provides color as to the continuing significance of Tiananmen Square: "All of this constituted 'a crisis of legitimacy'. From the intellectuals to factory workers and peasants people did not question the need for reform, but the distribution of benefits. They began to ask in whose interests the state and the Party were acting."[13] Those same sentiments exist in the 2010s, with the CCP painfully seeking to balance the need for change with the need to maintain control.

China is hardly alone among state capitalist countries with the problem of income inequality. Saudi Arabia also has issues in this regard. Wealth has poured into the country because of its hydrocarbon exports, making the royal family some of the wealthiest individuals in the world. King Abdullah is estimated to be personally worth $18 billion. The government has been willing to pump some of its oil money into the betterment of living standards for the population. Yet the rise of the population from 6 million in 1970 to 28 million in 2013 has left millions of Saudis lagging behind the more well-to-do. It is estimated that between 2 and 4 million of the country's native Saudis live on less than about $530 a month—about $17 a day—considered the poverty line in the kingdom.[14] It is also estimated that a third of young Saudis are unemployed.[15] Part of the problem has been that some of the money earmarked for poverty reduction ends up in the pockets of the royal family through a web of nepotism, corruption, and cozy government contracts.

The Saudi government is aware of the corruption issue and has repeatedly sought to clean up the redistribution process, but bad practices continue, leaving a group of Saudis who are economically marginalized and politically alienated. This becomes more problematic considering the often extravagant lifestyles of the Saudi royal family and their often un-Islamic behavior outside of the Kingdom. After all, in 2010, Wikileaks revealed an alleged "raucous underground" culture of the Saudi royal youths where alcohol, drugs, and prostitutes were rampant. While the Western media is quite content to print stories about "bad" Saudi behavior, an anonymous

Twitter user, Mujtahidd, has actively reported the intimate details of members of the royal family back to Saudi Arabia along with criticism of various policies.

The Saudi government practices press censorship, but Mujtahidd is thought to have almost one million followers, indicating a ready audience in a country devoid of such information. Part of the issue is that Saudi Arabia is governed by Sharia law, is home to Mecca and Medina (two of the holiest cities in Islam) and is the birthplace of Wahhabism, a very strict fundamentalist interpretation of the faith. Religious leaders and the mutaween (vice police) enforce Islamic law and order. Consequently, the reported bad behavior of members of the privileged royal family (and not all members fit this description) strike a nerve in a society where much of the social world remains opaque and not everyone enjoys the same levels of petro-wealth. Alienation also extends to the kingdom's minority Shia Muslims, who are closely watched by the security forces because of concerns over possible subversive links to Shia Iran.

Another major autocratic state capitalist country with income inequality problems is Russia. According to a report from Moscow's Higher School of Economics (HSE) in 2011, the wealthiest part of Russian society doubled its wealth since the fall of communism, while close to two thirds of the population did not see much of a change, and the poorest actually lost ground.[16] The HSE report also made the following observations: income inequality is the country's major problem; the best-off 20 percent of the population is successfully participating in the rise of prosperity related to the market economy; and the cheaper pleasures (food, drink, and alcohol) were somewhat cheaper. The problem is that while the number of people under the poverty line in Russia has shrunk, income inequality is very evident in the conspicuous consumption of the super-wealthy and points back to the questionable manner in which some of that wealth was achieved. One of the authors of the report, Vladimir Gimpelson, noted that measures could be taken to rectify some of the more egregious aspects of income inequality. As he stated: "Many things are required to change this. We need more political and market competition, enforcement of property rights, rule of law, systemic change in labor market institutions and stronger social protection for the needy."[17]

The challenge in regard to income inequality in autocratic state capitalist countries is the weakness of civil society in monitoring the causes of income disparity, the relationships between the rich and powerful, and creating the means for some type of re-balancing. Although it can be argued that income inequality in the West is also a product of the cozy relationship between government (both elective and bureaucratic) and business (bankers often come into the line of fire on this), there are other elements of society that can respond. This includes elections where the voters can "throw the bums out," but also organizations that are vocal in their criticism of income inequality. In this regard, the United States had Occupy Wall Street and other protest movements that sought to point out huge societal income differences. Equally important, the U.S. government has a tradition of going after white-collar crime, which—though it may not always be satisfying to the public—has underscored that there are limits to financial abuse. In China, Russia, and Saudi Arabia, civil society is generally weak, many of the wealthy are also politically connected, and there is no option to vote them out of office.

The reason income inequality is such a problem in autocratic state capitalist countries is the implicit societal pact that in return for citizens' inactivity in politics, the leadership will provide economic benefits, including jobs, better living conditions, and some structure for old-age pensions and healthcare. Failure to deliver on the economic side of the social pact represents a major breakdown between rulers and the ruled. Indeed, the façade of electoral processes in some states is shown to be exactly what it is—a sop to the masses. Despite the problems inherent in democracies and the rise of interest groups, citizens in Western liberal democracies have the option to organize and throw the ruling party out of office. They also have the option to seek redress of grievance through the courts. In an autocratic government, those options are often not available—and to manifest discontent runs the risk of incurring the displeasure of the authorities. The option of more violent means becomes one of the few paths left to record discontent, which explains the large number of riots that annually occur in China, both recorded and unrecorded.

LEGITIMACY AND THE AUTHORITARIAN TEMPTATION

As pressures mount in terms of change derived from demographics, technology, and income issues, political institutions around the world will feel the stress. Indeed, it can be argued that these trends will complicate the creation of new bases of political association and challenge political legitimacy and effectiveness. Political scientist Samuel P. Huntington noted that this situation does not always end well: "The result is political instability and disorder. The primary problem of politics is the lag in the development of political institutions behind social and economic change."[18] Huntington also noted that governments command the loyalty of their citizens and thus have the capacity to tax resources, conscript manpower, and innovate and execute policy. But legitimacy relates back to the ability of the government to provide economic benefits. Without the ability to provide economic benefits, the state capitalist model runs the risk of being challenged.

In China the government's ability to maintain legitimacy in the eyes of its people has long been referred to as the Mandate of Heaven. In dynastic China, there was a cycle of government in which the ruling dynasty would become corrupt and ineffective in managing the empire's resources, leading to banditry and rebellions. Eventually a new leader would emerge, topple the old order, and establish a new dynasty, which would promptly address such issues as providing personal security (good for economic development), maintenance of canals and roads (good for trade and important in the movement of troops), and defense of the frontiers (keeping those pesky barbarians out of China). Although China is no longer the realm of family dynasties as of old, the government in Beijing still wrestles with many of the same challenges. Above all else, the Communist Party in China seeks to maintain its legitimacy in the eyes of its population. Likewise Putin and his court seek to provide many of the same services to the Russian population, to maintain their legitimacy. The same trade-offs are found throughout the Gulf States in the Middle East and even in governments of autocratic statist–leaning nations, as in Ecuador, Venezuela, and Argentina.

But legitimacy is a difficult thing to maintain. It is a challenge for even those governments that have long traditions of elective politics, adhering to the constitutional laws and having functioning civil societies. In many cases there is a tremendous attraction to a leader who has the ability to cut through what may appear to be the Gordian knots of political dysfunction and blocked economic policymaking. This was certainly the case in the rise of Hitler in Germany and Mussolini in Italy, and even provided support for dictators like Argentina's Juan Domingo Peron, Brazil's Getulio Vargas, and Portugal's Antonio Salazar. Considering the sweeping nature of challenges confronting leaders in the twenty-first century, there can be an attractiveness to strong-arm tactics to get things done, especially when confronted by legislative bodies and judiciaries that appear more intent on obstructing reforms than on helping in the governing process.

All of this points back to the issue of legitimacy. If governments are not able to deliver what they have promised, there is a risk of sociopolitical unrest and even rebellion. Governments in China, Russia, and Saudi Arabia are aware of this and are seeking to address it, though the results are likely to be varied. In this the strength or weakness of political institutions is clearly an issue. One of the saving graces of more open societies is usually that public discontent has outlets, either through the ballot box or through the media. The Republican Party in the United States paid the price for bad policies that led to the Great Recession, a factor that helped elect Democrat Barack Obama to the White House in 2008 and gave his party a majority in Congress. In the same fashion, the Labour Party was voted out of office in the United Kingdom in 2010. In India in 2014, the Congress Party was held accountable for economic mismanagement, corruption scandals, and an inability to make further headway with reform. Democracies are hardly exempt from the need to periodically reinvent themselves, especially at times when government (in the broad sense of head of state, legislative body, and judiciary) becomes increasingly dysfunctional in the eyes of the citizens, much like the U.S. Congress following the Great Recession. It should never be forgotten that politics—between domestic players and between different national systems and ideologies—has not gone away. John Micklelthwait and Adrian Wooldridge noted: "The twenty-first century is sure to be shaped by ever-fiercer competition between states to figure out which innovations in governing yield the best results. The liberal democracies of the Western world still enjoy a significant leg up in terms of wealth and political stability. But it's not clear whether the West will be able to summon the sort of intellectual and political energy that, for the past four centuries, has kept it ahead in the global race to reinvent the state."[19]

The authoritarian temptation is likely to be more manifest as the nature of international relations becomes less cordial and many governments and leaders feel a more urgent need to reform their economies. That is certainly the case in China, where the political purges of 2014 are consolidating power for President Xi and his clique, with an eye to massive challenges. The view from inside the ruling elite is that if control is not fully established over the levers of power, then they will not be able to impose the reforms badly needed to restructure the economy and deal with the more macro-level changes being pushed by demographics, technology, and the management of national resources. In the Chinese case, there is also a fear that if political controls are eased and the economy is not reformed, the Communist Party will fail and the country will be engulfed in chaos. Consequently, political power is being concentrated in the office of the president, and Xi has already become a more powerful leader than other Chinese presidents possibly as far back as Deng Xiaoping.

Even India, the world's largest democracy, faces these currents. The idea of a strongman leader has some degree of appeal, considering how

India's political system makes reform very difficult. As *The Economist* noted of the attraction of Narenda Modi, who became prime minister in 2014: "This is because India is an extraordinarily hard place to govern. Much power is devolved to the states; the fissiparous nature of its polity means that deals have constantly to be done with a vast array of regional and caste-based parties; and a colonial and socialist past has bequeathed India a bureaucracy whose direction is hard to change."[20] *The Economist* added that the danger "is that Mr. Modi's strength will go to his head, and he will rule as an autocrat, not a democrat—as Indira Gandhi did for a while." In all democracies that is the risk: strong leaders often challenge democratic checks and balances, but that is why those checks and balances are there. Supreme Court justices, legislative leaders, and chief bureaucrats are there to uphold the law of the land. In autocratic states this is usually not the case, which can be a huge weakness.

STATE CAPITALISM AND CRONY CAPITALISM

The most difficult challenge for autocratic state capitalist regimes is avoiding the slippery slope that morphs the system from the mix of intelligent state guidance and market discipline to a self-aggrandizing arrangement in which the political elite either interlink with the business elite or are one and the same. Singapore is an example of a country that has been able to maintain a dynamic balance between state businesses and the political system, creating one of the world's highest standards of living. Anyone visiting Singapore finds it clean, efficient, and safe. Moreover, the city-state's leadership has repeatedly demonstrated a sense of vision, pertaining to everything from the nature of the commanding heights of the economy to food security issues. Equally important in this is that the country's government is not perceived as corrupt. There is a higher degree of transparency in Singapore than in most emerging market countries and certainly when compared to China, Russia, and Saudi Arabia. One of the lasting criticisms about Singapore is that its society is overly programmed; the ruling elite has set the guidelines as to how society will be run. Along these lines, consensus is key, dissent is not appreciated, and the ruling People's Action Party (PAP) overwhelmingly wins the elections for parliament on a regular basis. But Singapore is a high standard for autocratic state capitalist regimes.

One of the most significant challenges to any political system is the type of linkages developed between the government (in the broad sense) and economic interests. Stated in another way, how do autocratic governments avoid giving up the efficiency and discipline of the market for the coziness of crony capitalism? Considering the sensitivity to income inequality that many countries face, the issue of crony capitalism is a major point of concern, which in the past has been a factor in the downfall of governments. That was certainly the case in the revolutions that toppled autocratic regimes across North Africa in 2010–2012. China, Russia, and Saudi Arabia are painfully vulnerable to this risk if social issues are not dealt with. In particular, autocratic states tend to be strongly wed to the ideas of political order and stability, while promoting economic development, with a substantial share of it earmarked for the elite. Yet that economic development and accompanying technological changes and innovations are what threaten political order and stability. The fundamental issue is that when such forces collide, social turmoil often occurs. As *Der Spiegel* journalist Dirk Kurbjuweit observed: "Revolutions arise from obstinacy. People are dissatisfied with what they are told and develop new ideas."[21]

The authoritarian nature of some state capitalist regimes also inhibits their ability to respond to certain socially delicate issues, such as deadly diseases. This was evident in the initial outbreak of SARS (severe acute respiratory syndrome) in southern China and Hong Kong in 2002–2003. Symptoms of this respiratory illness include fever, muscle pain, lethargy, coughing, and sore throat. Although Chinese authorities eventually moved to contain the disease and have since become more competent in disease control and identification, SARS caught Chinese officialdom flat-footed and reluctant to act. The disease made its first appearance in November in Guangzhou. Millions of migrant workers lived there and some fled, helping spread the virus to Beijing and Shanghai. It was not until February that China officially notified the World Health Organization (WHO)—and even then the action was perceived by many as the work of a high-ranking doctor, Jiang Yanyong, who leaked the information to Chinese media, who leaked it to the West. By then the disease had spread to a number of countries, including Vietnam, Canada, and the United States. Although the number of those infected was a little over 3,000, it was estimated that 9.6 percent of people who got SARS died.[22]

It was painfully obvious to the Chinese public that their government had withheld information from them and had failed to take action in the early stages of the crisis. In the aftermath of the epidemic, it was revealed that lower-level officials had blocked the flow of information, fearing that it would hurt their promotion prospects. Indeed, Beijing municipal authorities hid the actual SARS situation in the nation's capital from the Party center until April. Seton Hall University's Yanzhong Huang found the reasons for this state of affairs in the country's bureaucracy, which had become fragmented and disjointed between local and national levels, poor inter-governmental communications (as between local and national levels), and slowness in the leadership in being made aware of the grave nature of the crisis. Huang also noted: "By early April, it was evident that SARS was being taken very seriously at the top level. Yet the government's ability to formulate a sound policy against SARS was hampered as lower-level government officials intercepted and distorted the upward information flow. For fear that any mishap reported in their jurisdiction might be used as an excuse to pass them over for promotion, government officials at all levels tended to distort the information they passed up to their political masters in order to place themselves in a good light."[23]

Huang also observed that such bureaucratic problems are reduced in democratic societies by "decentralized oversight," which empowers citizen interest groups to check up on government actions. As he noted: "Because the general public in China is not enfranchised to oversee the activities of government agencies, however, lower-level officials can fool higher authorities more easily than their counterparts in liberal democracies." The argument can be made that the response to SARS was slow and disjointed until it became an embarrassment to the authorities.

While China has made an effort to improve its ability to respond to deadly diseases, another autocratic state, Saudi Arabia, is having similar problems in containing the spread of Middle East Respiratory Syndrome (MERS). The disease was first discovered in Saudi Arabia in 2012, and it has since spread to Yemen, Oman, Qatar, Jordan, and the UAE. According to the U.S. Centers for Disease Control and Prevention, MERS kills about 30 percent of those who become infected. As in China, the emergence of MERS as a serious health threat was given a slow response by officialdom, and valuable time was lost. Indeed, Reuters observed: "Saudi health sources and international virologists said poor communication and a lack of accountability in government departments, inadequate state oversight and a failure to learn from past mistakes have all hindered Saudi Arabia's battle against the SARS-like virus."[24]

POLITICAL SUCCESSION

One last issue that complicates the life of autocratic regimes—clearly a major limit—is political succession. Autocratic states are intended for control, which is meant to be the path to political order and stability. However, the changes occurring in the world in the early twenty-first century represent massive challenges to the ability of all governments to respond. Autocratic states often have a higher degree of brittleness than non-autocratic states when difficult crises, in particular economic ones, hit. That said, the critical challenge for all regimes is political succession. The more personalized the regime, the greater the potential for problems in the form of princelings battling to assume the leadership. Along these lines, China has created a process of political succession, from president to president, where the intramural jousting for dominance occurs behind the screen, usually away from the public's eyes. Russia's political succession has worked well for the past decade, but a post-Putin Russia leaves the door open for fierce factional infighting. Saudi Arabia's political succession could be even more challenging, considering that the fight is between family members.

While political succession in China has become a more formulaic event—at least in the public's perception—it is a more complicated issue in Saudi Arabia and potentially in Russia. In Russia the political and economic elite are most likely to close ranks quickly and rally behind someone who can be constitutionally anointed within a short period of time if something were to happen to Putin. That something could be his becoming "diplomatically ill" or "having an accident." If nothing else, Russia has a constitutional form and structure, and day-to-day running of the government can sit in the hands of the premier. The challenging issue in Russia is what happens if there is increased opposition to President Putin. Although he was popular in the aftermath of the occupation of Crimea in 2014, Putin's problem will be in maintaining a lifestyle for middle-class Russians, a group that is particularly vulnerable to deterioration in economic ties with the West.

Saudi Arabia's political succession has been a point of concern for years. Their 1992 Basic Law of Governance is relatively vague on political succession, stating that "rule passes to the sons of the founding king and their children's children." Additionally, in 2006 an Allegiance Council was created to help select crown princes. This process soon became complicated with the placement of various princes; when Crown Prince Sultan died in 2011, followed by Crown Prince Nayef in 2012, it was the king who appointed the successor, without input from the council.

Another potential source of competition for the throne was thought to possibly come from a younger generation of princes, who are patiently waiting for the older generation to die off. The younger generation is aware of the undercurrents of resentment against them in Saudi society. These range from Al-Qaeda sympathizers who favor a violent overthrow of what they see as a corrupt regime, to a growing middle class frustrated by roadblocks to socioeconomic mobility created by royal corruption and privilege. Saudi political succession is a major question that influences the region's future, especially as the autocratic lid runs the risk of being blown off when there is a change in leadership.

Saudi Arabia's political succession underwent a substantial revamping in 2015, following the death of King Abdullah, who was in ill health. The new King Salman moved in April 2015 to restructure the succession system. The Saudi leader sought to remove any ambiguity by appointing his son second in line to rule. In this, King Salman elevated Interior Minister Mohammed bin Nayef, 55, to crown price and Defense Minister Mohammed bin Salman, 30, became deputy crown prince. Succession over the past several decades has not moved from father to son, but rather older brother to younger brother among the Ibn Saud male siblings of King Abdulaziz—of which there were 44, and 35 of whom survived him when he died in 1953. With the changes in 2015, the uncertainty hopefully (from a Saudi standpoint) has been reduced.

CONCLUSION

While autocratic state regimes have made progress in a number of areas and maintain a degree of legitimacy with their citizens, this model of government has limitations, some of them quite serious. These limitations, mainly political in nature, often upend hard-won socio-economic gains. The most significant problem is the expansion of political elites into the business sphere, favoring cronies and crowding out entrepreneurs. Critical in this process of balancing political and economic demands are such questions as how to deal with official corruption, allow the venting of some degree of dissent or frustration against the system, and take into consideration what may be better ideas. State capitalist governments have achieved considerable gains in the betterment of their citizens, with millions being pulled out of poverty. Yet the ability to continue economic momentum runs the risk of favoring control over innovation. This is one of the major challenges facing countries like China, Russia, and Saudi Arabia in the decades ahead. This touches upon everything from new technology in the energy industry to the free flow of capital needed for business development. Control helps provide stability and keeps the ruling class in power, but it can also, over the long run, set the stage for social malaise and political decay. Western liberal capitalist countries confront similar issues and tend to go through periods of decline and anemic leadership, but have thus far demonstrated an ability to reinvent themselves. One of the limitations for autocratic state governments is that once legitimacy is lost, it is often substituted by the use of force. The use of force ultimately leads to political upheaval and overthrow of the old order. This risk places a large question mark over the future regime survival of autocratic governments—and technology is only accelerating the pace of change.

NOTES

1.   Moody's Investors Service, "Announcement: Moody's Will Reduce Economic Growth Worldwide in the Next Two Decades," August 6, 2014.

2.   Data noted in Weiyi Lim, "China Baby Boom Wagers Go Bust on Child Cost Burden," *Bloomberg*, August 21, 2014.

3.   Ibid.

4.   Ibid.

5.   Ilan Berman, *Implosion: The End of Russia and What It Means for America* (Washington, D.C.: Regnery Publishers, Inc., 2013), p. 14.

6.   David Brooks, "The Fertility Implosion," *International Herald Tribune*, March 12, 2012, p. 10.

7.   Leslie Parker and Fox Hu, "Alibaba Said to Plan to Stop Taking Orders for IPO Early," *Bloomberg*, September 12, 2014.

8.   Viktor Mayer-Schonberger and Kenneth Cukier, *Big Data* (New York: Houghton Mifflin Harcourt Publishing Company, 2014), p. 19.

9.   The National Intelligence Council, *Global Trends 2030: Alternative Worlds* (Washington, D.C.: the National Intelligence Council, December 2012), p. iv.

10.   World Bank, *Making the Most of Scarcity: Accountability for Better Water Management Results in the Middle East and North Africa* (Washington, D.C., World Bank, 2007).

11.   Keshar Petal, "China's Food Policy Dilemma," World Policy Institute, June 4, 2014. http://www.worldpolicy.org/blog/2014/06/04/chinas-food-security-dilemma.

12.   "Income Inequality Now Greater in China than in U.S.," *Michigan News*, April 28, 2014. ns.umich.edu/new/releases/22156-income-inequality-now-greater-in-china-than-in-us.

13.   Gerard Lemos, *The End of the Chinese Dream* (New Haven, CT: Yale University Press, 2013), pp. 49–50.

14.   Kevin Sullivan, "Saudi Arabia's Riches Conceal a Growing Problem of Poverty," *The Guardian* (Manchester), January 1, 2013. www.theguardian.com/world/2013/jan/01/saudi-arabia-riyadh-poverty-inequality.

15. "Time for the Old Men to Give Way," *The Economist,* June 23, 2012. http://www.economist.com/node/21557330/print.

16. Study noted in Tom Parfitt, "Russia's Rich Double Their Wealth, But Poor Were Better Off in 1990s," *The Guardian,* April 11, 2011. http://www.theguardian.com/world/2011/apr/11/russia-rich-richer-poor-poorer.

17. Ibid.

18. Samuel P. Huntington, *Political Order in Changing Societies* (New Haven, CT: Yale University Press, 1968), p. 5.

19. John Micklethwait and Adrian Wooldridge, "The Global Contest for the Future of Government," *Foreign Affairs* (July/August 2014), p. 132.

20. "India's Strongman," *The Economist,* May 24, 2014, p. 11.

21. Dirk Kurbujweit, "The Merkel Effect: What Today's Germany Owes to Its Once-Communist East," *Spiegel Online International,* October 2, 2014. www.spiegel.de/international/germany/how-east-germnay-influences -modern-day-german-politics-a-994410.html.

22. World Health Organization, "Summary of probable SARS cases with onset of illness from 1 November 2002 to 31 July 2003." www.who .int/csr/sars/country/table2004_04_21/en.

23. Yanzhong Huang, "The SARS Epidemic and Its Aftermath in China: A Political Perspective." From the Institute of Medicine (U.S.) Forum on Microbial Threats, S. Knobler, A. Mahmoud, S. Lemon, et al., editors, *Learning from SARS: Preparing for the Next Disease Outbreak: Workshop Summary* (Washington, D.C.: National Academic Press, 2004).

24. Reuters, "How Saudi Arabia Let the Deadly MERS Virus Spread," *Newsweek,* June 12, 2014. http://www.newsweek.com/how-saudi-arabia -let-deadly-mers-virus-spread-254579. Also see the U.S. Centers for Disease Control and Prevention.

EIGHT

Conclusion: An Uncertain Future

The geopolitical landscape stretching out into the twenty-first century will be defined by a more fragile form of globalization, competing models of development between autocratic state capitalism and democratic private sector–led capitalism, and greater shocks to the system caused by the inherent instability of autocratic states. This is not to say that the next several decades will necessarily be ones of ongoing political upheaval. However, the potential for chaos is likely to grow, not shrink. While all governments have an interest in creating a world based on trade and investment, and improvement in the standard of living for their citizens, not all are going to seek those goals—at least beyond mouthing the necessary rhetoric. A major difference between democratic and autocratic political systems is how each addresses the need for some sense of vision about the future. In this not all governments are created equal. While democracies have their set of problems, autocracies operate with the handicap that their political systems offer fewer peaceful outlets for frustration and aspirations. This leaves both political economic models with considerable uncertainty in the years ahead but puts more onus on autocratic states—as, when they come to an end, there tends to be a more violent upheaval.

What makes managing these challenges more difficult is a serious disjoint in worldviews between autocratic and democratic states, especially when it comes to defining the rules of the game. This is increasingly evident in how countries like China and Russia approach foreign affairs, in contrast to the United States, Europe, and Japan. For the former, long-standing borders are no longer sacrosanct, and conflict resolution is not all about arbitration and meetings but increasingly considers military force and coercion. Among the latter, such changes raise fundamental questions over the rules and regulations governing international business, and criticism over those not being "responsible shareholders" in the world order. The new geopolitical norm is one of greater friction between states, companies, and peoples, pushed along by technologically driven closeness and the self-interest of trade and investment. It is less driven by Western norms and more nudged along by other voices, many of them uncertain of what they actually want from the global order. Above all else, the new geopolitical norm is one of uncertainty, which signals greater volatility to come for global markets and national economies.

REFLECTIONS ON THE JASMINE REVOLUTION

While China, Russia, and Saudi Arabia's autocratic governments appear to be permanent features of the geopolitical landscape, much the same used to be thought of the regimes in North Africa, where local leadership elites were firmly entrenched. In Tunisia, Libya, and Egypt, autocratic strongmen and their allies in the security forces and big business held the levers of power. Despite periodic efforts to reform their economies, each of these countries became examples of crony capitalism and were increasingly less able and willing to meet the needs of their people. The deep-set problems of making a living in Egypt, Libya, and Tunisia for hard-pressed middle- and working-class families ultimately set the stage for angry mobs willing to end crony capitalism. Tunisia's dictator was the first to slink out of the country, followed by the more protracted and violent ousters of the Mubarak regime in Egypt and the Gadaffi family in Libya.

Although the revolutions did not lead to full-fledged democratic governments in North Africa, Tunisia's experiment holds promise. Its economy, once the domain of crony capitalists, is in a state of flux, and some good things might actually emerge. Meanwhile, Egypt's democratic experiment ended in the return of the deep state, that secular-minded combination of the military, bureaucracy, judiciary, and business. In Libya, the political system fragmented, with various groups seeking to gain control of oil assets and port facilities. Despite the seeming dead-ends in Egypt and Libya (dictatorship and chaos, respectively), the aspirations of the 2011 uprisings are worth remembering, as they remain symbols that cut across geographic frontiers and touch on what citizens want and, when given the option, demand. Michele Dunne, a senior associate at the Carnegie Endowment for International Peace, astutely observed of the Jasmine

Revolution, or Arab Spring: "In Egypt, for example, the rallying cries were 'aysh, hurriya, adala ijtima'ia': bread, freedom, and social justice. Another frequent demand in several Arab Spring countries was 'karama', dignity. What the revolts all boiled down to was a call for a different relationship between citizen and government: a rejection of corrupt, repressive regimes that treated citizens as subjects without rights, paired with outrage at the capture of most economic benefits by government officials and their cronies."[1]

In many regards, there is something timeless about the demands mentioned by Dunne. Edmund Burke, the Irish-born conservative author of *Reflections on the Revolution in France* (1790), believed in the idea of a social contract that the French radicals failed to live up to, instead being motivated by self-interest and greed. In Burke's view, the social contract derives from the belief that good government is a gift from God. Because government is a divine gift to creation, morality and government cannot be separated. No person should act out of selfish desires, as a member of a governing body. Indeed, legislators should consider the potential repercussions on future generations, of legislating for the moment. From this premise, Burke believed society was a contract between the living, the dead, and the unborn—and, as such, was transcendental. Good government should seek to uphold the social contract between generations. In North African Arab Spring countries, the ousted regimes had not lived up to their end of the social contract and, as such, lost their legitimacy, especially with the younger generations.

Events in the Arab world loom as a possible path for other autocratic states that run the risk of pervasive corruption and creeping crony capitalism. There are lessons here for leaderships in China, Kazakhstan, Russia, and Saudi Arabia—and even Turkey and Hungary, where strong leaders have demonstrated authoritarian tendencies. The test of balancing societal needs versus the wealth and power of a few is not easy to handle. At some point the spoils of the system diminish, and competition increases. The disparity between those who are a part of the system and those who are not becomes painfully evident. That was the way of the French Revolution, as well as other revolutions in Russia, Mexico, and China. The willingness and ability of autocratic governments to deal with this issue will define the new geopolitical norm. In all likelihood, many autocratic states will face difficult socio-economic problems that have a transcendental element. Considering how deeply embedded some of these state-owned companies are in global markets, this represents a potentially disruptive force. The major risk for private sector companies is that state-owned companies or closely state-allied private companies from autocratic nations may be used as economic weapons to destroy what may be perceived as rivals. If nothing else, this leads to a breakdown in trust, which undermines confidence in the international system to sustain trade and investment.

While autocratic states probably represent the biggest challenge to the international system in the years ahead, the problems of democracy add to the great cloud of uncertainty that hangs over the global landscape. While democracy has much to recommend it, when it loses its direction or lacks a sense of mission, it has a tendency to fall in on itself, and the caliber of leadership declines as parliamentary deadlocks suffocate initiative and increase alienation. Governmental dysfunction, as reflected by Washington in the early 2010s or Europe's inability to introduce meaningful economic reforms, points to a failing in democracies to provide outlets for real change. Indeed, it can be argued that the heavy reliance on financial capitalism in the lead-up to 2008 indicates that the American and British democracies had lost their way, with moneyed interests narrowing the scope for sharing the national wealth.

The frustration and drift in democracy also makes alternative paths of action more attractive, including strong nationalism, leading to confrontation or revolution based on strong ideological convictions that a different type of society can be won. Many people still desire some sense of action or momentum. This explains the popularity of President Putin's 2014 annexation of Crimea among Russians, and the ability of the Islamic State of Iraq and Syria to attract recruits from the West. In the latter case, many of the recruits are disillusioned young men seeking to find a purpose and make their mark on society. Staying in France, Germany, or the United Kingdom has little to offer them except poverty, alienation from the society around them, and possibly a life of crime. In those cases, Western democracy and capitalism are not working. While this should not be overstated, both Russia and ISIS resort to force to get what they want, moves calculated to make Western democratic capitalism look weak and ineffective.

The problematic nature of democratic capitalism in many ways is similar to the period prior to the First World War in 1914—increasingly dominated by a wealthy few, growing urban populations struggling to make a living, and a buying of influence among political parties and leaders to halt reforms. There was a crisis in Western civilization in the decade before 1914, in the form of widening income disparity, international crises, and fast-paced wars—and much of the same landscape today negates the best of democracy. In many regards it is the internal crisis in democracy that has built up the idea of a threat from autocratic capitalist regimes. Burke's idea of a trans-generational sense of responsibility is very much at risk of breaking down and desperately needs to be restored. Ward Wilson, writing in *Foreign Policy* in 2014, observed: "The widespread sense that government fails to reflect the concerns of the government gives rise to protest movements such as the Occupy campaigns and the Tea Party. Europe has its own worries about the deepening 'democratic deficit', reflected in the rise of UKIP and other anti-immigration movements. Many voters share the belief that government responds only to narrow (mostly moneyed) interests that are unwilling to countenance new ideas or fresh approaches."[2] Sadly, a degree of upheaval may be needed to break the impasse in democratic capitalism, and this may be in evidence in the period ahead—either from external challenges such as autocratic states or from internal frustration boiling over and demanding better government. Critically, the democratic path can achieve change, and the system in North America and Europe is battle-tested. New battles are looming.

THE NEW GEOPOLITICAL LANDSCAPE

The world prior to 2008 was based on border-shrinking developments in business, technology, and politics, that implied that nationalism—or at least the nation-state—was over. The *Financial Times'* Gideon Rachman observed: "The emergence of the internet bolstered the idea that borders no longer matter. In a borderless world of bits and bytes the traditional concerns of nations—territory, identity and sovereignty—looked as anachronistic as swords and shields."[3] This was upheld by a certain smug sense of cultural superiority in which Western political correctness was imposed on the global system. Opposition to political correctness was dealt with by sharp-edged letters of warning, backed by verbal condemnation at international forums. What was papered over in the rush to globalize was that the very process of stripping away barriers between people exposed differences—a disorienting process for parts of the world, such as the Middle East and Africa, as well as parts of the Western world where old proto-nationlisms like those of the Scots and Catalonians percolated not far from the surface. The Great Recession, induced by Western financial capitalism, aggravated the suspicion of globalization and international finance. It made people look back to common history, languages, ethnic mix, and borders for comfort. In this tectonic change, there was comfort in the idea of a strong state leading the way, in both political and economic life—at least for some regions in the world.

The Jasmine Revolutions and other events since 2008 reflect the fact that the new geopolitical environment is increasingly fractured along the lines of autocratic state capitalist regimes and democratic capitalist governments. In this, there is a risk of other failures in autocratic capitalist regimes causing disruption to trade, capital flows, and economic growth. The political chaos that hit Libya in 2013–2014 factored into international oil prices. At the same time, sharp differences over foreign policy issues inject another disruptive factor into global business. A good example of this is Russia's annexation of Crimea in 2014, which resulted in sanctions against Russia by the West, and Russian counter-sanctions against the West in 2014. China's aggressive stance in the South China Sea sparked riots against Chinese companies operating in Vietnam in 2014. None of this is positive for international peace, global growth, and business development.

In June 2014, Russian President Vladimir Putin paid a visit to his Chinese counterpart, President Xi Jinping. This was an important visit. Russia had recently annexed Crimea from Ukraine and was facing Western economic sanctions aimed at high-ranking and wealthy Russians, many of them cronies of Putin. What came out of the trip was a re-affirmation of China and Russia's "strategic partnership," based on expanding trade, resolution of border disputes, and a mutual interest in impeding U.S. hegemony—or, at the very least, containing Western influence (in the broader sense) in the world at large. The meeting was sweetened by the announcement of a $400 billion deal involving Gazprom, meant to pump Russian natural gas to China. This convergence of Russian and Chinese interests clearly raised concerns in the Western intelligence community that the invigoration of the Sino-Russian relationship threatens to consolidate into an anti-American alliance.[4] Does this represent a new development in which the autocratic state capitalist states band together to counter the private sector–driven economies of the democratic West?

While Putin's regime has demonstrated a willingness to incur economic pain in its fight against what it saw as an encroachment of the West in Ukraine, China has demonstrated a far more cautious approach in confronting other countries. Its actions in the South and East China Seas have rankled Southeastern Asian countries and Japan. Nations must walk a fine line to keep the global economy in motion. It was China, after all, that stepped up in 2008–09 with a substantial stimulus package that pushed up Chinese economic growth and maintained a high level of imports from around the world. As the United States and Europe stumbled, China became the responsible partner among the largest global economies. Significantly China proved itself as a shareholder in the global economy. That shareholder status derives from the engagement of both its state-owned companies and privately owned companies. Despite the sometimes prickly nature of Chinese policy out of Beijing, there has been a high level of consistency in doing what it takes to bolster international trade and capital flows. China is highly interconnected with the West and Japan, which it needs to maintain its own experiment of autocratic state capitalism. The same can be said for Saudi Arabia, the Gulf States, and other countries with substantially high levels of state company involvement, like Brazil and India. Even horribly managed Venezuela has a stake in the system.

Yet globalization is under acute pressure. This is painfully evident in the Eastern Question—what to do with Russia and Ukraine? While sanctions against Russia are justified by its use of military force in Crimea and aid to eastern Ukrainian separatists, punishment of the Russian economy, in the long term, does not help keep the global economy on track for growth, the sharing of ideas, and the betterment of societies via cultural exchanges. Indeed, an economic collapse of Russia would do considerable damage in terms of mutual disengagement between West and East. It would also encourage Moscow to seek an alternative world order, formed of like-minded regimes and based more on a more macho form of nationalism, supported by military hardware and state-owned companies. One alternative path would be the development of a Sino-Russian alliance, spanning much of Eurasia and incorporating a number of allied regimes around the world, like Cuba, Venezuela, Nicaragua, and Zimbabwe. It would face a counter-alliance of the West and Japan, with its own set of allied states in Africa, the Middle East, and Latin America. This polarization was the road traveled by the European powers in the decade leading up to 1914.

While the return of aggressive nationalism is a force pulling against globalization, it is not alone in offering a different path for the world. Indeed, the emergence of a militant form of Islam has created a new ideology that offers a clear and radical alternative to both globalization and nationalism. It is based on a fundamentalist interpretation of Islam and provides a moral outlook that has no shades of gray, but a very black and white world. Good and bad are sharply bifurcated, and nuances are not appreciated, though technology (Twitter, videos, and social media) is used. The concept of jihad, its deadly use by the Islamic State, and the political decay of governments in Syria and Iraq have left fertile ground for greater political upheaval. Indeed, the old order of regional alliances was disrupted, and national borders are no longer sacrosanct. These national borders, after all, were the product of the Sykes-Picot Agreement, a secret deal between the governments of the United Kingdom and France to define spheres of influence. Those spheres of influence became set as the borders for the Middle East, which have remained largely intact into the early twenty-first century—until 2014, when the Islamic State spread its insurgency and the borders of its "caliphate" across what had been the international borders of Syria and Iraq. The Islamic State was very vocal in its desire to destroy the colonially imposed borders.

It is important to clarify that the appeal of an aggressive form of Islam is not limited to the Middle East. The Islamic State, Al-Qaeda, and the Taliban (in both Afghanistan and Pakistan) are transnational in their mission. The same could be said about some of the Islamic extremist groups operating in the Saharan and Sahel region (as in Mali) and forces in Somalia (happy to create problems for Kenya, with its Muslim minority). Nigeria's Boko Haram has yet to operate outside of Nigeria, but is supportive of a broader-based anti-Western movement. Taken together, the desire of these extremist organizations is to uproot the corrupt established order, disrupt the corrupting influence of the West (and increasingly China) and impose a rule of law based on Sharia. In this they are often helped by corrupt and inefficient governments weakened by crony capitalism. Radical Islam and its appeal should not be underestimated, as it remains a major force in defining the new geopolitical norm.

In a sense, the first part of the twenty-first century is defined by a growing competition between Western liberal democracy complemented by economies that are private sector–led, autocratic state capitalist regimes, and radical Islamic movements, largely based in the Middle East but with global reach into advanced economies like the United Kingdom and France as well as autocratic states like China and Russia. While the first two find common ground in a global capitalist system, the last is increasingly disruptive, as it refutes international borders, relies on military force, and has an open dislike and suspicion of non-Islamic people and cultures. Radical Islamic movements also have a disruptive element that leave no middle ground for life between Sunnis and Shias in the Middle East. In 2014 the Islamic State was active in its efforts to eradicate unbelievers, with a particularly genocide-driven approach to groups like the Yazidis in remote parts of Iraq, who were shot, buried alive, or sold into slavery.

The new geopolitical norm, therefore, is defined as a more sharp-elbowed world, in which an aggressive form of nationalism is competing with democratic norms and practices, while radical Islamic forces seek to disrupt the global system. This leaves a world system that is likely to find geopolitical disruption at a higher level than before 2008—the new norm. It will also increasingly be a world system in which autocrats and democrats will be forced to continue to cooperate; the alternative being a more polarized planet, with globalization in retreat and the means of maintaining a healthy degree of economic expansion in decline. If not properly managed, the major danger is that competition between the two systems will intensify, a development that could be mutually damaging. In this, international business leaders face a tough landscape, driven by political factors that are difficult to quantify and forecast.

MANAGING TECTONIC CHANGES

For economic policymakers, business managers, and citizens, the shifts in the global system since 2008, in particular the rivalry between two broadly defined political-economic models, are impinging on day-to-day reality. It becomes even more daunting when other factors are added: Islamic terrorism, continent-crossing diseases like Ebola, longstanding border disputes, a surplus of available weapons in places like Africa, and climate change, with major swings in the weather. For the average citizen, this translates into employment, health, and lifestyle issues. Is public transportation safe? Does a political struggle elsewhere end up being fought in their neighborhood shopping mall? Is it safe to fly during the holidays, or is a bomb likely to go off? Do pollution problems elsewhere end up affecting the local weather or result in flooding of coastal areas? Does another government's support for the local state-owned company translate into the loss of a job elsewhere by someone working for a private sector company? As the public grapples with these issues, so do economic policymakers, seeking to find solutions. In turn, finding solutions has its own set of political considerations that can determine the economic outcome. When people are angry, they are more likely to vote against those sitting in office.

For many large multinational companies that have benefited from globalization, increasing revenues and profits have come hand-in-hand with greater risk factors. Many management teams in the past have opted to ignore political risks or not put their companies into those markets. In this they have either exposed their companies to greater risk or missed substantial opportunities for growth—which means the generation of jobs. However, being in business today has exposed companies to wars, expropriation, and abrogation of contractual obligations, including debt repayment. We must add that this is not just a problem for private sector companies, but hits at many state-owned companies active in foreign markets.

Major private sector companies must enhance their ability to identify political risk. This entails a commitment to having the right people or groups in place to screen and interpret considerable data and correctly measure the nature of particular geopolitical risks. This is not just a matter of understanding politics and economics, but also of being able to assess the strategic challenge of a competitive business coming from an autocratic state capitalist company. Questions that need to be answered include what level of support is given to the company by its government, what access to credit the company has, including the ability to tap government banks and sovereign wealth funds, and how competitive the products are that such companies offer. This takes a combination of political science, economics, and business acumen, particularly credit analysis. As for the last, data necessary includes how revenues are generated, how debt is managed, and how management is selected. Equally significant is how transparent the company is in its financial statements and how willing it is to disclose that data. Investing in foreign markets therefore embraces an approach of the macroeconomic, political, and business environments. For doing business in autocratic states, the added risk is that the rule of law can be selective and regulatory enforcement targeted.

Companies conducting business overseas or competing with foreign companies in their own markets face a world driven by tectonic changes. Russia's actions against Ukraine leap out in this regard, considering the adoption of sanctions by both sides against businesses. The major change was that Russia pushed back against what it perceived as the relentless Western advance in its traditional sphere of influence. This was played out between European, American, Ukrainian, and Russian governments, but as the Eastern Crisis became an extended affair, it was businesses in all of these countries that ended up on the firing line: losing sales and being forced to close down operations and seek new customers to make up for the loss of old business. Also affected by these measures are people: the workers who depend on salaries to feed their families and pay their rent or mortgages. The risk is that while policymakers wrestle, it is the citizens that are hurt.

Sadly, the geopolitical and economic changes are not going to fade away; they are more likely to expand in number and become more complex in nature. It is often said that the world has become a smaller place, but it is equally true that problems seem to be getting bigger. A hard economic landing in China would be a global event, hitting everyone from the United States and Europe to most developing countries, in particular commodity exporters. China's economic slowdown in 2013–2015 was accompanied by declines in a number of commodity markets. Similarly, an extended recession in the Russian economy is not a good thing for the global economy, in particular for Europe and its businesses. It would also be problematic for China, with which Russia has a growing trade and investment relationship. There are equally difficult questions concerning what would happen if Saudi Arabia's government falls. Although 2014 observed a collapse in international oil prices, Saudi Arabia remains the swing state in global production, and any change in regime would have an impact felt from Tokyo and Seoul to Berlin and Caracas. This was indeed something that was closely watched as the Arab country changed monarchs in the middle of the Saudi campaign to maintain its market share in global oil exports in 2015.

It would be wrong to leave the outlook for competition between state capitalism and private sector capitalism on a dark and gloomy note. There are positives. Global trade continues to be a major factor in the intercourse between nations. Investment in other economies has not dried up; capital flows between Western democracies, with economies dominated by the private sector continuing to put money into autocratic state capitalist–dominated economies. China continues to invest in Europe and North America. This leaves some degree of hope for the future. The friction between competing models of development does not have to overcome mutual benefits.

To the above we must add that advances in technology continue. Indeed, they serve to maintain a degree of interdependence that remains critical for a world where both autocrats and democrats have a stake. Martin Wolf, writing for the International Monetary Fund, observed: "Technology will continue to drive integration. Soon, almost every adult and many children are likely to own a smart mobile device that offers instant access to all the information available on the World Wide Web. It will make the transmission of everything that can be digitized—information, finance, entertainment, and much else—essentially costless. An explosion of exchange is certain."[5] While this raises issues of control for the autocratic states, it also holds out the possibility that the exchange of ideas can help in the managing of tectonic shifts in the global economy in the years ahead. It can also provide opportunities for businesses and peoples.

CONCLUSION

In the early twenty-first century, globalization will struggle to remain the dominant force. The headwinds against this have multiplied, the most significant being tensions between autocratic state capitalism and private sector–led economies with democratic systems of government. This was evident in the tensions between Russia and the West over Ukraine in 2014 and in Saudi Arabia's oil campaign the same year. While cleavages between these two competing systems can be substantial, the framework for international relations is being increasingly pushed back into the realm of realpolitik and moving away from a Western-imposed political correctness that served to generate friction over a number of issues, ranging from gay rights, free speech, and religious freedom to pollution, climate change, and food security. Although the democratic West may believe that it has the moral high ground in this debate, there is considerable pushback from other parts of the world that do not accept many of these tenets as core beliefs.

The challenge ahead will be to find common ground between competing systems, to contain problems that may be highly disruptive to global trade and investment, and to preserve many of the gains derived from globalization. Attention will also need to be paid to political transition issues in autocratic states, with a view to political succession and, in extreme cases, regime change. These last can be highly disruptive affairs. The fact that many political transitions in autocratic states can be disruptive plays to the strengths of democratic capitalism, a factor that leaves us more confident over the long term about how political systems will evolve and the central significance of the private sector as the generator of wealth and income in the future. Without responsible governments, with checks and balances and some degree of transparency, it becomes easy to shift into crony capitalism and political decay, which often ends in a violent changing of the guard. At the same time, democratic capitalist countries need their own upheavals to rectify problems, including income disparity and political drift. This is going to be the challenge of the decades ahead: how to manage change and encourage innovation and the free flow of ideas. Along these lines, democratic capitalism will eventually triumph over autocratic state capitalism, as the former has a tendency to stress order and stability over ways to improve the status quo—even if some of the options are potentially disruptive in the short term. It was the American statesman Thomas Jefferson who asserted: "I hold that a little rebellion now and then is a good thing, and as necessary in the political world as storms in the physical." The ability to generate those little rebellions now and then is the saving grace of democracy; autocratic states lack that option in their ultimate brittleness of control.

NOTES

1. Michele Dunne, "Storms of the Arab Spring," *Current History*, December 2013, p. 364.

2. Ward Wilson, "The Age of Frustration," *Foreign Policy*, November 13, 2014. http://www.foreignpolicy.com/article/2014/11/13/the_age_of_frustration.

3. Gideon Rachman, "The Dangerous Revival of Nationalism," *Financial Times*, September 22, 2014. http://www.ft.com/intl/cms/s/0/dfOaDDLE-3FEF-11E4-936B-00144feable.

4. Michael Lumbers, "What Should the US Do About Closer Sino-Russian Ties?" *The Diplomat*, June 6, 2014. http://thediplomat.com/2014/06/what-should-the-us-do-about-closer-si.

5. Martin Wolf, "Shaping Globalization," *Finance & Development* (International Monetary Fund), September 2014. http://www.imf.org/external/pubs/ft/fandd/2014/09/wolf.htm.

Selected Bibliography

PRIMARY SOURCES

Devlin, Robert, Antoni Estevadeordal, and Andres Rodriguez-Clare, editors, *The Emergence of China: Opportunities and Challenges for Latin America* (Washington, D.C.: Inter-American development Bank, 2004).

International Monetary Fund, *Regional Economic Outlook Update Middle East and Central Asia* (Washington, D.C.: International Monetary Fund, 2015).

International Monetary Fund, *World Economic Outlook, October 2014: Legacies, Clouds, Uncertainties* (Washington, D.C.: International Monetary Fund, 2014).

International Monetary Fund, IMF Survey *Regional Economic Outlook: Mideast Sees Fragile Recovery amid Conflicts and Transitions* (Washington, D.C.: International Monetary Fund, October 27, 2014). http:www.imf.org/external/pubs/ft/survey/so/2014/CAR102714A.htm.

International Monetary Fund, *Russian Federation: Concluding Statement for the 2014 Article IV Consultation Mission* (Washington, D.C.: International Monetary Fund, April 30, 2014).

International Monetary Fund, *Saudi Arabia 2013, Article IV Consultation,* IMF Country Report, No. 13/229. (Washington, D.C.: International Monetary Fund, 2013).

McKinsey & Company, *Lean Russia: Sustaining Economic Growth Through Improved Productivity* (Moscow: McKinsey Global Institute, 2009).

Moody's Investors Service, Announcement, "Population Will Reduce Economic Growth Worldwide in the Next Two Decades," August 6, 2014.

Moody's Investors Service, *Population Aging Will Dampen Economic Growth over the Next Two Decades: Special Comment*, August 6, 2014. (New York).

National Intelligence Council, *Global Trends 2030: Alternative Worlds* (Washington, D.C.: National Intelligence Council, December 2012).

Organisation for Economic Cooperation and Development, *Society at a Glance 2014: The Crisis and Its Aftermath* (Paris: Organisation for Economic Cooperation and Development, 2014).

Organisation for Economic Cooperation and Development, *Latin American Economic Outlook 2015* (Paris: Organisation for Economic Cooperation and Development, 2014).

Organisation for Economic Cooperation and Development, *OECD Economic Surveys: Russian Federation*, January 2014. (Paris: Organisation of Economic Cooperation and Development, 2014).

Organisation for Economic Cooperation and Development, *State-Owned Enterprises in the Middle East and North Africa: Engines of Development and Competitiveness?* (Paris: OECD, 2013).

Powell, Andrew, Coordinator, *The Labyrinth: How Can Latin America and the Caribbean Navigate the Global Economy* (Washington, D.C.: Inter-American Development Bank, 2015).

Rhee, Changyong, "Asia: Achieving Its Potential," *Finance & Development* (Washington, D.C.: International Monetary Fund), June 2014, Vol. 51, No. 2.

World Bank, *Making the Most of Scarcity: Accountability for Better Water Management Results in the Middle East and North Africa* (Washington, D.C.: World Bank, 2007).

SECONDARY SOURCES

Articles

Bhagwati, Jagdish, "Global Trade's Uncertain Course: Dawn of a New System," *Finance & Development* (International Monetary Fund), December 2013. www.imf.org/external/pub/ft/fandd/2013/12/bhagwati.htm.

Brooks, David, "The Fertility Implosion," *International Herald Tribune*, March 12, 2012: 10.

Busvine, Douglas, Stephen Grey, Roman Anin, and Himanshu Ojha, "Russian Railways Paid Billions to Secretive Private Companies," *The Globe and Mail* (Toronto), May 23, 2014. http://www.theglobe andmail.com/report-on-business/internationalbusiness.

Castaneda, Jorge, "Latin America's Left Turn," *Foreign Affairs,* May 2006: 28–43.

Charap, Samuel, and Jeremy Shapiro, "How to Avoid a New Cold War," *Current History*, October 2014: 265–271.

Dunne, Michele, "Storms of the Arab Spring," *Current History*, December 2013: 364–365.

The Economist, "Hong Kong and Taiwan: Losing Hearts and Minds," *The Economist*, December 6, 2014: 46–47.

The Economist, "India's Strongman," *The Economist*, May 24, 2014: 11.

The Economist, "Sheiks v Shale," *The Economist*, December 6, 2014: 17.

The Economist, "State Capitalism in the Dock," *The Economist*, November 22, 2014: 12. http://www.economist.com/news/business/21633831 -performance-state-owned-enterprises-has-been-shockingly-bad -state-capitalism-dock.

The Economist, "The Long Game," *The Economist*, September 6, 2014: 15.

The Economist, "Time for the Old Men to Give Way," *The Economist*, June 23, 2012: 34. http://www.economist.com/node/21557330/print

The Economist, "Venezuela's Oil Diaspora: Brain Hemorrhage," *The Economist*, July 19, 2014: 31.

Economy, Elizabeth C., "China's Imperial President: Xi Jinping Tightens His Grip," *Foreign Affairs*, November/December 2014: 80–91.

Eremenko, Alexy, "Russia's Rising Middle Class in for a Scare," *The St. Petersburg Times*, May 23, 2014. http://sptimes.ru/index. php?action_id=39916.

Fidler, Stephen, "Ukraine Crisis Clouds Russian Policy Forum," *The Wall Street Journal*, October 23, 2014: A13.

Fleischhauer, Jan, "Putin's Not Post-Communist, He's Post-Fascist," *Spiegel Online*, May 2, 2014. http://www.spiegel.de/international/ world/speeches-by-russian.

Fukuyama, Francis, "America in Decay: The Sources of Political Dysfunction," *Foreign Affairs*, September/October 2014: 5–26.

Gill, Nathan, "Socialist Correa Seeking to Boost Capital Markets in Ecuador," *Bloomberg*, April 19, 2013.

Gray, Nathan, "Rail Still at the Heart of Russia's Economy," *The Moscow News*, April 22, 2013. http://themoscownews.com/business/2013 0422/191459818/Rail-still-at-the-heart-of-Russia's-economy.

Haass, Richard N., "The Unraveling: How to Respond to a Disordered World," *Foreign Affairs*, November/December 2014: 70–79.

Henderson, Simon, "Saudi Succession Change Risks Royal Family Squabble," Policy Analysis, The Washington Institute, March 27, 2014. http://www.washingtoninstitute.orgpolicy-analysis/view/saudi-succes.

Horne, John, "The Global Legacies of World War I," *Current History*, November 2014: 299–304.

Kimmet, Robert M., and Stephen A. Myrow, "The Economic Levers That Might Stop Putin," *The Wall Street Journal*, March 4, 2014: A19.

Laruelle, Marlene, "Russian Nationalism and Ukraine," *Current History*, October 2014: 272–277.

Li, Cheng, and Ryan McElveen, "Can Xi's Government Strategy Work?" *Current History*, September 2013: 203–209.

Mitter, Rana, "History's Unfinished Business in East Asia," *Current History*, September 2014: 218–223.

Munoz, Sara Schaefer, "Despite Riches, Venezuela Starts Food Rations," *The Wall Street Journal*, October 23, 2014: A15.

Nakhleh, Emile, "Propaganda and Power in the Middle East," *Current History*, December 2013: 360–362.

Ostroukh, Andrey, and Alexander Kolyandr, "Russian Economy Faces Contraction Threat," *The Wall Street Journal*, March 27, 2014: A8.

Perry, Elizabeth J., "Citizen Contention and Campus Calm: The Paradox of Chinese Civil Society," *Current History*, September 2014: 211–217.

Rachman, Gideon, "The Dangerous Revival of Capitalism," *Financial Times*, September 22, 2014. http://www.ft.com/intl/cms

Reuters, "How Saudi Arabia Let the Deadly MERS Virus Spread," *Newsweek*, June 12, 2014. http://www.newsweek.com/how-saudi-arabia-let-deadly-mers-virus-spread-254579.

Rodrik, Dani, "The Paradoxes of the Successful State," *European Economic Review*, 1997: 41: 411–442.

Schipani, Andres, and John Paul Rathbone, "Venezuela Loses Faith in Socialist Government," *Financial Times*, December 11, 2014: 14.

Shevtsova, Lilia, "The Next Russian Revolution," *Current History*, October 2012.

Sun, Yan, "The Roots of China's Ethnic Conflicts," *Current History*, September 2014: 231–237.

Tuttle, Robert, "Qatar Shifts Foreign Policy after Supporting Revolts," *Bloomberg*, August 13, 2014.

Vinocur, John, "Why Europe Wobbles before Russia's Challenge," *The Wall Street Journal*, March 4, 2014: A19.

Waldman, Peter, "Buying Time: The Saudi Plan to Extend the Age of Oil," *Bloomberg Markets*, May 2015: 26–35.

Ward, Karen, and Frederic Neaumann, "Consumer in 2050: The Rise of the EM Middle Class," HSBC Global Research, October 15, 2012.

Wilson, Andrew, "The High Stakes of the Ukraine Crisis," *Current History*, October 2014: 259–264.

Wolf, Martin, "Shaping Globalization," *Finance & Development* (International Monetary Fund), September 2014. www.imf.org/external/pubs/ft/fanold/2014/09/wolf.htm.

Yanzhong Huang, "The SARS Epidemic and Its Aftermath in China: A Political Perspective," Institute of Medicine (U.S.) Forum on Microbial Threats. Knobler, S., Mahmoud, A., Lemon, S., et al., editors, *Learning from SARS: Preparing for the Next Disease Outbreak—Workshop Summary* (Washington, D.C.: National Academic Press, 2004).

Books

Angell, Norman, *Europe's Great Illusion* (London: Simpson, Marshall, Kent & Co, 1909).

Appleby, Joyce, *The Relentless Revolution: A History of Capitalism* (New York: W. W. Norton & Company, 2010).

Berman, Ilan, *Implosion: The End of Russia and What It Means for America* (Washington, D.C.: Regnery Publishers, Inc., 2013).

Bremmer, Ian, *The End of the Free Market: Who Wins the War Between States and Corporations?* (New York: Portfolio Trade, 2011).

Bulmer-Thomas, Victor, *The Economic History of Latin America Since Independence* (New York: Cambridge University Press, 2014).

Burke, Edmund, *Reflections from the Revolution* (New York: Oxford University Press, 2009 edition).

Burns, James MacGregor, *Fire and Light: How the Enlightenment Transformed Our World* (New York: Thomas Dunne Books, 2013).

Davidson, Christopher M., *After the Sheikhs: The Coming Collapse of the Gulf Monarchies* (New York: Oxford University Press, 2013).

Economy, Elizabeth, and Michael Levi, *By All Means Necessary: How China's Resource Quest Is Changing the World* (New York: Oxford University Press, 2014).

French, Howard W., *China's Second Continent: How a Million Migrants Are Building a New Empire in Africa* (New York: Knopf, 2014).

Fusfeld, Daniel R., *The Age of the Economist* (Glenview, IL: Scott, Foresman and Company, 1977).

Gallagher, Kevin P., and Roberto Porzecanski, *The Dragon in the Room: China and the Future of Latin American Industrialization* (Stanford, CA: Stanford University Press, 2010).

Geesen, Masha, *The Man Without a Face: The Unlikely Rise of Vladimir Putin* (London: Granta, 2013).

Goldman, Marshall I., *Petrostate: Putin, Power and the New Russia* (New York: Oxford University Press, 2010).

Gustafson, Thone, *The Wheel of Fortune: The Battle for Oil and Power in Russia* (New York: Public Affairs, 2011).

House, Karen Elliott, *On Saudi Arabia: Its People, Past, Religion, Fault Lines—And Future* (New York: Alfred A. Knopf, 2012).

Huntington, Samuel P., *Political Order in Changing Societies* (New Haven, CT: Yale University Press, 1968),

Kamrava, Mehran, *Qatar: Small State, Big Politics* (Ithaca, NY: Cornell University Press, 2013).

Kamrava, Mehran, *The Revenge of Geography* (New York: Random House, 2012).

Kaplan, Robert D., *Asia's Cauldron: The South China Sea and the End of a Stable Pacific* (New York: Random House, 2014).

Kissinger, Henry, *World Order* (New York: Penguin Press, 2014).

Krane, Jim, *City of Gold: Dubai and the Dream of Capitalism* (New York: St. Martin's Press, 2009).

Lemos, Gerard, *The End of the Chinese Dream* (New Haven, CT: Yale University Press, 2013).

Levitsky, Steven, and Lucan A. Way, *Competitive Authoritarianism: Hybrid Regimes After the Cold* (Cambridge, UK: Cambridge University Press, 2010).

Lind, Michael, *Land of Promise: An Economic History of the United States* (New York: Harper Collins Publishers, 2012).

MacDonald, Scott B., and Jonathan Lemco, *Asia's Rise in the Twenty-First Century* (Santa Barbara, CA: Praeger, 2012).

Matthiesen, Toby, *Sectarian Gulf: Bahrain, Saudi Arabia and the Arab Spring that Wasn't* (Stanford, CA: Stanford University Press, 2013).

Mayer-Schonberger, Viktor, and Kenneth Cukier, *Big Data* (New York: Houghton Mifflin Harcourt Publishing Company, 2014).

McGregor, Richard, *The Party: The Secret World of China's Communist Rulers* (New York: Penguin Books, 2012).

Mickelthwait, John, and Adrian Wooldridge, *The Company: A Short History of a Revolutionary Idea* (New York: Modern Library, 2003).

Naughton, Barry, *The Chinese Economy: Transitions and Growth* (Cambridge, MA: The MIT Press, 2007).

Niblock, Tim, and Monica Malik, *The Political Economy of Saudi Arabia* (London: Routledge, 2007).

Pei, Minxin, *China's Trapped Transition: The Limits of Developmental Autocracy* (Cambridge, MA: Harvard University Press, 2006).

Piketty, Thomas, *Capital in the Twentieth Century* (Boston: Belknap Books, 2014).

Reid, Michael, *Brazil: The Troubled Rise of a Global Power* (New Haven, CT: Yale University Press, 2014).

Reynolds, Lloyd G., *Economic Growth in the Third World: An Introduction* (New Haven, CT: Yale University Press, 1986).

Richard, Alan, and John Waterbury, *A Political Economy of the Middle East: State, Class, and Economic Development* (Boulder, CO: Westview Press, 1990).

Roett, Riordan, and Guadalupe Paz, editors, *China's Expansion into the Western hemisphere: Implications for Latin America and the United States* (Washington, D.C.: The Brookings Institute, 2008).

Santiso, Javiet, editor, *The Visible Hand of China in Latin America* (Paris: Organisation for Economic Development and Cooperation, 2007).

Schard, Mark Lawrence, *Vodka Politics: Alcohol, Autocracy, and the Secret History of the Russian State* (New York: Oxford University Press, 2014).

Smith, Adam, *The Wealth of Nations* (New York: Bantam Classics, 2003).

Victor, David G., David R. Hults, and Mark Thurber, editors, *Oil and Governance: State-Owned Enterprises and the World Energy Supply* (New York: Cambridge University Press, 2012).

Wiarda, Howard J., *Corporatism and Comparative Politics* (Armonk, NY: M.E. Sharpe, 1997).

Yergin, Daniel, and Joseph Stanislaw, *The Commanding Heights: The Battle for the World Economy* (New York: Free Press, 2002).

Yu, Lianne, *Consumption in China: How China's New Consumer Ideology Is Shaping the Nation* (Cambridge, UK: Polity Press, 2014).

Yu Zheng, *Governance and Foreign Investment in China, India, and Taiwan: Credibility, Flexibility, and International Business* (Ann Arbor: University of Michigan Press, 2014).

Index

About the Authors

Scott B. MacDonald, PhD, is the Head of Research for MC Asset Management Holdings LLC, which is a wholly owned subsidiary of Mitsubishi Corporation. Before joining MC Asset, Dr. MacDonald was a principal and the Head of Credit & Economic Research at Aladdin Capital Holdings (2000–2011); prior to that having served as the Chief Economist for KWR International, Director of Sovereign Research at Donaldson, Lufkin & Jenrette; Sovereign Risk Analyst and Director at Credit Suisse; and International Economic Advisor, Office of the Comptroller of the Currency. He has also been an adjunct professor of Political Science at the University of Connecticut, where he taught European Politics and Comparative Politics. Dr. MacDonald has authored, coauthored, or edited 18 books, including nine with Praeger or Greenwood Press on international economic, financial, and geopolitical issues. Dr. MacDonald earned a BA in History and Political Science from Trinity College (Hartford), an MA in Area Studies (Far East) from the University of London's School of Oriental and African Studies, and a PhD in Political Science from the University of Connecticut.

Jonathan Lemco, PhD, is a principal and senior sovereign risk analyst at The Vanguard Group, one of the world's largest mutual fund companies. Before joining Vanguard in 2000, Dr. Lemco headed the sovereign research effort at the Credit Suisse First Boston Corporation. He also served for five years as director of the National Policy Association, providing public policy forums and publications related to the NAFTA region; and for four years as a professor at The Johns Hopkins University School for Advanced International Studies, teaching courses in sovereign risk, public policy, and North American economic and political issues. Dr. Lemco has authored or coauthored 11 books, including six with Praeger, and many articles on international economic, geopolitical, and financial issues. A native of Montreal, Canada, Dr. Lemco earned a BA at Clark University and an MA and PhD in political science at the University of Rochester.